G000080536

By the same author

Before the Echoes Die Away
(The story of a Territorial Gunner Regiment)

GUNNERS AT LARKHILL

A History of the Royal School of Artillery

GUNNERS AT LARKHILL

A History of the Royal School of Artillery

N. D. G. James

GRESHAM BOOKS

in association with

THE ROYAL ARTILLERY INSTITUTION

© N.D.G. James 1983

First published in 1983 by

Gresham Books
P.O. Box 61
Henley-on-Thames, RG9 3LG
Oxfordshire, England

All rights reserved. No part of this publication may be reproduced, stored in a retrieval system or transmitted, in any form or by any means, electronic, mechanical, photocopying, recording or otherwise, without the prior permission of The Gresham Press.

ISBN 0 946095 07 8, hardback edition
ISBN 0 946095 08 6, soft cover

Typeset in IBM Baskerville by Academic Typesetting Service
Gerrards Cross, Buckinghamshire
Reprographics by Litho Production Services,
Farnborough, Hants.
Printed and bound by Staples Printers Rochester Ltd.

Contents

List of Illustrations   vii

List of Maps   viii

Acknowledgements   ix

Foreword   xii
    by The Master Gunner, St James' Park,
    General Sir Thomas Morony, KCB, OBE

Preface   xiii

  1   The Evolution of the Practice Camp   1
  2   The Establishment of Larkhill and West Down   7
  3   Flying at Larkhill   20
  4   The First World War   31
  5   Between the Wars   54
  6   The Second World War   73
  7   The Changing Scene   90
  8   The Latter Years   117
  9   The Wings   127
10   The Ranges   159
11   Larkhill and the Territorial Army   181
12   Larkhill Garrison   189
13   The Royal School of Artillery   211

References   234

Appendices

I   Commandants   250
II   Colonel Commandants   251
III   Deputy Commandants and Garrison Commanders   251
IV   Camp Commandants, Larkhill and West Down   252
V   Commandants, School of Instruction,
       Larkhill   252
VI   Chaplains at Larkhill   253
VII   Depot and Support Regiments   254

VIII	The Origins of the Royal School of Artillery	254
IX	Some RA Schools and Practice Camps	255
X	Larkhill Days and Artillery Days	256
XI	Guns and Equipment of Historical Interest	257
XII	Buildings and Roads Bearing Commemorative Names	259
XIII	Plantations Bearing Commemorative Names	262
XIV	Plantations on the Ranges in 1903	264
XV	Farms Extinguished by Formation of the Ranges	266
XVI	Masters, Royal Artillery Hunt	267
XVII	Notable Events in the History of the School	268
Index		270

List of Illustrations

1	RHA Battery firing at Okehampton	3
2	131 Battery, RFA, firing at Okehampton	10
3	Drawing by Col. E.A. Hobday	15
4	1st Balloon Section during the Boer War 1900	21
5	Old balloon hangars at Rollestone Camp	22
6	A balloon being prepared for ascent	25
7	Moraine monoplane over Stonehenge, 1912	27
8	Original hangars in Wood Lane	29
9	View, during construction of the camps, 1915	34
10	Larkhill Military Railway	37
11	HM King George V's train	38
12	The Packway in 1915	41
13	The Packway in 1982	41
14	Stonehenge after the First War	44
15	Notepaper heading of 1916	49
16	Traction engines hauling baggage, 1914	51
17	Larkhill Sports Day, 1922	60
18	50th Anniversary of the School. Painting by Miss Joan Wanklyn	69
19	A battery of 9.2 in. howitzers firing on the Ranges	76
20	Their Majesties King George VI and Queen Elizabeth at Larkhill, 3 April 1941	81
21	Cover of Race Card, 1947	93
22	Mr 'Taffy' Gould being presented to HM The Queen	97
23	Demolition of the old huts, 1959	100
24	FM Lord Alanbrooke laying the foundation stone of the new buildings, 1960	103
25	The Foundation Stone, 1983	103
26	'A' Mess, 1915-68	109
27	50th Anniversary 'First Day Cover'	113
28	50th Anniversary of the School. Painting by Miss Joan Wanklyn	115
29	The County Badge	119
30	Visit of HM The Queen to Larkhill, 1973	121
31	Greenlands Farm, 1975	167

32   The last inspection of the Salisbury Plain Range
     Detachment, 1960   170
33   Greenlands Farm, 1983   173
34   Territorials with 15 pr BL field gun, c. 1909   182
35   The camp newspaper, 3rd West Lancashire Brigade
     Territorial Force, 1914   184
36   Territorials firing 15 pr BLC, 1912   186
37   Silver centre piece, presented to
     HRH The Duke of Connaught   192
38   Silver statuette commemorating the Mountain
     Artillery   194
39   Drawing by Gilbert Holiday – 'The Scent'   196
40   Drawing by Gilbert Holiday   198
41   'The RA Hunt' by Lionel Edwards   200
42   The Warrant Officers' and Sergeants' Mess, 1983   201
43   Model of 6 in. howitzer and limber   202
44   Garrison Church of St Alban, 1982   204
45   Roman Catholic Church of St Barbara and
     St Anthony, 1982   206
46   The Larkhill Point-to-Point Course, 1974   209
47   Original School Headquarters   213
48   The Newcome Hall   221
49   Aerial view of the School Headquarters, 1982   225
50   Artillery Day   229
51   A letter of appreciation   230
Flags flown at Larkhill   facing pages 224 and 225

List of Maps

                                                     facing page

1   Acquisitions of land on Larkhill and West Down
    Ranges: 1897–1936   8

2   Larkhill Garrison area showing the boundaries
    of the 1914–15 camps, nos 1–30   55

3   Rollestone area showing the boundaries of the
    1914–15 camps, nos 31–4   56

Acknowledgements

It would be impossible to write a book of this kind without the help and assistance of a large number of people, and I would like to take this opportunity of thanking all those who have so readily provided me with information and reminiscences.

I am very grateful to the Commandant, Brigadier J.B. Bettridge, CBE, and his predecessor, Brigadier D.M. Jones, for allowing me to visit various parts of the School and the Garrison and I also wish to thank the Deputy Commandant, Colonel J.M. Browell, MBE, for all his help and advice. In order to obtain information on such a variety of subjects, it has been necessary to carry out a considerable amount of research and to contact many of those associated with the School, both in the past as well as the present. This has only been possible with the constant and unfailing help of Colonel P.R.R. de Burgh, OBE, the Librarian of the Badley Library, for whom nothing has been too much trouble and to whom I am extremely grateful.

I am also very much indebted to Lieutenant-Colonel J.R. Guy who has allowed me to make extensive use of his book, *A History of Gunnery Wing*, which I have found indispensable. I also wish to thank members of the School Headquarters; Gunnery, Tactics, Signals, REME, and Guided Weapons Wings; the late Administrative Wing and its successor, the Support Regiment, RSA; and members of the Larkhill Garrison.

I would like to thank the following for their help in various ways. Brig. J.S. Badley; Mr C. Bayliffe; Maj.-Gen. A.J.C. Block, CB, CBE, DSO; Oberstleutnant J.W.K. Böthling; Mr E. Bowden; Maj. P.R. Bowker, RA; Maj. J.D. Braisby, RA, Editor of *Gunner* for permission to use extracts from a number of articles and reports; BSM (AIG) retired R.W. Bray; Mr T.D. Bridge; BSM (AIG) retired J. Bridle; Maj.-Gen. W.D.E. Brown, CB, CBE, DSO; Col. D.S. Brown, MBE; WO2 (SMIG) G.R. Brown; Mr P.W. Browne; Maj. J.D.C. Cadogan, RA; WO2 R. Carmen; Mr J. Carver; Lt.-Col. G.P. Chapman, DSO; Brig. C. Childs, CBE; Maj. R.A. Chilton, WRAC; Mr E.J. Chivers; Messrs W.E. Chivers & Sons, Ltd; Lt.-Col. S.M. Cleeve; Col. B. Cocks, GM, TD; Brig. C.J. Codner, CBE, MC, (and for his permission to use extracts from *The Journal of the Royal Artillery* and other publications of the Royal Artillery Institution); Maj.-Gen. G. de E. Collin, CB, MC; Maj.-Gen. Sir Cyril Colquhoun, KCVO, CB, OBE; Maj. C.E. Corke, MBE; Maj. G.S.C. Cornish, REME; Maj. T.F. Couper, RA; Mr J.G.E. Cox, Keeper of the Records, St Albans Cathedral; Lt.-Col. R.C.F.Craven, RA; Capt. J.R. Cross, AAC; Maj.-Gen. J.H. Cubbon, CB, CBE; Mrs K.P. Cummins; Brig. A.B. Davies, CBE; Flg. Off. A.F.P. Dezonie, RAF; Capt. M.M. Double, RA; Col. G.E. Drought; WO2 L. Emanuel; Maj. J.L. Etherington; Col. J. Fairclough, OBE; Maj. M.H. Fallon, RA; Mrs M.H. Fallon for the loan of several photographs; Col. J.S. Fielding, MBE; Lt.-Col. T. FitzGibbon; Mrs G.G. Ford including the loan of photographs; Maj.-Gen. P.B. Foster, MC; Lt.-Col. L.J. Frost, RA; Mr T.L. Fuller for permission to use several photographs; Air Cdre A.J.W. Geddes, CBE, DSO; Maj. P.M. Gell; Maj.-Gen. Sir Peter Gillett, KCVO, CB, OBE; Maj.-Gen. P.J. Glover, CB, OBE; WO1 (RSM) J.A. Green; Mr P.R.G. Gutteridge; Brig. H.A. Hardy, MBE, MC; Col. A.J.W. Harvey; Mr T.H.J. Heffernan; Maj. A.S. Hill, RA; Mrs H.N. Hooper; Lt.-Gen. Sir Edward Howard-Vyse, KBE, CB, MC; Lt.-Col. L.W. Huelin, OBE, RA; the Editor, *Illustrated London News* for permission to include an illustration of a balloon; the Keeper of the Department of Photographs, Imperial War Museum, for permission to use a photograph; Mr R.A. Jones; Mr P.J. Lambert; Col. C.E. Lane; Maj. D.L.S. Langley, MC; Maj. P.J. Lawrence, RAA; Maj. P.J. Lee, MBE; Brig. R.J. Lewendon; Brig. J.E.F. Linton, DSO; Maj. T. Lynch, ACF. Col. M.G. McComas, MBE; Lt.-Col. A.M. Macfarlane, RA; Maj. C. McNaught; Maj.-Gen. K.J. McQueen; Mr M. McRitchie; the Rev. D.O'L. Markham; Col. C.H. Martin, OBE, TD, ADC; the Rev. H.W.H.B. Martin, SCF; Maj. F.J. Millar, RA; the Ministry of Defence: Air Historical Branch (5RAF), Chief Surveyor, Defence Lands Directorate, Chief Librarian, Whitehall Library; Mrs Jean Morrison; Mr T. Neate; Maj. J. Newcome; Lt.-Col. R.W. Nye; Brig. E.N. Oldrey, OBE; Lt.-Col. W.A. Owen; Mr B.A. Painter, MBE; Mr N.C. Parker; Lt.-Col. J. Pasquier; Maj. E.C. Peasley, TD; Maj.-Gen. P.J.M. Pellereau; Mr F.N. Pettifer; Lt.-Col. D.W.O. Price; Lt.-Col. J.H.G. Price; the Librarian, Prince Consort Library, Aldershot; the Editor of *Punch* for permission to reproduce part of *In Flanders Fields*; Maj. D.L. Radnoti, U.S. Army; Lt.-Col. P. de N. Ramus, OBE; Mrs E. Rhodes; Brig. J.H.W.G. Richards, OBE; Maj. F.M. Robertson, MC; Maj. D. Rollo; the Commanding Officer, No. 3 (F) Squadron, RAF (and for the loan of photographs); the Royal Aircraft Establishment; the Warden, Royal Army Chaplains'

Department; the Officer in Charge, Royal Artillery Manning and Records Office; the Librarian, the Royal Engineers Corps Library; Brig. D.F. Ryan, OBE; the Editor, *Salisbury Journal and Times* for permission to use a photograph; the Curator, Salisbury and South Wiltshire Museum; Col. C. Scott; Maj. G.D.C. Scott, CD, RCA; Maj. P.H. Scott, RA; Mr A.G. Sills; Brig. J.H. Slade-Powell, DSO, OBE; Col. G.N.C. Smith; Maj. W.R. Stacey; Lt.-Col. P.M.R. Stacpoole, RA; Maj. E.G. Stadward, TD; the Librarian, the Staff College, Camberley; Maj.-Gen. C.H. Stainforth, CB, OBE, Editor, *The Army Quarterly and Defence Journal*; Maj. A.F. Stevens; Mrs S.M. Stirling, Librarian, the Devon and Exeter Institution; Mr R.E. Tanswell; Maj. A.O. Taylor; Maj. G.D.B. Thatcher, RA, MFH; Miss Alice Thompson; Mrs K.A. Timbers; Mr T. Neate; Brig. B.E. Watson; Major M.G. Watson, RA; Mrs M.G. Watson; Maj.-Gen. R.H.L. Wheeler, CB, CBE; Maj. J.H. Whitcombe; Capt. G.P. White, RA; Dr R.J. Whitney; Col. J.F. Williams-Wynne, CBE, DSO; Mrs W.A. Wilson; Lt.-Col. R.G. Woodhouse, the Light Infantry Office, (Somerset).

I also wish to record the help that I have received from Mrs Alix Bremridge who has drawn the maps and the illustrations both of the flags flown at Larkhill and for the jacket.

Finally, I would like to thank my son, Capt. T.D.R. James, RHA, for many valuable suggestions and for all the help that he has given me on numerous occasions.

Foreword

By The Master Gunner, St James' Park,
General Sir Thomas Morony, KCB, OBE

Larkhill lies very near to the heart of the Royal Regiment. Woolwich with all its history, tradition and panoply is of course our home, but Larkhill is our school, our University and our workshop. I am therefore delighted to have been invited to write this Foreword.

I do not doubt that the inhabitants of Woolwich were also pleased when – in the 1870s – the firing of live ammunition on the Common ceased and our training area on Salisbury Plain was subsequently bought. For this purchase ended the danger of damage to houses on the edge of Woolwich Common inflicted by rogue cannon balls: contrariwise it also began the story of Larkhill.

Today's world presents us all with problems that become evermore sophisticated and difficult; intellectually athletic or not, we all have to learn to take technological leaps, bounds and even quantum jumps in our stride, and it is to Larkhill that we come to learn to do it. The Gunnery Staff at Larkhill have moreover become the standard bearers and custodians of our Gunner skills.

This admirable archive records our story for almost a hundred years on Salisbury Plain. In all the changes that we can be certain will lie ahead, the importance to Gunners of Larkhill and all it stands for will not diminish.

Preface

My first visit to Larkhill was in August 1937 when the Territorial Brigade to which I belonged, attended Practice Camp. We occupied bell tents on Knighton Down just to the north of 'A' Mess. At this time the 9.2 in. howitzers of Hamilton Battery were in position and horses were still very much in evidence.

My next visit was in November 1939 when the Brigade, now a Regiment, was based at Greenlands Farm and spent three days on the ranges before leaving for France. Except for attending a course in August 1940 (when, on more than one occasion, we occupied slit trenches adjoining the Gun Park, during air raids) I did not see the School again until after the war.

Many changes have taken place since then and few who knew the School in the old days, would recognise it now. However, *plus ça change, plus c'est la même chose* – the more things change, the more they are the same and Larkhill still retains its indefinable character. I hope it always will.

N.D.G.J.
Blakemore House,
Kersbrook,
Budleigh Salterton,
Devon

May, 1983

1. The Evolution of the Practice Camp

The decision to acquire land on Salisbury Plain for military training was implemented in 1897 by the appointment of a War Office Committee,[1] but the need for better training facilities had been apparent for a number of years. This was especially so in the case of the artillery which, because of the nature of their equipment, needed a large area on which to manoeuvre and practise. For the infantry it was a less urgent matter: so long as they continued to fight in close order and were equipped with smooth-bore muskets, they were able to conduct their exercises and firing within a comparatively small compass.

By the middle of the last century, artillery training comprised gun drill, which could be carried out on the gun park; manoeuvres, which required a far larger area; and target practice, which demanded the most land of all. At first, use was made of commons and other open spaces which happened to be situated within a convenient distance of the barracks, and in the first half of the nineteenth century manoeuvres and the firing of live ammunition took place on Woolwich Common. Presumably some form of safety precaution was taken, but it is recorded that on one occasion a gentleman cadet, who was watching from a point near the gates of the Academy, was killed by a ricocheting cannon ball, and it was not unusual for buildings that stood on the edge of the Common to be hit.[2] However by 1860 the only two locations where the firing of live ammunition was permitted were Plumstead Marshes at Woolwich and Shoeburyness where the School of Gunnery had been established on 1 April 1859. A less exacting form of practice sometimes took place at seaside towns where the target was a barrel, moored a little way off shore.[3]

Not only were the activities of the artillery restricted by a shortage of land for firing and manoeuvres but for many years it had been required to 'conform to infantry'. There seems to have been some doubt as to the precise meaning of this term but in effect it demanded that the artillery should march with the infantry. Shackled by an invisible yet unbreakable bond, when the

1

infantry moved, the artillery moved and when the infantry halted, the artillery halted.[4] The adverse effect of such a policy on the tactical use of artillery can be readily appreciated and in 1871 a memorandum was issued by HRH the Duke of Cambridge, as Colonel of the Royal Artillery, which gave commanders far greater scope in the deployment of their batteries.[5] While this enabled the artillery to enjoy greater mobility in the field, it also reflected the need to provide more land where their new-found freedom could be exercised.

The year 1871 was also notable for two events which had a marked influence on the military opinion of the day. The first was the defeat of France by Germany at the conclusion of the Franco-Prussian War, as a result of which the reputation of the French Army suffered a heavy blow. The second was the holding of the Aldershot manoeuvres under the command of the Duke of Clarence which excited considerable public interest, stimulated no doubt by the defeat of the French. Three divisions took part and from a tactical point of view the occasion was of particular importance: it was the first time that a comparatively large force consisting of various arms had taken part in such an exercise. In his report on these manoeuvres the Duke remarked on the noticeable improvement in the deployment of the artillery which he considered to be the result of his earlier memorandum on the subject.[6] The success of the Aldershot exercises led to others being held on Salisbury Plain and Dartmoor during the next two years and these can be seen as the shadows of coming events.

The decision to acquire a new practice area was taken as a result of the recommendation of a committee appointed in 1874 with Major-General F. Eardley-Wilmot as President. It was concerned with certain trials which had been conducted at Shoeburyness and during the course of its deliberations, the Committee had become very much aware of the fact that the conditions which existed there were far removed from those that might be expected on active service. It therefore recommended that steps should be taken to deal with this problem and its report which had been sent to the Director of Artillery, was submitted to the Secretary of State who immediately approved it. As a result, two members of the committee visited Dartmoor on 23 June 1875 and subsequently reported that they preferred the moor in the vicinity of Okehampton because of its climate, excellent water supply and railway connections with Exeter and Plymouth. With commendable promptness all matters relating to the use of the land were settled by 17 July and the new camp was established on 2 August

PLATE 1: RHA Battery firing at Okehampton. Fall of shot is observed by telescope sited behind the guns while the teams wait to bring the guns out of action, 1897.

1875 under the command of Lieutenant-Colonel Tod Brown, Royal Horse Artillery.[7]

Thus, discounting Shoeburyness, Okehampton became the first practice camp for horse and field artillery and its establishment proved to be the turning point in the quest for larger and more realistic areas where the theory of fire and movement could be put into practice. The demand for more practice areas continued however and until permanent practice camps were eventually established local ranges of a temporary nature were employed. These local ranges were not always welcomed by the local inhabitants, as may be gathered from the following report which appeared in a contemporary issue of the *Shrewsbury Chronicle*:

> The greatest consternation was caused on Friday in the little village . . . by the booming of cannon, and the unwelcome arrival of shot after shot from the Royal Artillery stationed on the Church Stretton Hills. Upon this lofty eminence the guns are fixed, and incessant firing continues from morning until night. Whether the gunners miscalculated their distance is not known, but visitors were disconcerted by the whizzing of cannon balls over their heads when walking on the hills, the balls falling in the village of Minton nearly two miles off, to the great danger of that peaceful locality. The greatest damage was the destruction of a barn . . . The women ran screaming from the houses carrying their children with them.[8]

This period was also marked by a growing enthusiasm amongst the recently formed Artillery Volunteers and in 1863 the National Artillery Association was formed. Its purpose was to encourage efficiency in gunnery by means of competitions and the first meeting was held at Shoeburyness during the summer of 1865. Further details of the work of the Association will be found in Chapter 11.[9]

In their report, Major-General Eardley-Wilmot's committee included the following recommendation as regards practice camps:

> The Committee strongly urge that the conditions under which the annual practice of batteries is carried out be revised, and that endeavours be made to procure several land-ranges in different parts of the United Kingdom, where two or more batteries could be encamped for practice.[10]

However twenty-four years elapsed before this recommendation produced any worthwhile results and it was not until 1899 that additional practice camps were established at 'Salisbury Plain' (now Larkhill) and at Glen Imaal in Ireland.[11] These were followed in 1903 by Trawsfynydd in Wales and, in 1912, by Ad Fines which was later renamed Redesdale.

The schools of gunnery which had been set up were closely concerned with the provision of practice areas. The first was founded by Sir William Congreve the elder in the Royal Military Repository at Woolwich in 1778. However, as the power and range of guns increased, the value of Woolwich Common as a practice range declined, and consequently a new school of gunnery was established at Shoeburyness. As a result of this, the Repository became an ancillary school and the centre for instruction in siege work. It was finally closed in May 1900 after a committee under the chairmanship of Lieutenant-General J.F. Owen (afterwards General Sir John Owen, KCB) recommended that the school at Lydd should be extended.[12]

The establishment of the School of Gunnery at Shoeburyness was authorised on 1 April 1859 and Regimental Standing Orders laid down that the School was to consist of two branches, 'of which that at Shoeburyness provides for the instruction of Horse, Field, Mountain and Garrison Artillery, while that at Woolwich is in addition intended to train the Militia and Volunteer Artillery'.[13]

At first the new ranges proved to be of the greatest value and the instruction that was provided covered the needs of the whole Regiment. However as new thoughts and ideas on the use of artillery began to emerge, so it became increasingly clear that the training requirements of horse and field units were very different from those which operated in a comparatively static role. The successful establishment of an inland practice camp at Okehampton in 1875 lent further weight to these arguments but it was not until 1891 that the School of Gunnery for Horse and Field Artillery was formed at Shoeburyness. After 1875 the Commandant of the School moved to Okehampton each year for the summer practice season where he continued to act as commandant, returning to Shoeburyness in the winter. However this arrangement was never very satisfactory as it was still necessary to carry out a limited amount of instruction at Shoeburyness during the summer while the annual move was the cause of considerable inconvenience to those who were involved.

It was therefore an event of the greatest importance to the Regiment when, in 1897, the first purchases of the land which now forms part of the West Down and Larkhill ranges were completed. By the end of 1899, an area of some 22,000 acres had been acquired and the first practice over this land took place during that year. The subsequent use and development of Larkhill and the adjoining area of West Down as practice camps is described in Chapter 2.

Lydd had been established as a practice camp in 1882 although it was not considered to be entirely suitable for the purpose. 'Selected originally for the 'Lydd Experiments' . . . on account of the absence of inhabitants, it had drifted into being a summer practice camp and a place for Ordnance Committee experiments.'[14]

When the Repository at Woolwich was closed in 1900 the staff were transferred to Lydd, although a link already existed between the two establishments. Since 1890 the commandant of the Repository had acted as Commandant at Lydd during the practice season. In 1900 Lydd became the Siege Artillery Branch of the School of Gunnery but was later renamed the Siege Artillery School and remained as such until 1921 when it was amalgamated with the School of Artillery and moved from Lydd to Larkhill. In 1919 the Heavy Artillery Centre of the School of Gunnery was transferred from Winchester to Larkhill to become a part of the new School of Artillery. Further information on this point will be found in Chapter 5.

As the nineteenth century drew to a close, a fundamental change took place in the constitution of the Regiment when, under an Army Order of 1899, it was divided into two separate branches.[15] One was composed of the Royal Horse Artillery and the Royal Field Artillery, and the other of the Royal Garrison Artillery which included mountain artillery, and this division continued for the next twenty-five years until it was terminated in 1924.

2. The Establishment of Larkhill and West Down

The history of Salisbury Plain stretches back into the distant past that lies in the Stone and Bronze Ages and much evidence of this is to be found in the vicinity of Larkhill. Stonehenge, Woodhenge, Durrington Walls, the Cursus and innumerable barrows provide outstanding examples of the activities of the people of those remote days. As the succeeding centuries wore on these early inhabitants were followed by Celts, Romans, Saxons and Normans. For centuries much of the Plain was regarded as little more than a rather wild and inhospitable region but as the population increased and agriculture developed, its value for sheep-and-corn husbandry came to be appreciated. John Evelyn, an associate of Samuel Pepys and the diarist and author of *Sylva*, one of the earliest books on forestry, visited Stonehenge in 1654. He later described the surrounding countryside as 'that goodly plaine . . . which I think for eveness, extent, verdure, innumerable flocks to be one of the most delightful prospects in nature'.[1]

Before the process of acquiring land for military purposes had begun at the end of the nineteenth century, the area which now forms the Larkhill and West Down ranges included a substantial number of farms. These were shown on an Ordnance Survey map of 1872–84, revised in 1894–9.[2] A comparison with a map of the same area, published in 1980,[3] gives some indication of the effect that the purchase of this land must have had on the local farming community, since none of the twenty-three farms shown on the earlier map existed in 1980. (Further details of these will be found in Appendix XV.) Of the few roads which crossed the area, by far the most important was the turnpike which ran from Salisbury to Devizes. The southern length of this road is still in use as the A360 as far as its junction with the A344, from which point it continues as a part of the B3086 to the crossroads adjacent to Rollestone Camp and then on to the Bustard Hotel. From Honeydown Copse, about one and three-quarter miles beyond the Bustard, until it reaches Redhorn Hill some five miles south-east of Devizes, the road forms the boundary between the West Down

and Larkhill ranges. In 1912 a new road was built through Shrewton, Tilshead and West Lavington, on the line of what previously
had been little more than a footpath,[4] and on its completion the
old road across the ranges was closed to the public.[5]

In 1892, under the provisions of the Military Lands Act of that
year, the Secretary of State was given power to purchase land in
the United Kingdom for military purposes.[6] Subsequently, in
August 1897, the first property was bought and this marked the
beginning of the acquisition of the Larkhill and West Down ranges.
This was Grove Farm which amounted to some 364 acres on Ball
Down at the southern end of what is now the West Down impact
area, the grid reference of the centre of the land being 048511.[7]

During the succeeding three years extensive areas were purchased
and by the end of 1899 more than 22,000 acres had been acquired,
of which some 5,400 lay in the area of West Down range and
17,000 acres in the Larkhill area. After 1899 the purchases of land
decreased substantially and only a little over 3,000 acres were
bought during the ten years from 1900 to 1910. The last major
acquisition took place in 1911 when some 3,200 acres were added
to West Down while the last purchase took place in 1936.

In 1982 the total area of West Down range amounted to 11,274
acres (4,563 hectares), Larkhill Camp occupied 803 acres (325
hectares) and Larkhill range with the adjoining areas as far as the
Amesbury–Upavon road (A345) covered 17,297 acres (7,000
hectares).[8] An indication of the urgent need for such an area is
the fact that in August 1899 an exercise for the artillery of an
entire corps together with that of three divisions was held under
Major-General G.H. Marshall at West Down on the land that had so
far been acquired.[9]

The value of this new area was immediately appreciated and the
hope that one day the School of Gunnery for Horse and Field
Artillery might move from Shoeburyness suddenly became a
feasible proposition. Accordingly, in January 1900, the Assistant
Adjutant-General of Artillery, Colonel E.O. Hay (afterwards
Major-General E.O. Hay) put forward a proposal that the School
should be transferred to Salisbury Plain. The suggestion received
the support of both the Adjutant-General, Sir Evelyn Wood, VC
(afterwards Field Marshal), and the Secretary of State, the Marquis
of Lansdowne, and in June of that year it was recommended that
the School should move to Netheravon and also take over Syrencote House. However objections were raised by the School largely
on the grounds that the proposed accommodation was, for various
reasons, unsuitable and also on account of the distance from the

WESTDOWN AND LARKHILL AREA SHOWING SUCCESSIVE ACQUISITIONS OF LAND

Dates indicate years of purchase.
— shows extent of each purchase.

Scale: 0 ___ 1 mile

ranges. In fact, the distance from Netheravon village to Newfoundland Farm Wood is two and a half miles if the road and track past Wexland Farm is used. Discussions and negotiations continued over the next three years but in the end the matter was dropped, because of objections raised by the School, and it was not until 1915 that it finally moved to Larkhill.[10]

The postponement of the transfer from Shoeburyness did not however delay the establishment of a practice camp at Larkhill and West Down, and in 1899 the new camp was recorded in the Annual Report of the School of Gunnery under the title of 'Salisbury'.[11] As Sir John Headlam observed,

> At last the field artillery were in possession of a range on which the usual 'practice camp conditions' were conspicuous by their absence, for the space was ample, and the ground, without being featureless, allowed of movement in all directions. Here, for the first time, brigade commanders could be given a free hand in the application of the accepted principles for the employment of artillery to an actual problem on the ground; here battery commanders could select their positions in accordance with their task unfettered by considerations of safety; here battery leaders could devote their attention to the use of the ground in accordance with the tactical requirements unhampered by the necessity of finding a practicable route between bogs and boulders; and here, finally, it was possible to demonstrate that fire discipline in a battery involved not only the accurate discharge of their technical duties by all ranks, but also the exercise of their intelligence and powers of observation.[12]

Batteries which came to practice at Larkhill were quartered in what were described as 'the new Bulford hut barracks' and, because this involved a daily march of between four and five miles each way, the range party was stationed at Newfoundland Farm, 'which affords good accommodation for about 20 men and horses . . . it is most conveniently situated and there is a large barn which makes an excellent storehouse for targets, etc.'.[13]

Although Newfoundland Farm no longer exists, its position is marked on the modern range maps as Newfoundland Farm Wood (grid reference 107478). For the first year, 104 Battery RFA acted as the 'permanent or depot battery' while, as regards safety arrangements, it was recorded that 'Electric communication was put up round the northern half of the danger area to enable the vedettes to communicate rapidly with the splinter proof . . . No trouble was experienced in keeping the ranges clear.'[14]

However, in the following year the 'electric communication' was 'dispensed with'. As more land was acquired it became possible to enlarge the range area and in so doing, to increase its value for training purposes. The 1901 Annual Report records

> The extension of the artillery ranges to the westward as far as the Salisbury-Devizes road has been a marked success, and has given such an increased manoeuvring area that this range now, more than any other, fulfils the requirements of modern field artillery. It is possible to fire here at ranges up to 7,000 yards.[15]

The first practice camp at Larkhill, held in 1899, is referred to in the Annual Report of the School of Gunnery for that year. However the 1900 Report does not contain any reference to Salisbury Plain and it would not appear that a practice camp was held at Larkhill during that year. The first camp commandant was Lieutenant-Colonel H.B. Jeffreys but in 1901 he was succeeded by Col. L.W. Parsons (afterwards Lieut.-Gen. Sir Lawrence Parsons).

PLATE 2: 131 Battery, RFA firing 15 prs at Okehampton. Probable date 1903.

He had fought in the Boer War and was recognised as being especially suitable for this position; General Sir Evelyn Wood who was
commanding the II Army Corps at the time considered that he
was 'one of the best, if not the best, instructor I have met in the
army'.[16] From 1901 until 1910 a single commandant was placed
in charge of 'Salisbury Plain' practice camp but from 1911 until
1913 separate commandants were appointed for Larkhill and West
Down. The names of those who held this position until 1913 are
given in Appendix IV and it will be seen that these included several
distinguished members of the Regiment, amongst whom were
Brigadier-General E.J. Phipps-Hornby, VC, CB.

The summer practice camps provided a unique opportunity for
passing on the latest developments in gunnery, for practising new
procedures and for a general exchange of ideas. The first year in
which practice took place at Larkhill also marked the beginning
of the Boer War which had started in October 1899 and was not
to end until June 1902. It provided many valuable lessons which,
backed by personal experiences, were to stand the Regiment in
good stead during the First World War. One of the most important
was the introduction of indirect fire which arose out of the need
to deploy the guns in concealed positions, out of sight of the
enemy. This in turn created a demand for a system of communications between the observing officer and the guns.

> There still remained the difficulty of communications between
> the observing station and the battery. Megaphones were found
> too limited in range, a chain of orderlies repeating messages
> proved quite unreliable, and signallers had been abolished for
> horse and field artillery in 1899. Naturally enough battery
> commanders were reluctant to quit their guns for the observing
> station for fear of losing touch. So the Regiment took the mat-
> ter into its own hands: amateur signallers sprang up as if by
> magic: their official recognition followed: the semaphore
> proved admirably adapted to the requirements; and the 'double
> chain' solved the problem until displaced by the telephone
> which in 1903 was still 'under consideration'.[17]

Another lesson of the Boer War which the commandant was
anxious to emphasise was the need to co-operate with other
arms, since he felt that the new practice area could 'afford an un-
rivalled field for tactical instruction'. This was difficult to arrange
however, since the units which might have taken part were, as
often as not, engaged in their own regimental training. In his

report for 1901, Colonel Parsons made the following comment:
'Although every day's practice was carried out under a pre-arranged
tactical scheme, the want of the actual presence of other arms,
even in the form of a weak skeleton force, was much felt.'[18]

The only batteries which co-operated regularly with other arms
appear to have been those of the Honourable Artillery Company,
and in 1902 the Dorset Imperial Yeomanry and infantry units
took part in field firing practice. 'A most interesting and realistic
scheme was well carried out by the combined force under the
command of Colonel the Earl of Denbigh, commanding the
Honourable Artillery Company.'[19]

In 1905 the Prime Minister, Sir Henry Campbell-Bannerman
appointed R.B.H. Haldane (afterwards Viscount Haldane of Cloan)
as Secretary of State for War. A man of boundless energy and
great ability, he devised an 'Expeditionary Force' which would be
available should an emergency arise in Europe, and his shrewdness
and foresight were fully vindicated by the events of 1914. In 1907
he undertook the complete reorganisation of the volunteers and
militia which resulted in the passing of the Territorial and Reserve
Forces Act.[20] In addition, he established the General Staff and
created the Officers' Training Corps, the latter continuing until it
was superseded in 1939 by the Junior Training Corps, while the
University Officers' Training Corps was replaced by the Senior
Training Corps. In 1948 the Junior Training Corps became the
Combined Cadet Force; the Senior Training Corps later reverted
to the University Officers' Training Corps and became a part of
the Territorial Army.

Much information relating to the history of the ranges and their
immediate surroundings can be obtained from a study of successive maps of the area, one of the earliest of which, 'Ordnance
Survey. War Department Land on Salisbury Plain', is dated 1903.
Drawn to a scale of two inches to a mile, it was surveyed during
the twelve years from 1872-84, revised between 1894 and 1899
and published in 1903. It shows an area marked 'Artillery Range'
the northern boundary of which ran from Redhorn Hill to Caster-
ley Camp while the eastern boundary was much the same as it is
today, terminating on the Packway at grid reference 144441. The
southern boundary followed the Packway westwards to the Rollestone crossroads where the boundary turned north along the line
of the old Salisbury–Devizes road, past the Bustard and back to
Redhorn Hill. To the west lay an area which now forms part of
West Down range, its southern boundary running westward from

the Bustard past Keepers Farm to a track junction at reference 054475. At this point the boundary line changed direction, following the course of the track which runs northwards past West Down Plantation and the site of Candown Farm (reference 044504) until it reached Phillpots Farm (033521). It then followed a north-easterly line past Easterton Farm (038531) to meet the Ridgway on Urchfont Hill at grid reference (046556) and so back to Redhorn.

No buildings are shown in the vicinity of the Packway over the whole of its length from the Stonehenge Inn to the Rollestone crossroads, the only buildings to the south being Down Barn, later Down Barn Destructor (reference 132439) and Fargo Barn (116437) which has since disappeared. The map marks three camps, the first lying to the north of – and obliquely adjoining – the Packway which is inscribed 'R.F.A. Practice Camp'. The approximate centre of the area is grid reference 134444 which is the open ground that lies between the present RA Mess and the Garrison Church. Two other camps are shown to the west of the Old Salisbury–Devizes road which now forms the boundary between the two ranges. The first, which was named West Down Camp North, was situated near Barrow Plantation, the reference of the centre of the area being 063494 while the second was West Down South Camp with its centre at 063480. The sites of these camps are in no way related to the present West Down Camp which lies some 2,100 metres (2,300 yards) due west of the old South Camp.

During the Boer War a weapon which had made a rather unwelcome appearance as far as British troops were concerned was the 37 mm Vickers Maxim gun. This fired belts of one-pound shells and, on account of the noise which it produced was known as the 'pom-pom'. Steps were immediately taken to provide a similar gun for the British Army and, although issued to batteries in the first place, it was subsequently transferred to the cavalry.[21] The North and South Camps were established in 1902 for the accommodation of two cavalry brigades to enable them to carry out firing practice with their pom-poms on West Down. In his report for 1906 the Camp Commandant, Colonel W.F.L. Lindsay, remarked

Pom-pom sections of five Cavalry Regiments carried on their annual practice at Larkhill during the season, viz:-

King's Dragoon Guards
5th Lancers

8th Hussars
16th Lancers and
21st Lancers.

They arrived at the camp in my opinion insufficiently prepared
to derive full advantage from their practice. Their rapidity of
movement, when mounted, was undeniable, but rapidity of
ranging, service of gun, hooking and unhooking, and the advan-
tages of cover, seemed to have been but slightly considered.[22]

In 1909 a map to the scale of one inch to one mile was published by the Ordnance Survey under the brief title of 'Salisbury
Plain' which included the revision of War Department property up
to 1908. The boundaries of Larkhill range, which was described as
'Artillery Danger Zone' were similar to those shown on the map of
1903 except in the case of the southern boundary. After following
the line of the Packway as far as grid reference 138442, the boundary turned north-west to reference 136446 and then continued in
a straight line to a point (reference 095454) which is approximately
midway between Rollestone crossroads and the Bustard.
   It would appear that the re-alignment of the southern boundary
to the north of, and further away from, the Packway was made in
order to provide space for additional camps adjacent to the road.
A comparison of the two maps also shows that there had been a
substantial increase in the number of camps since 1903, the
'R.F.A. Practice Camp' having been renamed Durrington Camp
while to the west, Larkhill Camp is shown straddling the Packway.
The section on the north side of the road is now occupied by
Roberts Barracks and that on the south side by the Packway Mess
and the adjacent area as far east as Lightfoot Road. A little to the
north of Fargo Plantation, and in prolongation of it, was Fargo
Camp; to the north and east of Rollestone Bake Farm was Rollestone Camp. To the north the Bustard Camp was situated on either
side of the old Devizes road and a short distance beyond the
Bustard Hotel. The West Down North and South Camps were still
in use, and two and a half miles to the north Pond Farm Camp had
been established, the grid reference of the centre of its area being
055534.
   Another map, to a scale of two inches to a mile, was published
in 1914 under the same title as that of the 1903 map. It was in
fact a reprint of the earlier map together with the revisions that
had been made in 1911 and 1914. Two ranges were shown on it,

PLATE 3: A familiar situation. One of the humorous drawings in *The Gunner's ABC* by Col. E.A. Hobday which was published about 1901.

'Larkhill Artillery Range' and, adjoining it, 'Rollestone Artillery Range' which later became known as West Down. The limits of the Larkhill Range were the same as those that had been marked on the earlier maps except for the following changes to the southern boundary: from grid reference 136446 or thereabouts, the boundary extended in a straight line to a point (reference 100440) that lay a little to the east of Rollestone Bake Farm and, after avoiding Rollestone Camp, terminated on the Bustard road at reference 095455. The main distinguishing feature between the two earlier maps and that of 1914 is the addition of Rollestone or West Down range. This had been extended in 1911 and the Report for that year states: 'A new range at West Down was opened this season and should, when extended as proposed, form a valuable addition to the few areas available for gun practice.'[23]

The southern boundary ran westwards from the Bustard to a track junction (066467) a little to the south of Greenland Camp. At this point it turned south to a road and track junction at grid reference 060459, about 320 metres north of the church in Orcheston St Mary and then turned due west to join the Shrewton-Tilshead road at reference 043459. From there the boundary followed the road as far as The Island at Tilshead, where it passed to the east and north of the village to rejoin the road at 019488. After continuing beside the road for some 800 metres to reference 016494, it turned north-east and then north-west past St Joan à Gore Farm to grid reference 012509. Bearing north-east from the this point the range boundary continued close to Brazen Bottom Farm and, after a slight deviation to the north-west, continued in a north-easterly direction past Lime Kiln Farm to Urchfont Hill, reference 044558, and so to Redhorn Hill. With a few minor exceptions the range boundary was virtually the same in 1982 as it was in 1914.

By the end of 1913, the number of camps at Larkhill and West Down had increased to nine and this figure included Hamilton Camp as well as those already mentioned. This camp lay on the north side of the Packway, opposite the present Fargo Ammunition Compound and occupied a rectangular area, the map coordinates of the centre being 108448 or thereabouts. A further change which had taken place since 1909 was the renaming of Fargo Camp as Fargo Down Camp and so, at the beginning of 1914, the following camps had been established at Larkhill and West Down.

Bustard Camp	Pond Farm Camp
Durrington Camp	Rollestone Camp

Fargo Down Camp   West Down North Camp
Hamilton Camp   West Down South Camp
Larkhill Camp

However it might be more accurate to describe these as camp sites since they were, in effect, simply locations for tented camps.

As Larkhill increased in importance and popularity as a practice camp, so the body of opinion which favoured a transfer of the Headquarters of the School of Gunnery for Horse and Field Artillery from Shoeburyness began to reassert itself. In his report for 1909, Colonel S.C. Smith, Chief Instructor, Horse and Field School of Gunnery, put forward the following reasons for moving:

> It has for sometime been recognised that Shoeburyness has ceased to be a suitable place for the training of Horse and Field Artillery. As the headquarters of the School of Gunnery, Horse and Field, it becomes less and less suitable every year.
>
> The only practice ground is (as has always been the case) the sands. The only available position at our own disposal, from which to practise, is from among a number of trees at an angle of some 30° to the line of fire.
>
> To enable an 'undercover' position to be used, we are dependent on the good nature and kind offices of the Superintendent of Experiments for the occasional use of the New Ranges, as a favour . . .
>
> Even for such drill purposes, as laying at natural objects . . . the ground at our disporal is quite unsuitable.
>
> It appears to be high time that the question of the removal of the School of Gunnery (H. and F.) to some more suitable locality should be seriously considered.[24]

Although Colonel Smith did not specifically refer to Larkhill as a suitable location, his next report for 1910 makes this very clear.

> each year the necessity for a move to a more suitable neighbourhood and for expansion, so as to meet the increased demands, becomes more and more pressing.
>
> What appears to me to be the most useful direction in which this establishment should be improved is by making it into an 'Artillery School', whereat lectures in Gunnery can be supplemented by a certain amount of mounted drill and manoeuvre.
>
> Many Territorial officers coming here seem to have been

under the impression that they would get practical instruction in these matters, and have been disappointed to find that such was not the case.

The advantage to the Territorial Artillery, could such a school be established, would be incalculable, and the money spent on it would be well spent.

A position in the vicinity of the new Salisbury Ranges, near Tilshead, or in that neighbourhood, would probably be suitable. I trust that this subject will be strongly urged.[25]

In the following year Colonel Smith made a further reference to the subject while in 1912 he once again drew attention to the urgent need to provide a new location, adding, 'I know of course that a War Office Committee has enquired into the matter and put forward proposals, and I hope that something may be done in the matter.'[26] Finally in his report for 1913 he remarked, 'I understand the Army Council has approved in principle the removal of the Horse and Field School, and I hope that before very long a move may be made towards putting this principle into effect.'[27]

In the meantime the headquarters of the School had moved to Larkhill for the summer of 1912, instead of to Okehampton, where it had normally taken up residence during the practice season. Finally, in 1914, approval was given for the School of Gunnery for Royal Horse and Royal Field Artillery to move to Larkhill and the events which followed this decision are considered in Chapter 4.

The Annual Reports for 1912 and 1913 included a list of the staff appointments at Larkhill and West Down, although these varied to some extent as regards the number of officers who held them. It would however appear that the staff in respect of each of the camps was based on a strength of a commandant, two staff officers, a gunnery instructor, an assistant staff officer, a recording officer, two range officers and a quartermaster. In his report for 1913 Colonel the Hon F.R. Bingham, who was 'Chief Instructor, Horse and Field School of Gunnery', remarked,

I hope that the present Larkhill Camp will be moved to the site of the aeroplane sheds. It would then be off the manoeuvring area, and the aeroplane sheds could be used as institutes which are very much wanted, and the camp will be close to the proposed site of the School of Gunnery when it is moved to Salisbury Plain.[28]

On the maps of 1909 and 1914, Larkhill Camp occupied the site of Roberts Barracks, on the north side of the Packway, and the area between the Packway Mess and Lightfoot Road, on the south side. Steps were also taken in 1912 to improve both the Larkhill and West Down ranges by providing extra 'splinter proofs', additional telephones and 'permanent field works'.[29]

3. Flying at Larkhill

Although as a young general, Napoleon Bonaparte had used balloons for observation in the French Army as early as 1794, the first occasion when they were employed on active service in the British Army was during the Bechuanaland and Sudan Expeditions of 1885.[1] Later, in the Boer War they were used on a number of occasions, particularly at Lombard's Kop, Paardeburg and Kimberley.[2] Although authority had been given for the production of balloons and accessory equipment at Woolwich Arsenal in 1878, it was not until 1890 that the first Balloon Section was formed in the British Army. In the following year the section moved to Aldershot and the Balloon Factory which incorporated the School of Ballooning was established there in 1892 under Major L.R.B. Templer as 'Instructor of Ballooning'.[3] Though he was not a gunner himself, two of his successors have been notable members of the Regiment – Brigadier C.R. Templer and his son, Brigadier J.R. Templer. In 1909 the Balloon Factory and the Balloon School were divided into two separate establishments, the former being placed in charge of a civilian engineer. Further reorganisation took place in April 1911 when the Balloon School became the Air Battalion, Royal Engineers[4] while in December of that year the Balloon Factory became the Army Aircraft Factory.[5] In 1912 the name was changed once again to that of the Royal Aircraft Factory.[6]

Balloons were introduced into the British Army so as to enable observation to be carried out from the air if, for some reason, observation from the ground was either difficult or impossible. Consequently balloons were of the greatest importance to the artillery and were frequently used at Larkhill during the practice season as the Annual Report for 1906 shows.

A balloon section was present in camp during the greater part of the season. Work was carried on between batteries and the balloon section with great intimacy. Valuable lessons were learnt. Many R.A. officers observed practice from the balloons, both as spectators and as taking part in the tactical scheme for

20

PLATE 4: 1st Balloon Section near Kronstaad during the Boer War 1900.
(*Illustrated London News*)

the day. The general conclusion came to was that the balloon observation was good and valuable under summer conditions and that observation of percussion rounds was more reliable and easier than in the case of time shell.[7]

The Report for the following year notes that 'The balloon was kindly placed at my disposal by the R.E. section and usually an artillery officer telephoned or megaphoned his observations from it, with useful results when the target was concealed'.[8]

It is a recognised fact that as soon as a new weapon is produced, steps ought to be taken to render it ineffective, should it be used by the opposing force. In the case of observation balloons it was considered that the most effective counter-measures would be obtained by shooting them down with artillery fire. The Report for 1902 contains the following account of the method adopted which must be one of the earliest examples of anti-aircraft procedure.

The General Officer Commanding 2nd Army Corps kindly obtained . . . the loan of two old balloons. Colonel Templer, Superintendent Balloon Factory, was good enough to bring these balloons himself from Aldershot, and assisted in every way to make the practice successful and realistic. Two observing parties were used with signallers lent by the Royal Garrison

Artillery. In the first series the height of the balloon was 1,500
feet.

Range from guns . . . . . 3,300 yards.

Angle of sight . . . . . 8 degrees 30 minutes.

The third shell wounded the balloon, but it did not collapse
until 25 minutes elapsed, during which 46 rounds were fired.

In the second series the height of the balloon was 1,700 feet.

Range from guns . . . . . 4,450 yards.

Angle of sight about .1 degree 30 minutes.

The battery commander bracketed with a low and a high shell,
and then poured in a bouquet at the mean elevation of the bracket. In six minutes the balloon was seen to be badly wounded
and was brought down.[9]

By 1907, possibly on account of the cost of balloons, kites were
introduced as targets and it was reported that 'A kite was fired at
by a 60-pr. battery, good practice being made. The method
adopted was ordinary time shrapnel ranging, with the result of
20 hits.'[10] Two years later balloons were still being used as targets
at Larkhill – 'captive balloons were engaged on Salisbury Plain
with considerable success' – while at Glen Imaal 'a target to repre-
sent an airship was used . . . but gave little information as to the
possibility of engaging a real one'.[11]

PLATE 5: The old balloon hangars at Rollestone Camp built in 1916 for the
Royal Flying Corps. (*RSA Reprographics*)

The use of balloons for observation continued and in 1916 the Royal Flying Corps took over some 50 acres of land on the west side of the Bustard road, opposite Rollestone Bake Farm. On this site No. 1 Balloon School was established and erection of the balloon hangars, which soon became a noticeable feature of the landscape, began in the same year. In 1920, after the formation of the Royal Air Force, the station became part of No. 7 Group RAF and was renamed the School of Balloon Training. However this designation was changed in 1929 to the Larkhill Kite Balloon Station, in 1932 to the RAF Balloon Centre and in 1936 to No. 2 Balloon Training Unit. This belonged to No. 22 (Training) Group RAF which ceased to exist on 1st December 1940. In 1939 Rollestone Camp became the RAF Anti-Gas School but in 1946 the Royal Air Force gave up the site,[12] and in 1967–8, when the Fargo Ammunition Compound was being rebuilt, Rollestone Camp was used as a temporary ammunition centre. From November 1980 until December 1981, except for a short interval, it was adapted as a civilian prison. When this came to an end it returned to its former use as a camp to accommodate units visiting the area for training purposes. Until 1931 married quarters were provided in the buildings of the old Military Hospital at Fargo, for the RAF officers who were stationed at Rollestone.

The hangars which were still in existence in 1983 consisted of two large sheds built side by side, each of which measured approximately 105ft in length, 40ft in width and 40ft to the top of the roof ridge. In that year they were in a very good state of repair but recently the original sliding doors at the east end or front of the hangars had been replaced by doors on the north side. There is, in addition, a small aircraft hangar which stands a little to the north of those provided for balloons. Some of the large iron rings which had been fixed in concrete blocks so as to anchor the balloons could still be seen in 1982, amongst the beech trees on the south side of the hangars. These trees had been planted in the form of the letter 'E', presumably in order that the spaces between the horizontal bars of the letter could provide sheltered anchorage space for additional balloons. The use of balloons for observing artillery fire continued until 1935 and, up to that year, all those who attended courses for Battery Commanders and Young Officer's and the Gunnery Staff Courses, were required to conduct shoots from balloons.[13]

The balloons were not inflated on site but arrived tethered to their lorry. On one occasion we were being taken up in pairs but

as the day was drawing on the balloonist took the last four of us
up together. As we started on our way up he said something
like 'Listen to me – firstly don't touch that red rope or you will
open the bag and we'll go down quicker than we are going up
and secondly, will you all hold on to the ropes as this basket is
only meant to hold two and the bottom may drop out'. I think
this somewhat marred our enjoyment of an interesting and
somewhat eerie experience.[14]

During 1909 an event took place at Larkhill which although it
was probably thought to be of little importance at the time, can
be claimed to be the first step towards the subsequent formation
of the Royal Air Force. In June of that year a leading pioneer in
British aviation, Horatio Barber, rented a small area of land close
to the point where Tombs Road joins the Packway, and built a
shed on it. In this he housed his first aeroplane. Shortly afterwards
the War Office erected an additional shed adjacent to Barber's
which was intended to be used by the Hon. C.S. Rolls in order
that he could instruct army pilots but owing to his death this
did not materialise.[15] Subsequently this shed was let to Captain
J.D.B. Fulton, Royal Field Artillery, who owned a Bleriot aeroplane and was serving in 65 (Howitzer) Battery of the 8th (Howitzer) Brigade, RFA, which was stationed at Bulford.[16] Shortly
afterwards he was joined by another leading figure in the embryo
world of flying – G.B. Cockburn – who erected another shed close
by and in which he kept his Farman biplane.[17]

By 1910 the Army had become increasingly interested in flying and in the spring of that year three military hangars were
erected some 250 metres to the south of those referred to in the
previous paragraph. The reason for building these hangars in this
position was due to what is known as the 'sun gap'. This is a 'path'
some 64 metres wide along which, on the morning of the Summer
Solstice, the sun could be seen from Stonehenge rising above the
horizon. The solstices occur when the sun is furthest from the
equator and in the northern hemisphere this is on or about 21
June (the Summer Solstice) and 22 December (the Winter Sols-
stice). No buildings were permitted to be erected on the line of
this 'path' in a position that would obstruct the natural horizon
above which the sun rose. As this was some 20 metres to the east
of Tombs Road the land between Wood Road and Tombs Road
which lay in the 'path', was accordingly kept free of buildings.

In June 1910 a three-bay hangar and, a little later, a two-bay
hangar, were built by the British and Colonial Aircraft Company

PLATE 6: A balloon being prepared for an ascent outside the Bristol Flying
School hangar which now faces Wood Road. (*T.L. Fuller*)

of Bristol which later became The Bristol Aeroplane Company and
subsequently The British Aircraft Corporation. These were built
so as to accommodate the machines which were used by the
Company's newly established flying school and are still in exis-
tence. They occupy a site in Wood Road opposite the entrance to
Colquhoun Road and, although now used by the Royal Army
Ordnance Corps as the Accommodation Exchange Store for
Larkhill, are probably the oldest aeronautical buildings in Britain.
All these hangars were erected on the west side of what is now
Tombs Road and, as neither Wood Road nor the houses and build-
ings which form Goodbody Road, Colquhoun Road and Lawson
Road had been built, they faced an open area of land which
stretched as far as Down Barn. Seven hangars are shown on the
Ordnance Survey map of the area published in 1914, and are
marked 'aeroplane sheds', but there was one exception to this. In
August 1912 Military Aircraft Trials were held at Larkhill and in
order to house the aircraft that were taking part, twenty temporary hangars were erected behind those described above and nearer
to Tombs Road. After the trials were completed these hangars
were dismantled and later re-erected at Farnborough.[18]
   The Bristol Flying School held a position of considerable
importance since those who wished to take up military flying were

required to learn at their own expense before the War Office would consider their application. However, after they had qualified and had been accepted, they were given a grant of £75 by the War Office towards their expenses. This system continued until the formation of the Royal Flying Corps on 1 April 1912 when pilots were then trained at the Central Flying School at Upavon.[19] By this time far more attention was being paid by the Army to activities in the air, although at first this was mainly concerned with balloons. Their use at Larkhill has already been described and they were apparently based on the Army hangars in Tombs Road; Plate 6, a photograph taken in 1912, showing a balloon next to the Bristol Flying School hangar, is reproduced on page 25. From time to time there have been references to the 'Balloon School' at Larkhill but it never appears to have achieved the status of an official army school. The flying of balloons was entrusted to the Sappers and the Army List for November 1910 contains an entry in respect of the 1st Balloon Company, Royal Engineers, which was stationed at Aldershot. During the army manoeuvres which were held in September 1910, the War Office obtained the use of two privately owned Bristol Boxkite aircraft and the results proved to be so successful that the Balloon Company of the Royal Engineers were instructed to provide 'opportunities for aeroplaning'.[20] By the end of January 1911 the Balloon School at Larkhill had been allotted four heavier-than-air aircraft.[21]

Under an Army Order issued on 28 February 1911, the Air Battalion of the Royal Engineers was formed and this consisted of two companies. No. 1 Company which operated balloons, airstrips and kites was located at Farnborough where the Balloon School and Balloon Factory were situated, while No. 2 Company which was concerned with fixed-wing aircraft, moved from Farnborough to Larkhill towards the end of April.[22] At the same time Captain Fulton transferred to the Air Battalion and was given the command of No. 2 Company and in December 1911 his name heads the list of 'Officers of the Battalion'.[23] In June of the following year he is shown as being attached to the Royal Flying Corps[24] and in September 1913 as an Instructor in Flying at the Central Flying School at Upavon.[25] By June 1915 he had joined the Aeronautical Inspection Department as Chief Inspector, had been appointed CB, had been granted the rank of temporary lieutenant-colonel and belonged to the Royal Flying Corps Reserve.[26]

At the present time when thousands of people travel by air every day without mishap, it is not easy to appreciate the problems and difficulties which faced those who flew during the early years of this century. Lack of experience and, in some cases, unreliable aircraft inevitably resulted in accidents and two are commemorated at Larkhill. On 5 July 1912, Captain E.B. Loraine and Staff-Sergeant R.H.V. Wilson were killed near the junction of the roads from Amesbury to Shrewton and from Longbarrow crossroads to the Bustard – that is, the A344, A360 and B3086. They were flying a 70hp Gnome-engined Nieuport Monoplane and when making a tight turn the machine side-slipped inwards and

PLATE 7: Moraine monoplane over Stonehenge, 1912.
(*No. 3 (F) Squadron, RAF*)

crashed. This was the first fatal aeroplane accident on Salisbury Plain and those who died were both members of the Air Battalion, Royal Engineers. Exactly one year later a stone cross which had been erected to their memory was unveiled by General Sir Horace Dorrien-Smith. It stands besides the crossroads close to where the accident took place (grid reference 098429) and is now often referred to as Air Man's Cross,[26] or Airman's Corner. The inscription on the memorial reads.

TO THE MEMORY

OF

CAPTAIN LORAINE

AND STAFF-SERGEANT WILSON

WHO WHILST FLYING ON DUTY, MET WITH

A FATAL ACCIDENT NEAR THIS SPOT

ON JULY 5TH 1912

ERECTED BY THEIR COMRADES.

Twelve months afterwards another accident occurred when Major A.W. Hewetson, RFA crashed as he was making a figure-of-eight turn which he had to undertake as part of the test for his licence – or brevet, as it was then known. The machine, a Bristol Monoplane Sociable (so named because the two seats were side-by-side) which was powered by a 50hp Gnome engine, crashed on the flying field between Wood Road and Down Barn.[28] Today the site of this tragedy is marked by a stone slab (grid reference 139439), enclosed by four rather dilapidated white posts and rails beside which a hawthorn bush is growing. The memorial incorporates a carved cross at the foot of which is an inscription, but in June 1982 this was difficult to read; many of the letters were missing although Major Hewetson's name was still legible. From what remained, it would seem that the inscription was similar to that on the memorial cross which has been erected in the south-east corner of Fargo Plantation adjoining the Amesbury-Shrewton road (A344). Originally this cross was some little distance from the road but over the years successive road widening operations have brought the road very much nearer. The memorial bears the following inscription:

IN MEMORY

OF

MAJOR ALEXANDER WILLIAM HEWETSON

66TH BATTERY ROYAL FIELD ARTILLERY

WHO WAS KILLED WHILST FLYING

ON THE 17TH JULY 1913 NEAR THIS SPOT

As a matter of interest, the 66th Battery to which Major Hewetson belonged was in the same brigade – the 8th (Howitzer) – as the 65th Battery of which Captain Fulton was a member.

With the formation of the Royal Flying Corps, the Air Battalion which had only been in existence for a little over a year became part of the new Service on 13 May 1912. As a result, No. 1 Company at Farnborough became No. 1 Squadron RFC, No. 2 Company at Larkhill became No. 3 Squadron RFC while a new No. 2 Squadron was formed from a core of pilots at Farnborough. However No. 3 Squadron was the only one equipped with aeroplanes and so became the oldest unit in the United Kingdom to fly heavier-than-air machines.[29] The Squadron's first commanding officer was Captain H.R.M. Brooke-Popham who later became Air Chief Marshal Sir Robert Brooke-Popham who died in 1953. Now, after seventy years the Squadron – No. 3 (Fighter) Squadron, Royal Air Force – is still very much in existence and living up to its proud motto *Tertius Primus Erit*, The Third shall be First.

PLATE 8: Original hangars in Wood Lane now used by RAOC as Accommodation Store (see illustration on page 25 for comparison).

By 1913 those concerned were becoming increasingly aware of the value of aircraft and the Report of the School of Gunnery for that year contained the following paragraph:

On a considerable number of occasions aeroplanes located hidden targets and observed and reported each round. The experiments were very successful and should be continued. We began in May with primitive methods but by August we had made much progress. A detailed report on the subject is being submitted by the Officer Commanding No. 2 Royal Flying Squadron.[30]

However flying at Larkhill was now rapidly coming to an end. Horatio Barber had already moved to Hendon in October 1910 where he opened his own flying school and aircraft factory. In June 1913 No. 3 Squadron moved to fresh quarters at Netheravon where a new aerodrome had been built, although it continued to make use of Larkhill until May 1914, when the flying field closed. At the same time the Bristol School moved to Brooklands.[31] After the declaration of war in August 1914 it was not long before a large part of the original flying field was used for the provision of hutted and tented camps which occupied the eastern portion while two branches of the military railway from Amesbury were built across it.

The events of these years have been briefly recorded on a plaque fixed to a stone block that stands on the east side of Wood Road some 26 metres north of the old Bristol Flying School hangars. The wording on the plaque is as follows:

ON THIS SITE THE FIRST AERODROME
FOR THE ARMY WAS FOUNDED IN 1910 BY
CAPTAIN J.D.R. FULTON R.F.A. AND MR. G.B. COCKBURN
THIS LATER BECAME 2 COY AIR BN R.E.
THE BRITISH AND COLONIAL AEROPLANE COMPANY
FORERUNNERS OF THE BRISTOL AEROPLANE COMPANY
ESTABLISHED THEIR FLYING SCHOOL HERE IN 1910
THE FIRST MILITARY AIR TRIALS
WERE HELD HERE IN 1912

4. The First World War

Today, nearly seventy years later, it is difficult to appreciate the tremendous changes which took place at Larkhill during the autumn of 1914, for when war was declared on 4 August the transformation of this area of open country into what has been described as 'a new hutted town' had scarcely begun.[1] In pre-war days, camps such as Hamilton, Fargo Down and Rollestone were simply sites on which tents were erected during the practice season and the Annual Report for 1904 observed that 'A small permanent camp for the staff in the vicinity of Down Barn would be a convenience',[2] but no action appears to have been taken on this. Consequently the first visible effect of the war on Larkhill was a tremendous acceleration in the construction of hutted camps. By the beginning of 1915, thirty of these had been built at Larkhill and four at Rollestone, each capable of accommodating an infantry battalion. The units which occupied them represented almost every arm of the British Army,[3] for it was not until after the School of Artillery had been formed in 1920 that Larkhill became almost exclusively a gunner establishment.

However Larkhill was only one of the centres which were selected in order to provide accommodation for Kitchener's New Army and for troops from overseas, and other camps included Belton Park, Blackdown, Catterick, Longmoor and Rhyl. The problem of finding suitable sites for these new camps was, in some cases, overcome by seeking the advice of local masters of hounds who had a unique knowledge of the country over which they hunted. In the case of Catterick the advice of the Master of Bedale Hounds proved to be of the greatest assistance.

The order for construction of hutted camps was issued on 12th August 1914 and by the 14th complete working drawings for a typical hutted camp of a battalion of infantry at war strength were complete and received the sanction of the Army Council. This rapid result, achieved by the energy and skill of Major B.H.O. Armstrong, R.E., and his chief assistant,

31

Mr. J.D. Michel and their small staff of draughtsmen working day and night, was remarkable.[5]

Major Armstrong later produced a pre-fabricated sectional hut which could be erected quickly and easily and was known as the 'Armstrong Hut'.

However the problem of erection was still to be settled and this was resolved in the following way: Sir John Jackson who was a civil engineer and one of the largest contractors for public works in the country, as well as being the Member of Parliament for Devonport, informed Lord Kitchener that he would be prepared to carry out any constructional work that was required, at cost price. His offer was readily accepted and he was immediately asked to undertake the building of a number of hutted camps of which Larkhill was one. The completion, early in 1915, of the camp at Larkhill was largely due to Sir John Jackson's organisation and efficiency. Since this was the period when railways were pre-eminent as a means of transport, it was decided to provide Larkhill with a railway connection so as to facilitate the construction of the camp and to provide it with transport facilities after its completion. The building of this line was also carried out by Sir John's firm but since he had already built a railway across the Andes from La Paz, the capital of Bolivia, to Arica on the Pacific Coast, it is unlikely that the Larkhill line presented any great difficulties.[6]

Some years before the construction of the railway to Larkhill had begun, the London and South Western Railway – which in 1923 became the Southern Railway – had been granted powers in September 1898 to construct the Amesbury and Military Camp Light Railway. This was built by J.T. Firbank, civil engineering contractors of London and ran from a connection with the main Waterloo–Salisbury line one mile south-east of Newton Tony to Amesbury a distance of four and a half miles. The line was opened in June 1902 and it was intended to continue it to Shrewton but this was never done. However, in anticipation of this extension, the initial engineering work for the proposed branch was carried out for some distance to the west of Amesbury Station, but when it was ultimately decided not to proceed with the line, the site was used to accommodate four sidings. The signal box at Amesbruy was also provided with two levers which were marked Shrewton Box 1 and Box 2 and these remained in position, although unused, until the station was demolished in 1965.[2] Although the Shrewton branch did not materialise, in 1906 the railway was extended for a further three miles through Ratfyn to Bulford and then on to Bulford Camp. During the First World War and in the years immediately preceding it, Amesbury was probably one of the busiest stations in the country and a considerable volume of passenger traffic passed through it at certain times. In June 1952, after 50 years of service, the line was closed to passenger traffic and although goods traffic continued for nearly eleven more years, the line was finally closed in March 1963 and the lifting of the track began in 1965.

When the route for the Larkhill Military Railway was being surveyed, it was decided that the most suitable point at which a connection could be made with the Amesbury-Bulford line would be near Ratfyn, some 640 metres north of Amesbury Station at grid reference 162424 or thereabouts. Although named Ratfyn Junction it was known to local railway workers as Wheelbarrow Junction and facilities were provided at this point for War Department locomotives to take over from those of the London and South Western Railway. From Ratfyn the line curved to the west and after continuing for about 275 metres it passed a loop, two engine sheds and some short sidings, before crossing the River Avon by a girder bridge about 180 metres in length. After passing over the bridge the track proceeded in a straight line for another 180 metres at which point the single track was increased to four but it became single again just before it reached an 'open' level-crossing on the Amesbury–Netheravon road, A345, known as Countess Crossing (reference 153424). Immediately beyond the road a short siding was provided on the north side of the line which swung to the north-west and proceeded in a straight line to grid reference 145431 which is now the south-east corner of Nine Acre Plantation that lies to the south of Fargo Road. At this point the track turned due west and after continuing for about 200 metres one of the main features of the railway was reached. This was a reversing triangle by means of which a locomotive was able to turn, so as to face the opposite direction. At the eastern apex of the triangle, the right hand arm curved northwards towards Larkhill while the left hand arm continued in a south-westerly direction. Approximately 90 metres from the most northerly of the Old King Barrows (reference 137429) this branch came to a dead end alongside which four sidings were built. From here two parallel tracks ran northwards but these became one before joining the line to Larkhill at grid reference 141433 and so completed the triangle.

Just to the north of this point a passing loop and siding were

PLATE 9: View looking north from the present junction of Fargo and Lawson Roads during construction of the camps in 1915. On the right hand skyline are the aircraft hangars. (*T.L. Fuller*)

provided but part of this site is now included in the gardens of some of the houses at Strangways. The line then crossed Fargo Road close to its junction with Lawson Road and after continuing for a short distance, reached a station the site of which is close to the western end of Colquhoun Road. One of the platforms was still in existence in 1983 and could be seen opposite the Strangway Stables which are adjacent to Colquhoun Road. Sidings were also provided at this station and a short branch continued northwards for 485 metres as far as the Packway where it terminated with a siding at reference 140442, that is, approximately opposite Biddulph Road. This branch ran between Camps 2 and 3 which had been erected on the old flying ground and it was presumably built not only in order to serve these two camps but also Camp 10 which was located on the north side of the Packway.

On leaving the station near Colquhoun Road the main line swung to the west but after covering a distance of about 485 metres it turned due north to cross the Packway at an oblique angle, immediately to the west of Lawrence Road and the present Garrison Church. Immediately before crossing the Packway, the line passed a depot and yard of the Royal Engineers which stood on the east side of the track, a loop line being provided so that waggons which were being loaded or unloaded did not obstruct the movement of trains. In recent years a young plantation has been established on the site of the original track bed for a distance of about 915 metres before reaching the Packway. From the road crossing the line followed a straight course towards the site of the present RA Mess but after some 210 metres it curved to the west, just cutting the southern edge of what is now the cricket ground and part of the old embankment could still be seen in 1983. A passing loop was provided on this length. The track then curved to the south to join the Packway at a point close to the entrance to Roberts Barracks and continued to run parallel to the road, on its north side, until it reached what is now the entrance to Ross Road. At a point opposite the junction of Whingates Road and the Packway, two parallel loop lines were built which extended for about 210 metres until the track became single again. Some 65 metres beyond that location, a dead-end siding ran back in a north-easterly direction for about 90 metres. The line then turned to the north and ran roughly parallel to the line of Ross Road for about 155 metres before curving away to the west. Shortly afterwards the railway passed Hamilton Battery (grid reference 121448) where a short spur was provided, presumably in order to transfer ammunition from the railway onto the light tramway which served the guns of the Battery.

Running almost parallel to the Packway the line continued in a westerly direction but at grid reference 116447 the main line turned due south to Druid's Lodge while a branch continued for about a quarter of a mile to Rollestone Camp. Shortly before reaching the camp the line again divided into two sections at reference 106449, one terminating in the Camp at 103449 while the other turned due south and then west to run parallel with the Packway for about 90 metres before it ended at 103446. This branch served the original Fargo Ammunition Depot which was situated on the north side of the Packway, about 200 metres to the west of the present depot. Immediately after crossing the Packway at grid reference 113445, the line became double track and continued as such to a point some 150 metres to the north of Fargo Hospital where a siding was also provided. Beyond the hospital the line curved to the west and cut through Fargo Plantation to cross the Amesbury-Shrewton road (A344) at grid reference 107428. Immediately after crossing the road a short spur some 365 metres long left the main line at 106427. This ran parallel to the road and served the Handley Page hangars of the Royal Naval Air Service which had been erected opposite the south-west corner of Fargo Plantation. From the Shrewton road the railway followed a straight course towards the south-west but at grid reference 102320 a branch some 1,830 metres turned east to Stonehenge Aerodrome which lay on either side of the Wylye Amesbury road (A303). This branch terminated in the aerodrome buildings at 117419. The main line, however, continued to the west of the group of tumuli at 101418 and after passing very close to the western corner of Winterbourne Stoke Clump (reference 101416) it crossed the A303 road immediately to the south. The track then followed an almost straight line until it reached the Salisbury road (A360) at 100408 from which point it ran beside the road for about 1020 metres to reference 100398 where it swung south-eastwards for a short distance to end at grid reference 101396. The object in extending the line to Druid's Lodge was to provide a connection with Lake Down Aerodrome which lay to the east of the point at which the railway terminated. In 1982 a massive water tower was still standing besides the main Salisbury road opposite Druid's Lodge and although several accounts have stated that this tower was erected in order to provide water for the locomotives of the Larkhill Military Railway, this was not in fact the case. It was built in connection with the water supply to the camp buildings and hangars[8] and the railway did not extend as far as the tower.

The total track length of the railway from Ratfyn Junction to Druid's Lodge including all the branches and the reversing triangle but omitting the sidings, amounted to approximately 17,360 metres (18,985 yards) or 10.78 miles. On the other hand the length of the main line alone, omitting the various branches and reversing triangle, covered a distance of some 11,765 metres (12,870 yards) or 7.31 miles. Construction of the railway began in 1914 and continued into the next year and owing to the urgency of the situation, as soon as a section was completed it came into operation. When HM King George V and Queen Mary inspected the Canadian troops at Larkhill in 1915, they travelled on the railway (see Plate 11, page 38).

The line was worked by a railway company of the Royal Engineers the personnel of which were accommodated in a small camp which was situated on the east side of the Amesbury-Upavon road (A345) at its intersection with the railway at Countess Crossing (grid reference 153425). Two engine sheds, a loop line and short sidings were built between Ratfyn Junction and the bridge over the river, the references of the two sheds being 159426 and 160425 respectively. Little information is available regarding the locomotives which worked on the line but photographs of two have survived. The first, which was used in the construction of the

PLATE 10: Larkhill Military Railway. 0–4–0 tank locomotive 'Queen Mary'.

railway was a 0-4-0 saddle tank named 'Queen Mary' (Plate 10, page 37) and was presumably retained for use on the line after it had been completed. This engine figures in a painting by Miss Joan Wanklyn which is now hanging in the RA Mess at Larkhill. It has been suggested that the locomotive received its name in commemoration of the Royal visit to Larkhill in 1915. The second engine was a 0-6-0 side tank (Plate 11, below) which appears to have a name-plate fixed to the tank but unfortunately the name is not discernible. It has not been possible to obtain any information as to the rolling stock which was used on the line, although there may have been a limited number of War Department wagons for local use. However, it is probable the great majority were either the property of the various railway companies or were privately owned and were used in the delivery of stores and materials to Larkhill.

PLATE 11: HM King George V with FM Lord Kitchener, leaving Larkhill after inspecting Canadian Troops. (*T.L. Fuller*)

As in other matters relating to the railway, there is little precise information as to its closure and the subsequent lifting of the track which took place over a number of years. Lieutenant-Colonel E. Woodhouse R.E. has recorded the position three years after the end of the war:

There were still two active Camp Railways in 1921, Catterick and Larkhill. About 140 men were on detachment working them. The organisation was troublesome under peace conditions, however well it worked during the War. The Northern Command in particular did not like the idea of the Catterick line being administered from Longmoor, and there was continual friction with the temporary officer in charge of it, whose methods were decidedly irregular at times . . . The Larkhill line was a smaller show, carrying no passenger traffic and gave less trouble; it was also run by a temporary officer. Negotiations for handing over the Catterick line to the L.N.E.R. were in hand when I left in 1924 and Larkhill closed down soon after.[9]

Although Colonel Woodhouse stated that the line did not carry any passenger traffic, there was one exception to this. In 1924 it was the normal practice for a passenger carriage to be standing just to the north of the Packway Crossing (near the church) every Saturday at 1300 hours. A small platform had been built at this point and anyone wishing to do so could board the carriage. On its arrival at Amesbury Station, the carriage would be attached to the Salisbury train. This was always a very popular arrangement with those who had weekend leave.[10] The first parts of the line to be closed were the sections from Fargo Hospital to Stonehenge Aerodrome and Druid's Lodge and these had been lifted by 1923.[11] The 1926 edition of the 6in Ordnance Survey (sheet Wiltshire LIV SW), revised in 1923, shows the railway terminating at the Fargo Hospital. Beyond this point the line of the trackbed which passed through Fargo Plantation is marked as 'Railway (Dismantled)'. Mr. E.J. Chivers of Messrs. W.E. Chivers & Sons Ltd., who was working at Larkhill during this period, recalls that in 1928 the railway had ceased to operate although much of the line was still in position.[12] One source stated that by 1932 most of the track had been lifted.[13] Any track that remained had been removed by 1937.

Although more than fifty years have passed since the Larkhill Military Railway ceased to function, in 1983 it is still possible to find evidence of its existence and this is especially so between Countess Crossing and the Packway. From the site of the bridge over the Avon to the Amesbury–Netheravon road, the course of the line is indicated by two parallel hedges but after crossing the road the old track bed can be seen even more clearly: because it is now a well-used footpath, the surface growth has been kept to a minimum. Cuttings and embankments are still well preserved and much of the reversing triangle to the south-east of Strangways can be easily recognised. Major (now Brigadier) D.F. Ryan has

referred to the apple trees growing along the side of the track
which are said to have grown from applecores thrown out by
troops from passing trains.[14] Whether this is true or not, the fact
remains that there are now a noticeable number of apple trees
growing in the hedges and on the embankments for much of the
length between Countess Crossing and Fargo Road. These are
scattered indiscriminately and show no indication of having been
planted, which would certainly lend support to the applecore
theory.

On the north side of Fargo Road the track bed has been planted
with trees but the old platform near the junction of Lawson and
Colquhoun Roads can still be found despite the dense growth of
bushes and brambles which covers it. Although the immediate
vicinity of the original station site is now part of a young plantation, the line of the track can be seen very easily beyond the
northern boundary of the wood.

On approaching the Packway, trees have again been established
on the line of the track while the footpath continues along the
eastern edge of the plantation. After crossing the Packway and
entering the main Garrison Area, little evidence of the railway
remains except for part of an embankment on the edge of the
cricket field, and it is only after passing the western boundary
of the Anti-Tank Compound (reference 118447) that signs of the
track appear again. From here the line of the railway is marked by
a track as far as grid reference 103449 and the embankment at
116447 which carried the line to Druid's Lodge can still be seen.
But to the south of the Packway no further evidence of this once
busy railway now exists.

As well as the many hutted camps which were constructed, a
number of shops and 'welfare buildings' were erected on the edge
of the Packway which were sited rather nearer to the Garrison
Church than they are at the present time. The shops included the
firms of Bollens Fruit Stores, Valters & Co., Newsagents, and
Sergeants Empire Stores and Restaurant, and among the welfare
buildings were the Young Men's Christian Association, more
generally known as the 'YMCA', the Salvation Army 'Soldier's
Home' and the Military Cinema.

Before the war the road system at Larkhill was very limited in
extent and an Ordnance Survey map, which had been revised in
1914,[15] only showed the Packway; a road from a point opposite
the south end of Glover Road to the south-east corner of Larkhill
Camp (reference 130438); Martinbushes Road and a track which
now forms Tombs Road and the eastern end of Fargo Road. The

PLATE 12: The Packway in 1915 looking east from a point near the site of the Garrison Church. The whiteness is caused by chalk dust blowing off the untarred road. (*T.L. Fuller*)

PLATE 13: The same view in 1982, seen from the Garrison Church.
(*RSA Reprographics*)

reason for this was the simple fact that until the beginning of the war there was little need for any additional roads. The horse was still the main source of motive power for the Army and, since Larkhill only functioned as a tented practice camp during the summer months, horse drawn vehicles and equipment could move across country without difficulty.

With the outbreak of war the position changed fundamentally; not only were thirty-four hutted camps built but these were in use all the year round, while the tremendous expansion in the number of personnel resulted in a proportionate increase in the quantity of rations and stores to be handled, quite apart from the continual movement of large numbers of troops. It was for these reasons that the railway was constructed but it was limited in its scope and extent, and roads were needed to move men and supplies between the railway and the various camps and in areas that were not served by the railway. The new roads were made almost entirely of chalk which became sticky in wet weather while in dry periods the passing traffic raised clouds of white dust that settled on guns, horses, clothes and tents. Plate 12 (page 41) showing the Packway in 1915 gives a good idea of the road conditions during this period.

For some years before the war there were signs that the mechanisation of road transport was not far distant and this appeared first in the form of steam traction engines and steam lorries, and subsequently as petrol-driven cars and heavy motor vehicles. At first these were used mainly for civilian purposes but in due course they were adopted by the War Department. Traction engines were used throughout the Boer War and Major J.L.B. Templer to whom reference has already been made in connection with the operation of balloons, was sent out to South Africa in November 1899 as Director of Steam Road Transport.[16] Further information on this subject will be found in *Military Traction Engines and Lorries 1858-1918*.[17]

In this changing scene, a not uncommon sight in and around Bulford, Tidworth and Larkhill were the traction engines, trailers and steam lorries belonging to Messrs W.E. Chivers & Sons of Devizes. Later this firm concentrated on building and civil-engineering work to the extent that they carried out the erection of most of the recent buildings at Larkhill. Although the firm had supplied both mechanical and horse-drawn transport to Bulford Camp before the war, this greatly increased when the War Department awarded the firm a contract in 1914. The work included the haulage of baggage and equipment, the delivery of rations, the supply of firewood to field kitchens and, at one period, the conveyance of ten tons of bread every night from Salisbury to Tidworth, in two large covered wagons hauled by a traction engine. Messrs Chivers also supplied motor buses and charabancs which can be described as open single-deck coaches, as well as petrol-driven lorries. All of these had to be started by hand and this could provide a considerable challenge on cold mornings when it was sometimes necessary for three men to haul on a rope attached to the starting handle.[18]

In addition to the massive constructional programme which was undertaken at Larkhill, three aerodromes were also built in the immediate neighbourhood. The first of these which has frequently been referred to as the 'Handley-Page Hangars' was a Royal Naval Air Service Flying School.[19] Built in 1915–16 on the south side of the Stonehenge–Shrewton road (A344) opposite the south-west corner of Fargo Plantation (grid reference 109427), its purpose was to train naval pilots to fly the 0/400 type Handley-Page bombers.[20] In 1983 the site of the hangars was still marked by an area of broken concrete on which scattered bushes were growing.

The second airfield known as Stonehenge Aerodrome lay some 500 metres to the south-west of Stonehenge, the camp being divided into two parts by the A303 road. On the north side of the road were situated the airfield, three hangars and the administrative buildings; the living quarters occupied the south side. This was the headquarters of the Royal Flying Corps' School of Navigation and Bomb Dropping. It was closed shortly after the end of the war and for a few years the buildings were used as a farm, being shown on the 1926 edition of the Ordnance Survey 6in map as 'Stonehenge Pedigree Stock Farm'.

In 1926 the buildings were purchased by Messrs W.E. Chivers & Sons, Ltd, and demolished in the following year since it was considered that they detracted from the amenity of Stonehenge.[21] For the same reason, a pair of cottages and a bungalow which stood some 300 metres to the east of Stonehenge were also pulled down. The third aerodrome, Lake Down, lay two miles to the south-west of Stonehenge on the east side of the Devizes–Salisbury road (A360) and a little to the north of Druid's Lodge. It was occupied by No. 2 Training Depot Station of the Royal Flying Corps which had been formed in August 1917 in order to train pilots in day bombing. Although it was only completed in 1917 it was closed soon after the end of the war and was demolished in 1919 or thereabouts.[22]

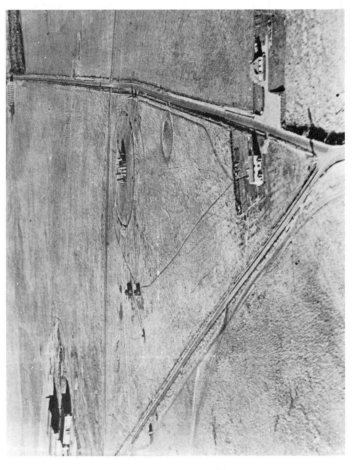

PLATE 14: Stonehenge after the First War. In the top left corner is the RFC, School of Navigation and in the top right, part of Fargo Plantation with the RNAS Flying School on the opposite side of the road. The pair of cottages and bungalow near the junction of the A303 and A344 roads have since been demolished. (*P.R.G. Gutteridge*)

With the tremendous influx of troops into the Larkhill area, action had to be taken to provide medical services and early in 1915 a military hospital was built immediately to the north of Fargo Plantation and partly on the site of the old Fargo Camp later known as Fargo Down Camp.[23] Apparently the site had previously been occupied by an isolation hospital for horses, but very little information is available on this point.[24] The name 'Fargo' was originally applied to a field that was 'in the far north-east corner' of the parish of Winterbourne Stoke which lies immediately to the west of Larkhill.[25] It is likely to have received this name because it lay a far distance or a 'far go' from the centre of the parish.

No sooner had war been declared than offers of help were received from those countries which were members of the British Empire and in a short time troops from many parts of the world were on their way to the United Kingdom. Amongst the first to arrive were the Canadians and the experiences of Major W.A. Wilson, taken from his diary, are given below. He had joined up in the ranks of the Victoria Fusiliers at Victoria, in Vancouver Island, on 8 August 1914 'as the artillery is up to strength' but by the end of September he had transferred as a gunner to the 2nd Battery of the Canadian Field Artillery (the prefix 'Royal' was not conferred until 1935).

We sailed from Gaspé Bay (Quebec) on October 2nd in convoy and landed at Plymouth on October 16th and went by train to Amesbury. As our horses had been so long on board they were not considered fit to pull any vehicles and we marched from Amesbury, leading our horses, to a tented camp at Westdown North, Salisbury Plain. It consisted of bell tents, 13 men to a tent and the horse lines were very muddy. The first thing as far as I was concerned was to get rid of the lice I had collected on the ship. My mother sent a complete change of under-clothing, I had a sort of bath and burnt the infected clothes, resulting in no more lice. We settled down to training.

King George V accompanied by Lord Roberts and General Kitchener reviewed us in terrible weather with squally rain. We paraded, mounted, at 7.00 a.m.; it consisted of Mount, Dismount, On Cloaks, Off Cloaks. His Majesty arrived at 2.0 p.m. We got back to camp about 4.0 p.m. wet through. I was now a gunner and one snag was doing Gun Park Guard.

By this time we had moved to Greenlands Farm and the Gun Park was on a very exposed hill, bitterly cold in January. From there we moved to billets in Devizes, what luxury! The town's inhabitants treated us royally. After a stay of a couple of weeks, we did a night march to a place where we entrained for Plymouth; there we were loaded on to a ship. On arrival at St. Nazaire we went by train to near Ploegstreet – 'Plug Street'.[26]

West Down North Camp, which is referred to in the above extract, was not on the site of the present West Down Camp but lay some 2650 metres to the north-east of it. Major Wilson was commissioned into the Special Reserve on 16 July 1916 and posted to 54 Battery which was then taking part in the Battle of the Somme.[27]

Another account of the weather which could be expected on the Plain during the winter has been left by Brigadier F. FitzGibbon who was commandant at the School from 1939 to 1942.

My first sight of Larkhill was in December 1915 when I took my (Kitchener) battery there to practice before going to France. We marched from a hutted camp at Fovant (9 miles west of Salisbury) to a tented one at Larkhill, practised from our position at Knighton Down the next day and back to Fovant again on the third day. I do not think it ceased to rain at all during that period.[28]

In February 1915, six months after the outbreak of war, an Army Council Instruction was issued of which the following is an extract:

It has been decided to establish, as a temporary measure, a new school of instruction for R.H. and R.F.A. near Larkhill, Salisbury Plain.

The new school will be on the lines of that already existing at Shoeburyness . . .

The G.O.C.-in-C., Southern Command, will arrange for the provision of temporary accommodation for the school in or near Camp No. 14, south of Knighton Down . . . In providing this accommodation the fact should not be lost sight of that it may ultimately be necessary to move the school to the site near Durrington Walls, to which it had been decided before the war that the School of Gunnery for Horse and Field Artillery at Shoeburyness would probably be transferred. New buildings should therefore be of a type which could be moved if necessary . . .

The GOC-in-C, Eastern Command, will arrange for one

section of the instructional battery now at Shoeburyness to be moved to Salisbury Plain as soon as the necessary accommodation is available. This section will form the nucleus of the instructional battery to be formed at the new school. The GOC-in-C, Eastern Command, will also arrange for the transfer to the new school of such portion of the instructional staff of the School of Instruction at Shoeburyness as the Commandant may decide he can spare without materially reducing the efficiency of the latter institution.[29]

At last the long-awaited establishment of a School for Royal Horse and Royal Field Artillery at Larkhill had been authorised and this proved to be a permanent arrangement rather than the 'temporary measure' envisaged by the Army Council Instruction. Camp No. 14 occupied the land which now lies between Brind Road, Glover Road and Knighton Down and forms part of Alanbrooke Barracks while the anticipated transfer of the School to Durrington Walls failed to materialise.

The Monthly Army List for May 1915 contains the first reference to this new organisation when, below the overall title of 'School of Gunnery', details of the new establishments were given under the following subheadings'

School of Instruction for Royal Horse and Royal Field Artillery
(Shoeburyness)
School of Instruction for Royal Horse and Royal Field Artillery
(Lark Hill)

At Larkhill the staff consisted of a chief instruction in gunnery, two major instructors, four captain instructors, and a quartermaster while Shoeburyness had a similar establishment except that there were five captain instructors. The first chief instructor at Larkhill was Brevet Lieutenant-Colonel W. Ellershaw, RA who had previously been an 'instructor of courses at Netheravon in the co-operation between artillery and aircraft'.[30] The commandants of the School are given in Appendix V.

The School provided courses for those who were already serving at the front as well as for those who had recently joined the Regiment.

My next experience was a course for B.Cs from active service during the winter 1916–17, the first part at Shoebury and the second at Larkhill. Safety precautions were much less stringent

than those of a later date and we were told that the course
before ours had had one or two casualties. One of the Instructors was Major – subsequently Major-General – Newcome who
did much to set the pattern for the post-war era of the School.
The spectators stood around well within the splinter area, to
watch bursts from 18-pr and 4.5 in. and 6 in. hows. It made a
pleasant break in a very cold winter in Flanders.[31]

Another glimpse of life on a course during the First World War is
given in the following letter which was written at Larkhill on
7 May 1916 by Lieutenant J.M. Couper, RFA to his sister. He was
wounded in March 1918 and died in German hands on 4 April.
This letter and also the letter heading on page 49 (Plate 15) are
reproduced by kind permission of Major T.F. Couper, RA.

> I have arrived here safely, but understand that the course
> only takes a week at the outside; there are only 15 of us, all
> back from the front, and we go straight back on completion of
> the course. It is quite comfortable here but very dreary and
> monotonous if you had to stay here any length of time.
>   It is not worthwhile sending anything here but could you
> please send me some summer underthings out to the Battery.
> If you send out my summer breaches too, I can get them
> mended free of charge. There is a professional tailor in the
> Forfar Battery.
>   This is a pleasant change. The Battery is still at Arras,[32]

Reference has already been made to the large number of overseas units which came to Britain's assistance after 4 August 1914
and, to assist in their training, an additional centre of instruction
was set up in October 1916 not far from Larkhill. At first it was
known as the Overseas Artillery School but after a short time the
name was changed to the Chapperton Down Artillery School.

> In the First World War Gunnery and Artillery schools sprang up
> all over the place in all theatres; and some of them taught some
> very queer gunnery. Then in the autumn of 1916, to meet the
> necessity for a degree of standardization of methods and
> terminology, a School was set up on Salisbury Plain called the
> Overseas Artillery School (shortly after renamed the Chapper-
> ton Down Artillery School). This School taught no observation
> of fire; a great deal of shooting took place but it all took the
> form of demonstrations. The School Headquarters was billeted

SCHOOL OF INSTRUCTION,

R.H & R.F.A.

LARK HILL,

SALISBURY.

PLATE 15: Notepaper heading of 1916. (*T.F. Couper*)

in extreme comfort in the thirteenth-century 'Old George Inn', still to be seen in the High Street, Salisbury. The courses used to motor out to Chapperton Down, on the present Imber Ranges, where firing was carried out.[33]

An Ordnance Survey map of the Chitterne area, dated 1916, shows a number of gun positions, observation posts and 'enemy trenches' which appear to have been used as targets and possibly for practising trench warfare.[34] The target areas, OPs and four gun positions are shown to the west of the Shrewton–Tilshead–West Lavington road (A360) and three gun positions to the east of the road. The names of these gun positions and their grid references were as follows:

East of A360 road

Fiddington Farm Position	028528
Field Barn Position	021497
Greenland Farm Position	066475

West of A360 road

Berril Position	996472
Barrow Position	003483
Rings Position	008487
Peels Position	018490

The target areas which were marked on the map and lay to the west of the road, were:

The Diamond	957458
Wonder Work	990478
Unnamed	971462

As the range from the Greenland Farm Position to the nearest marked target area (Wonder Work) was approximately 7,300 metres (8,000 yards) and to the furthest (The Diamond) 11,000 metres (12,000 yards), it is probable that this position was used when the heavier types of equipment were being fired.

Although it is recorded that the School at Chapperton Down was established in the autumn of 1916, no reference to it appears in the Monthly Army Lists until September 1918, when full details of the staff were given. This is probably because during the first two years of its existence Chapperton Down was considered to be a part of the School of Instruction for Royal Horse and Royal Field Artillery and that it was not granted independent status until August 1918.

The Army List for September gives an establishment of a commandant, a staff captain, a chief instructor of gunnery, a superintendent and assistant superintendent of experiments, three major instructors in gunnery, three captain instructors and a quarter master.[35] The first commandant was Brigadier-General W.B. Browell, CMG a great uncle of Colonel J.M. Browell, MBE who was appointed Deputy Commandant of the Royal School of Artillery and Deputy Garrison Commander in 1978. The second and last commandant was Colonel H.W. Newcome, DSO (afterwards Major-General H.W. Newcome, CB, CMG, DSO) who subsequently became the first Commandant of the new School of Artillery when it was formed in January 1920 and Chapperton Down was combined with it.[36]

During the early part of the war, probably in 1915, a mixed battery of heavy guns and howitzers was deployed in the area which is now (1983) occupied by the Anti-Tank Compound. The battery consisted of two 9.2 in howitzers on semi-permanent emplacements and one 8 in gun and one 6 in on wheeled carriages which could be removed to a gun park when not in use.[37] This was known as the Hamilton Battery and, although no records are available, it would seem very probable that both the Hamilton Battery and Hamilton Camp were named after General Sir Ian Hamilton, GCB, DSO who was GOC Southern Command from

PLATE 16: Traction engines belonging to Messrs W.E. Chivers & Sons hauling baggage for the Canadian Army, 1914.
(*W.E. Chivers & Sons*)

1905 to 1909. Though he was not a gunner, having been commissioned into the Gordon Highlanders, he took great interest in Larkhill and visited the Practice Camp on several occasions notably in 1905, 1907 and 1908.[38]

The battery was situated immediately to the north of the Larkhill Military Railway, the grid reference of the centre of the battery being 121448. Ammunition was brought up on a tramway which ran behind the guns in a south-west to north-east direction, crossing the railway at reference 110447. The main section of the tramway was 685 metres (750 yards) long with an additional loop line of 230 metres (250 yards) which ran through a storage shed. In the early 1930s the battery featured in a film entitled *Battle of the Somme* and although the tramway was lifted in 1936,[39] the 9.2 in howitzers were still in position in 1937 but had been removed by the end of 1939 when it is probable that they were transferred to the British Expeditionary Force in France.

In conclusion, some idea of life at Larkhill during the first war has been provided in an account by the late Brigadier B.G. Mason, from which the following extracts have been taken.

Up to 1918 the RA Practice Camp was used for newly formed RFA (Kitchener's) New Army Brigades of Divisional Artilleries prior to proceeding to France. These Brigades were located at Larkhill and in the neighbourhood e.g. Codford Valley, and shot under their C's RA, and under the very critical eye of the Inspector RA, General Brunker, who was a tiger and a fire eater of the top class, especially to young officers at the OP. He was greatly feared by all!

Officers went direct to the OPs in MT by 0900 where IGs put them through their paces. The battery position I remember best of all was the northern edge of Blackball Firs, firing over Shrewton Folly towards Slay Down. Imagine the picture in the winter - battery in the open in mud, to harness up and march out to Blackball Firs and to be laid on zero lines by 0900 (whatever the weather), while the course officers arrived at the OPs at the same time, and Range Parties (horsed) had to have the red flags up by then too. If it was foggy or snowy, as it often was, we had to stand and shiver (we certainly burned braziers of wood in Blackball Firs!) till the IG in charge opened the shooting and visibility was OK. The battery often did not get back in the winter till after dark, wet and weary. The command 'End of Practice' was music in our ears.

Larkhill in 1917-18 was virtually a camp cut off in the

middle of Salisbury Plain. Sunny and attractive for a horsed unit in the summer, but quite awful - mud and duckboards - in the winter. There was a ramshackle one-decker bus that plied to and from Salisbury and Tidworth (where the Reserve Cavalry Regiments Depot was). However it was the practice of young officers (like myself) to go for a night out to Salisbury mounted, with a horse holder between two or three of us, to the Chough Inn where we stabled our horses while we drank and fed at the Haunch of Venison, went to the local Hippodrome afterwards, and then rode home again, usually by the Avon Valley un-metalled road through Lake. It was, of course, all great fun to do just that - once I rode with others by moonlight across country back to camp. In the summer of 1917 there were local show jumping and horse show events - I remember competing with Colonel Gibbon on the horse show ground outside A Mess (the only mess then) on the south side.

As regards accommodation, the huts had corridors and rooms leading off to each officer's quarters, about six to eight to a hut. Heated by stoves, they were either red hot or stone cold as when the batmen drew fuel, they knew it was meant to be burnt and we all shivered the latter part of each week. It was not unusual to find unbreakable ice on one's ewer and jug in the morning in winter when reveille was always in the dark. There was no question of wearing gumboots - always field boots and spurs - but for early morning parades galoshs (bought from a shoe shop in Salisbury) or rubber overshoes were allowed over one's feet in Field boots, only when dismounted, i.e. at stables, without spurs.[40]

Finally, whilst admiring the tremendous efforts which brought about the development of Larkhill during the First World War, one should not forget the thousands who trained here before leaving for overseas. Many of them fought on the Western Front but did not return and it was of them and not of Larkhill, that Lieutenant-Colonel John McCrae wrote

> the crosses; row on row,
> That mark our place; and in the sky
> The larks, still bravely singing, fly
> Scarce heard amid the guns below.[41]

5. Between the Wars

As might be expected, the end of the war was followed by a feeling of anti-climax with thousands of men awaiting demobilisation and, in the case of overseas units, repatriation. Larkhill did not escape this atmosphere of decline and lack of purpose as can be appreciated from the following description.

A straggling sprawl of huts on both sides of the Packway, many in obvious need of repair, gave Larkhill, in early 1919, the appearance of a rather seedy, down at the heel, shanty town. It was indeed, a somewhat war weary encampment. The permanent Gunner enclave, on the high ground near Knighton Down, was the one area in which the various 'lines' had obviously been laid out in a purposeful way. Elsewhere it was all too evident that further groups of huts had been rushed up to meet the urgent needs of the moment, without any concerted attempt at overall planning. Away over towards Durrington there was a 'cage' still occupied by several hundred German POWs. South of the Packway a large incinerator displayed its presence by a slowly drifting plume of black smoke.

The Packway itself more or less bisected the camp, and along it could be found the Garrison Church, two Banks, the Post Office, the YMCA, as well as a collection of small shops. The only cinema had, a few days previously, been totally destroyed in a disastrous fire. Now only a few charred uprights marked the site. Canadian soldiers were everywhere, as all spare accommodation had been made available to them, as a vast transit camp, whilst ships were assembled for their repatriation. It was not exactly a prepossessing sight and yet . . . I soon came to have a great affection for Salisbury Plain, an affection that remains with me to this day.[1]

However, in spite of its rather depressing appearance action was being taken to concentrate instruction in gunnery at Larkhill. The first step was the amalgamation of the Chapperton Down Artillery School and the Heavy Artillery Gunnery School with the School

LARKHILL GARRISON AREA SHOWING THE BOUNDARIES OF THE OLD CAMPS OF 1914–15

N

1

Officers Married Quarters

4

5

Strangways

6

2

10

Stirling Barracks

3

School of Artillery

11

Church

12

Hockey Ground

13

14

Alanbrooke Barracks

Officer's Mess

8

9

Scale: 0 100 200 300 metres

20

18

Parade Ground

Roberts Barracks

15

School

21

24

19

16

22

26

25

28

17

23

29

Horne Barracks

The Packway

Officers Mess

27

30

of Instruction for Royal Horse and Royal Field Artillery in accordance with an Army Council Instruction dated 4 December 1919.[2] Under the title of 'School of Artillery' this laid down that 'The Schools named ... will be combined as The School of Artillery', and that 'In future all correspondence for these Schools will be addressed to the School of Artillery, Larkhill, Salisbury Plain.' Little has been recorded about the Heavy Artillery Gunnery School which is mentioned in the ACI, and what seems to be the first reference to it appeared in the Monthly Army List for September 1918, under the title of 'School of Gunnery – Heavy Artillery Training Centre'. This centre had been formed at Woolwich in September 1916 and had moved to Winchester in 1917 where it remained until it was transferred to Larkhill in 1919.[3] In September 1918 Lieutenant-Colonel H.E.J. Brake (afterwards Brigadier-General) was Commandant of the School. During the same year the School of Gunnery at Shoeburyness was renamed the Coast Artillery School[4] and in 1920 the recently formed Anti-Aircraft Artillery School was established at Ludgershall although it subsequently moved to Biggin Hill in 1923.

While the formation of the new School of Artillery was announced in the ACI of 4 December 1919, the date of its establishment is generally taken to be 1 January 1920. However as arrangements presumably had to be made regarding accommodation, organisation and administration, it was not until July that it became fully operative.[5] The full staff of the School, as shown in the Monthly Army List for January 1921 consisted of a commandant, brigade major, staff captain, adjutant, assistant adjutant, quarter master, two chief instructors in gunnery, six major instructors in gunnery (artillery), two major instructors in gunnery (survey), seven captain instructors (artillery), two captain instructors (survey) and a superintendent of experiments – a total of twenty-six. One of the chief instructors in gunnery and one of the captain instructors in gunnery (survey) were Royal Engineers and one of the major instructors in gunnery (survey) was a Royal Marine. The first commandant of the School was Brigadier-General H.W. Newcome who had been the last commandant of Chapperton Down while the first chief instructor who was responsible for gunnery was Lieutenant-Colonel P. Suther.

In 1916 the School of Instruction for Royal Horse and Royal Field Artillery occupied Camps Nos 11 and 14[6] but after the formation of the School of Artillery, instruction on the various types of equipment was allocated to different camps. Camp No. 11 dealt with the 9.2 in howitzer and also contained the lecture rooms; No. 14 was concerned with the 13 pounder, 18 pounder, and 4.5 in howitzer; No. 16 covered the 60 pounder and 6 in howitzer while No. 18 accommodated the Survey Section.[7] The boundaries of these camps are shown on the map facing page 55 superimposed over the present layout of the School. The work of the School at the time of its formation has been defined as follows:

> the School of Artillery, Larkhill, was responsible for providing qualified field artillery instructors for assisting in the training of Regular and Territorial units, for carrying out trials of new equipment, for staging fire-power demonstrations, and for writing artillery training manuals and pamphlets.[8]

During 1921 the Seige Artillery School at Lydd moved to Larkhill and became part of the School of Artillery.

Of the numerous courses which were run by the School between the wars, the basic one was the Gunnery Staff Course but as the School expanded and developed, so the number and type of courses increased and the following became available.[9]

Officers	*Soldiers*
Gunnery Staff Course	Gunnery Staff Course
Senior officers	Permanent staff instructors
Brigade commanders	Battery commanders assistants
Majors and captains	NCOs, Regular Army
Adjutants, Territorial Army	NCOs, Territorial Army
Subalterns	University Officers' Training
Gun position officers	Corps
Observation of fire	Other ranks battery staff
Counter bombardment	duties
	Survey

The NCOs Gunnery Staff Course which spent the first three to four months at Woolwich before moving on to Larkhill, was attended by representatives of all the branches of the Regiment and the following is an account of the 27th Gunnery Staff Course which arrived at the School in January 1935:

> However, Christmas was upon us; so farewell to Woolwich and we reassembled at Larkhill in the New Year. Here, at the Mecca of all Field Gunners, we left the general and got down to the particular. For the first month or so, we were lectured upon, or gave lectures ourselves on all the School's equipments. At that

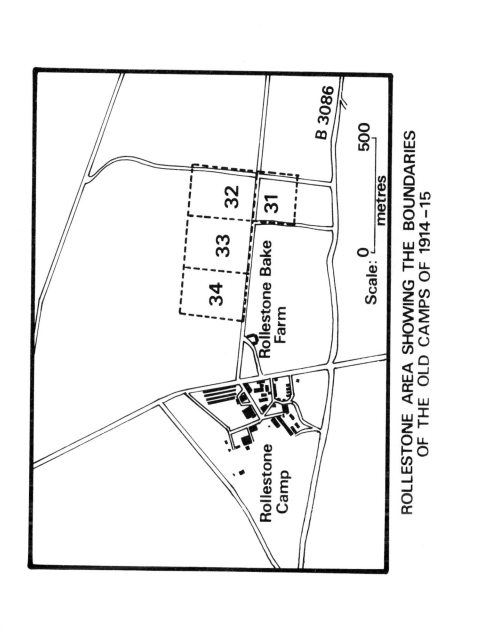

ROLLESTONE AREA SHOWING THE BOUNDARIES
OF THE OLD CAMPS OF 1914–15

time these were the 18 pr, 3.7 in and 4.5 in Hows, 60 pr, 6 in Mk XIX (I think), 8 in and 9.2 in Hows. We drilled on all these equipments until we could quote chapter and verse from all their drill books. We did Miniature Range and lectures on Fire Discipline until we knew Artillery Training Vol. II back to front and upside down. We surveyed our way round the Plain until we knew the six-figure co-ordinates of every tree, stone or building within sight (or almost).

Then, after about a month, we varied this by going out and firing on the ranges once or twice a week. Most of the shooting was done with 18 pdrs, presumably for economic reasons; however, we did shoot off every one of the weapons mentioned at one time or another. I think the ammunition allotted to the course was something like 1,200 rounds of 18 pdr per student down to something like perhaps half a round of 9.2in.

Naturally the Field Gunners on the course were in their element here. Coast Gunners, accustomed to their guns being bolted down, were a little surprised when they pulled the trigger to find themselves going backwards at the rate of knots. The firing platform for the 18 pdr (later used on the 25 pr) had only recently been introduced and was not always used. On one such occasion when one such individual had pulled the trigger on an 18 pdr and the gun had fired he, from his position as layer (No. 3), shouted 'Run-up' (the process for moving the gun back to its original position). The acting No. 1 wasn't having this and told him, in no uncertain terms, to 'Shut up. I'm the No. 1 on this shoot'. To which the response was yet another yell, agonised this time, of 'Run up, for . . . . . sake run up, the . . . . . gun's on my foot'.

Whilst at Larkhill we went up in an observation balloon a couple of times to see what it was like and to observe fire. We also had a trip round in an open cockpit aeroplane to let us see what problems the observation of artillery fire presented to a pilot. Apart from saying it looked as though he needed about eight arms to do all the things he was supposed to do, I'll leave it at that.[10]

In 1926 the first of the Young Officers' Courses was held at Larkhill for young newly commissioned officers and an account of these and of the Young Officers' Branch will be found in Chapter 9.

After the First World War life at Larkhill settled down to a regular peacetime rhythm and the fact that horses were still very much in evidence, added greatly to its attractions.

The weather had its ups and downs, and I soon discovered how wet and cheerless the Plain can be when it really tries. But there were many marvellous days too. One particular morning is etched in my memory. The omens were good. Nick had inspected the Section before we moved off, and had given us quite a pat on the back. During the night there had been just a touch of frost, and the going was crisp under hoof. The sun, rising behind us, was starting to break through the early morning mist. We trotted briskly along the down, and soon Rollestone could be seen ahead. The Section was in line, guns leading, followed by their respective wagons. I rode well out to a flank, as Richards had taught me, so that I could easily see the whole Section. 'Mischief', my Charger, her ears pricked forwards, had settled down by now, and was striding out with a beautifully level action. The Nos. 1 and Coverers had dropped back, and were riding alongside the limbers, from where they could keep an eye on their teams. Driver Rowell, my horseholder, brought up the rear. Gunners and Drivers all looked a bit bulky in Greatcoats, and they tended to lean forward, bracing themselves against the keen, leaping wind. The four, evenly matched, bay teams made a splendid picture. Here and there a horse snorted, sending a cloud of vapour over its head. Apart from this, I could hear, every now and then, the clip-clop-clop of fast moving hooves on rutted turf; the snap and clink as traces suddenly tightened hard on swingletrees; and, overall, the characteristic and peculiar noise of the wheels rotating on their bearings. Whitened headropes swinging from side to side in rhythmic movement seemed a perfect adornment for the trotting horses. The sun was a little higher now, and as we turned north for The Bustard, its slanting rays were beginning to highlight the strange looking camouflage on guns and limbers, and to reflect from highly burnished steel and polished brass.

I tell you it was pure magic as we trotted on our way that April morning. Now, over 60 years later, I can still see the scene in my mind's eyes, and conjure up the same thrill. Here (or should it be there?) was I, a subaltern with barely three months service, and these were my guns, my horses and my men. At the moment of which I write, I would not have contemplated changing jobs with anyone – no, not for all the tea in China. Of course there have been other nostalgic moments in my life, but none that can quite compare with that Spring day, so long ago, when my Section was swinging along towards Chapperton Down.[11]

Although the strength of the Larkhill Garrison had been considerably reduced after the war, it was still slightly larger in the 1920s, when it consisted of four major artillery units, namely, the School of Artillery, a field brigade, a medium brigade and a survey company, than it was in 1976.[12] The School occupied two of the original hutted camps which had been constructed in the early days of the war. One of these was known as North Lines or North Barracks and occupied the area between Brackenbury Road and the present Demonstration Area which now forms the major part of Alanbrooke Barracks. The other camp Stirling Lines, stood on the area which is at present occupied by the headquarters of the School together with that part of the present Alanbrooke Barracks which lies between Brackenbury Road and Glover Road. The field brigade was stationed in Roberts Lines which at that time lay in an area which today is bounded by Power Road, a line in prolongation of Cator Road, Brackenbury Road and the RA Mess. The medium brigade occupied Dickson Lines which were situated between Roberts Lines and Watson Road while the survey company was accommodated in Horne Lines which lay on the west side of Watson Road and opposite Dickson Lines.[13]

In 1919 RQMS G.W. Thompson was posted to Larkhill after serving in France for most of the First World War and the following description of life at Larkhill between 1919 and 1925, has been kindly provided by his daughters, Mrs G.G. Ford and Miss A. Thompson:

When we first arrived (in 1919) Larkhill was a wilderness – just horses and tin huts – even the Church and the Cinema were corrugated iron. There was no school and a soldier driver took the children to school in Amesbury in a coach drawn by two horses.[14]

The coach which had a hard top was provided with windows on each side and a door at the back which was also fitted with a window 'rather like a Wild West Mail Coach'. The more adventurous passengers frequently climbed out of the rear window and on to the roof so that they could sit with the driver. The Thompsons occupied a corrugated iron hut in 11 Camp, behind the Officer's Club and the Gun Park, the grid reference of the site being 138443.

This was a large hut containing nine rooms and having a passage along one side onto which the rooms opened. The kitchen had a coal burning range for cooking, a bathroom/scullery with

PLATE 17: Larkhill Sports Day 1922. Presentation of prizes by Lady Helen Newcome, wife of the Commandant, Maj.-Gen. H.W. Newcome who is on the left of the photograph. Standing immediately behind her is the Adjutant, Maj. J.E.T. Younger. (*Mrs G.G. Ford*)

a coal fired boiler for hot water, a sitting room, five bedrooms and a storeroom. As regards a garden we could use as much of the Plain as we cared to. My father built us a tennis court, gardens, chicken runs, etc., and also planted fruit trees.

Although it was very primitive we were all one happy family – General Newcome was the Commandant and Major J.E.T. Younger the Adjutant. Parties were held in the Sergeant's Mess at which all the family would attend – someone looked after the babies and small children. These parties took place about once a month - whist drive and dance and general get together which seemed to go on for hours. There was an orchestra which came from the Survey Company, I believe.[15]

Mrs Ford who married an AIG left Larkhill in 1925 but returned in 1939 when Mr Ford received his commission. In 1982 she remarked that she and her husband 'still remember "The School" with affection – to me it has always seemed like home'. There could hardly be a kinder appreciation of Larkhill than this.

In a letter written to *Gunner* in 1971 Major-General J.E.T. Younger, CB, who was adjutant of the School in 1921 and to whom Mrs Ford has referred, gave a further glimpse of life at Larkhill in the early days:

General Newcome was of course the creator of the School of Artillery and the founder of the great reputation which it now enjoys, he was a great Gunner and a fine administrator. He gathered in all the wartime schools like the Chapperton Down Artillery School, and formed them in one Artillery School. We all loved him and were proud to have him as our Commandant. He it was who obtained Major Macleod from the Sappers to teach us about Survey; a brilliant and charming man who laid the foundations of our well-known Regimental Survey. Indeed when saying good-bye to him some years later the Commandant remarked that he was so efficient and so nice that he might almost be a Gunner.

There were no civilians at the School in those days, so that the RSM had a large number of soldiers under him. One of them was the General's batman, known throughout India as 'Anderson Sahib' when the General was MGRA there. He was a Marine formerly, but was mobilised into a Field Battery and given a pair of horses to look after. He said 'Beg pardon Sergeant but how do I go about these 'ere, there weren't any of them in my last ship.'

We were true pioneers in those days, there were no shops at Larkhill, and the only available transport was Ranger's bus from Durrington. We did not enjoy the luxury of today, life was more simple, but we were very happy.[16]

One of the first changes to be seen after the war was the gradual removal of the old corrugated iron huts and the limited rebuilding of parts of the camp in a more permanent form. The first camps to be demolished lay to the south of the Packway extending from Tombs Road to Willoughby Road, that is to say, Camp Nos 1–9, 20–28, and also 31–4 which adjoined Rollestone Bake Farm.[17]

Shortly after the war a number of married quarters were built for the garrison as a whole, both for officers and other ranks. In the 1930s a further building programme was implemented to the benefit of the four major units, i.e. the School, the Field Brigade, the Medium Brigade and the Survey Company. As its share the School acquired its first brick buildings: two barrack blocks, a soldiers' mess, a canteen and a Sergeant's mess – all

North Barracks. The other three units received a similar alloca-
tion to their lines in this early rebuilding.[18]

In 1928, twenty-three officers' quarters were built on a piece of
land which lay between Fargo Road and the site of the reversing
triangle on the old railway. This was named Strangways after
Brigadier-General T. Fox-Strangways who commanded the Royal
Artillery in the Crimean War and was killed at Inkerman in 1854.
The houses were sited around the perimeter of an open piece of
land which was oval in shape and so provided a welcome alternative to the usual layout of squares and straight lines. Some of the
first soldiers' married quarters were also built in 1928 and 1929
and these comprised thirty-six semi-detached houses in Fargo
Road a little to the west of Strangways. Known as the Steel
Houses, the name originated from the fact that they are said to
have been constructed largely of steel sheets which would have
been used for building ships, if the First World War had continued.
These were followed by other married quarters for soldiers and by
1938 a further eighty-four houses had been built in twenty-one
blocks of four in Alanbrooke Road (then named Torrian Road),
Bingham Road, Gardiner Road and Wilson Road.
     In 1929, Brigadier A.F. Brooke, DSO, was appointed comman-
dant of the School, a position which he held until 1932. During
the Second World War he commanded the Second Army Corps of
the British Expeditionary Force (1939–40) and after serving as
Commander-in-Chief, Home Forces, he was appointed Chief of
the Imperial General Staff (1941–6). He was unquestionably one
of the most eminent gunners of all time and was promoted to
field marshal in 1944 and created Viscount Alanbrooke in 1946.
As well as being commandant he was garrison commander until
these two appointments were separated in 1931. During the time
that he spent at Larkhill he not only made an outstanding contribution to the technical and instructional work of the school but
he also brought about many improvements within the garrison
area. He was instrumental in accelerating the demolition of many
of the old camp buildings and was responsible for the improvement of several roads and the planting of a considerable number of
trees. His wishes and instructions were translated into action by
the garrison adjutant, Captain (afterwards Brigadier) J.H.W.G.
Richards, through the medium of the War Department Land
Agent, Lieutenant-Colonel H.L. Piggot, OBE.
     One of the most important tasks was the improvement of the
Packway in 1929 which entailed the filling in of deep ditches on

either side of the road before it was widened and the original chalk road resurfaced with tarmac. When this had been completed, the trees – which now greatly improve the appearance of the Packway – were planted. The choice of species and the work of planting them were carried out under the direction of Lieutenant-Colonel Piggott and the results which can be seen today, some fifty-four years later, are an admirable testimony of his work. The trees which were planted 18 feet apart in single rows consist for the most part of an assortment of beech, horse chestnut, lime and Norway maple. The shops on the Packway which had been built during the war, were constructed of corrugated iron and by 1929 were in a very poor condition. However, after Captain Richards in his capacity as garrison adjutant had personally called on the occupiers of the shops, it was agreed that all the premises would be rebuilt in brick as new leases were granted.[19]

At the same time, an experiment was carried out with a view to determining which road material would withstand the heaviest traffic. It is said that the CRE considered that bricks provided the most lasting surface and, with this in mind, he arranged for two sections of brick road to be laid. One length was put down on the Packway close to the junction with Brackenbury Road but this was replaced with tarmacadam sometime after the Second World War. The other section which was laid in Fargo Road, close to the entrance to Wells Road, was still in use and in good condition in 1983. Amongst the buildings which were constructed during this period was a new mess for warrant officers and sergeants which was completed in 1931,[20] while in 1938 two more mess buildings were added. For many years relics of the wartime hutted camps which had stood on the south side of the Packway existed in the form of two small blocks of officers' married quarters known as The Ark and The Stoep. The origin of the names is not known but 'stoep' was a South African word for a verandah or raised platform which extended along the front of a house and occasionally around the sides, and was commonly used during the Boer War (1899–1902). The name of the Ark was probably a humorous reference to Noah's temporary home and this building stood some 150 metres due east of Major A.W. Hewetson's memorial, its grid reference being 141439. The Stoep (reference 138439) was situated about 130 metres to the west of the memorial and although it was still occupied in 1963, it had been demolished by 1970.[21] The Ark was probably removed during the same period.

In the meantime life in the School and practice on the ranges continued in a regular succession of courses and practice camps, but this did not mean that life – for some at least – was always uneventful.

Major Richard Oldfield, in the very early days of the Great War, used his sword to kill two Germans who climbed the ladder in the church tower which he was using as his OP. He also had a very short fuze and abundant ambition.

At Practice Camp in the summer of 1930 on the Larkhill Ranges his turn had come to command a full War Establishment Field Battery. Each Battery Commander did this in turn and the whole Brigade contributed to make up a War Establishment for one day. I was the Battery Leader and my orders were to lead the battery without exposing it to the binoculars of the CRA who was inspecting us. That I exposed it to the enemy as far off as Marlborough town mattered not at all; my job was to move the battery without letting the CRA see it.

Actually I thought that I was doing pretty well. We trotted quietly along in one of those east-west little valleys so nicely scattered about the Plain. In my contentment I think I even hummed some tune. Then cheers from the battery behind me! What on earth was happening for had I not ordered quiet? I looked round and, horrors, bearing down upon me with sword flashing in the sunshine was our BC for the day, Major Richard Oldfield himself, who had, as we all knew, actually used his totally inappropriate Gunner sword to kill two Germans only sixteen years before. Never has anyone appreciated the situation so swiftly; luckily I had a faster charger than he had and I was away like a hare with a lead of two hundred yards and the troops whooping it up behind me. We made cover, in the shape of another small valley and I was able to shake off my pursuer without the CRA seeing anything at all. Major Richard Oldfield was congratulated; all was well. As for me I circled round at a quiet canter and, having made sure the BC for the day had vanished, I took over again from the subaltern who had very properly assumed the job of Battery Leader.

Now there is something that isn't likely to happen again! Not this year anyway.[22]

The building of a new officers' mess for the School, now generally referred to as the 'RA Mess', began in 1936 and after some delays it was eventually occupied in 1940, although it was not formally opened until 1941.[23] In 1938 the Packway Mess, which had been built in order to provide accommodation for officers who were not members of the School of Artillery, was finished and brought into use. The same year saw the completion of a new Warrant Officers' and Sergeants' mess at the eastern end of Brackenbury Road which was occupied in 1939. A more detailed account of these messes is given in Chapter 12. Since 1914 the Garrison Church had consisted of a small timber building that stood close to the site of the present church. However in October 1936 work began on a new building and on 22 January 1937 the foundation stone was laid by General Sir John Burnett-Stuart, KCB, KBE, CMG, DSO who was General Officer Commanding-in-Chief, Southern Command. Exactly sixteen months later, on 21 May 1938, the church was dedicated to St Alban the Martyr by the Chaplain General, the Reverend E.H. Thorold, CB, CBE, DD. Further information on the Churches at Larkhill will be found in Chapter 12.

After the School was established in 1920, steps were taken to ensure that the ranges were satisfactorily organised and operated and two aspects of this were of particular importance. The first was the appointment of a Depot Brigade in 1920 which in addition to providing the personnel and equipment for practice and demonstration shoots, also undertook the working of moving targets. The second was the establishment in 1924 of a Range Detachment at Greenlands Farm which was responsible for the maintenance of the ranges and their safety. A more comprehensive description of the Range Detachment and the Depot and Support units, will be found in Chapters 10 and 13 respectively. In matters of dress, the wearing of a red hatband by IGs originated at the School of Gunnery at Shoeburyness in about 1906. Colonel F.V. Bennett writing in *The Gunner* in June 1956 explained this custom as follows:

All officers had white jackets without rank distinctions, but Instructors wore their blue peaked forage cap with white linen cover over the crown and this continued up to the 1914–18 War for IGs at Schools of Gunnery but not in Commands or at defended ports. With the abolition of full-dress the red capband was presumably transferred to the Service dress cap.[24]

On 12 April 1926 it was agreed at a meeting presided over by the CIG (Colonel C.C. Armitage, CMG, DSO) that in future AIGs should wear white hat covers and that students on the GSC (NCOs) should wear white armbands although this was later discontinued. However, since 1939 white armbands have been

worn by safety officers during practice.[25] Sometimes, in spite of
the combined efforts of the IGs, AIGs, safety officers and the
Range Detachment, things could still go wrong and often when
least expected:

Having completed my YO's course in 1934 I was posted to
40 Field Battery (4.5 inch Howitzers) in 26 Field Brigade (as
regiments were termed in those days) which was the Depot
Brigade serving the School of Artillery. One of my first tasks
was to lead the Battery out on to the Ranges to provide the Fire
Unit for an observation of fire course at the School. Officially
the GPO was my senior subaltern, Lieutenant P. (Nobby) Clarke
(an officer with over 11 years' service!) but he had decided
that, since I was last from school, it would do me good to carry
out the duties of GPO and, at the same time, safety officer
(against all the rules!) whilst he withdrew to the wagon lines to
read a book.

The engagement of a number of targets went without any
noticeable hitch, when after three hours or more, the welcome
message 'End of Practice' came down from the OP. I summoned
up the gun and limber teams and led the Battery back to barracks. On arrival on the gun park the drivers dismounted, the
horses were led away to water, and the limber gunners came rush-
ing out with buckets of boiling water to sluice out the gun bar-
rels. This is where the trouble started. In the way that limber
gunners had, and probably still have, they swung the trails of the
guns round to a convenient position and disengaged the elevating
gears [a quick device on the 4.5 inch Howitzer to aid quick re-
loading without having to bring the piece level by operating the
elevating gear] thereby leaving the piece free to rotate about
the trunnions. It then appeared to be the custom, before opening the breach, to give the trigger a friendly pull, and on this
occasion, there was a loud bang, and one of my guns discharged
a round of HE from the centre of the gunpark! With the quick
release gear disengaged, the piece of this gun wobbled up and
down about the trunnions for quite some time, but, by some
remarkably happy coincidence, it was pointing in about the
only thirty degrees of arc where the least possible damage was
likely to occur; i.e. straight over Knighton Down as opposed to
the officers' quarters at Strangways, the barracks themselves, or
worse still, the Fargo ammunition dump! I've always said that if
my horses had not been clipped the day before, the shell would
have caught the backside of one of the last pair of wheelers on

their way to the water troughs. As it was, it missed the roof of the stables by no more than a foot or two and finally pitched and exploded in the middle of the second fairway on the golf course [at Alton Gorse in those days] just about where a reasonably good drive from the tee would end up. It was a little unfortunate that, standing on the second tee at that moment and about to drive off was Brigadier The Lord Malise Graham, The Commandant of the School of Artillery!

I was not, of course, in a position to observe the fall of shot, nor, at that moment, was I aware of the identity of the officer observing it, but it was not long before these gaps in my knowledge were fulfilled. Within an hour or so an inquiry was held in the Colonel's office and the main point at issue was whether or not 2nd Lieutenant Brown had given the order 'Empty Guns' before limbering up and moving off. I rather weakly said that I could hardly believe I had not but I could not remember doing so! It was then that the Number One of the gun in question, a Sergeant Belger who had earned distinction at Cambrai in 1917, came to my rescue by stating that I had given the order and that he had reported his gun as being empty when, as was to be revealed later, it was not! He subsequently was given a severe reprimand, a sentence which would have been more severe had it not been suspected, and rightly so, that he was covering up for this very young Section Commander.

At a Sergeants' Mess Dance a few weeks later, Sergeant Belger came up to me and suggested that I owed him a pint of beer; he said 'You know, Sir, that we were all agreed that you did not order "Empty Guns" but I couldn't have you getting into trouble after only a few weeks in the Service. I've had eighteen years in it and am more able to take a rap; in any case it was up to an old soldier to have shouted "Check Empty Guns" which would have saved some trouble.' Do we still breed NCO's of this calibre? I feel sure we do.[26]

The mid 1930s were also a time of change and development which began in 1935 when it was decided to replace the 18 pounder gun and 4.5 in howitzer, a decision which was to lead in due course to the production of the 25 pounder gun howitzer. In the same year, the use of shrapnel was discontinued and so the matter of shortening the corrector to raise the burst and the subaltern's *aide-memoire* of 'shortening your braces to raise your trousers' became things of the past. Another training event which came to an end in 1935 was the practice of conducting shoots from one of the balloons that were stabled at Rollestone Camp and a first-hand account of a balloon ascent has been included in Chapter 3. A further innovation was the introduction, in 1936, of a new map to the scale of 1 : 25,000 while at the same time changes were taking place in the administration of the School. In spite of all these changes, some things remained very much the same, including the old rule that time spent in reconnaissance is seldom wasted.

It was in the summer of 1936 that some sort of artillery fire power demonstration was organised by the School of Artillery for the benefit of some senior officers from the War Office and the Home Commands. Amongst the units taking part was 26 Field Brigade, the Depot Brigade serving the School. 40 Field Battery was part of this Brigade and it was led out to its gun position by Lieutenant P.T.N. Clarke, the senior subaltern with 12 years' service, with 2nd Lieutenant Brown as the only other officer present, whose allocated role was that of safety officer.

On arrival at the gun position, Lieutenant Clarke, having got his guns into action decided, and not for the first time, that Lieutenant Brown could combine the duties of safety officer with those of GPO whilst he retired to the wagon lines. Some while later a posse of horsemen, and very senior borsemen at that, appeared to the rear of the gun position on their way up to the splinter proof OP. They included the Commandant of the School and the GOC in C Southern Command (Sir John Burnett-Stuart); also Lieutenant Harry Slessor, the GOCs' ADC who rode up to 2nd Lieutenant Brown and announced that he wanted to borrow a pair of binoculars since his General had left his behind. Brown's comment that it would seem that it was Slessor who had left his master's binoculars behind was not received with much enthusiasm by an officer four or five years his senior! Be this as it may, Brown seeing Nobby Clarke's Sam Browne, with binocular case attached, lying on the ground

PLATE 18: One of two paintings by Miss Joan Wanklyn to commemorate the 50th Anniversary of the School. It covers the period 1920–45 and depicts the following scenes from left to right beginning in the top left hand corner. Locomotive 'Queen Mary' with 8 in. howitzers behind; 18 pr gun and 'Dragon' tractor; 9.2 in. howitzer. Horse lines; 4.5 in. howitzers at Netheravon Bake. Range finders; Brig. A.F. Brooke, Commandant 1929–32 in staff car; RHA Battery of 13 prs on the Packway; 2 pr anti-tank gun. The Gun Park with 25 pr, 60 pr and Morris Quad gun tower; the RA Mess; 5.5 in. gun near Honeydown Copse.

beside the artillery board, picked it up and handed the binocular case to Slessor. The posse of high ranking horsemen rode off to the splinter proof.

Shortly after this, Nobby Clarke arrived up from the wagon lines and announced that it was time for lunch. He asked for his binoculars to which Brown replied that he had just lent them to Harry Slessor for use by the GOC in C. 'I suppose you think that is very funny,' said Nobby, when, at that moment, a fairly hostile looking Slessor arrived at full gallop to announce that his General, having settled himself in the splinter proof, was peering out across the ranges and trying to extract what he assumed to be a pair of binoculars, when all he had been able to withdraw from the case was a packet of sandwiches, a hard boiled egg and a flask of brandy![27]

Between the wars, Larkhill had a unique atmosphere which those who experienced it are unlikely to forget. Many batteries were still horsed, the artillery board provided all the answers if the GPO knew his stuff, and a 'one inch map' was used for shooting from the OP. Moreover, the IGs of those days seemed to be a special breed whose comments added much to the enjoyment of the spectators if not to the unfortunate who was taking the shoot. On one occasion a young officer who was having some difficulty in ranging on a target, ordered 'Drop 100', followed by 'Drop 100' and again 'Drop 100'. At this piecemeal approach the IG who, it is said, was Major 'Ambrose' Pratt (afterwards Major-General F.W.H. Pratt, CB, CBE, DSO, MC) remarked 'For heaven's sake make your mind up and stop nibbling at your droppings'.[28] Although by the nature of things those responsible at the gun position may not have had the same opportunities for making such memorable comments, they had their own way of emphasizing a point.

A ploy the School had for demonstrating the accuracy of the 3.7 in. pack Howitzer was as follows. They would site a 3.7 and engage a pinpoint target at some modest range like 1500 yards. After getting a 50 yard bracket, they would go to 5 rounds fire for effect which would all go 'plus' or all 'minus'! They would correct 25 yards up or down as necessary and fire another 5 rounds. These would all do the same but on the opposite side of the target.

The instructor would then point out that 25 yards was the smallest division on the range scale. However, they could move the gun 12½ yards which of course they then proceeded to do and put the next 5 rounds all on the target and practically in the same hole![29]

Although tractors had been used for hauling heavy artillery in the latter years of the first war, it was not until 1923 that the mechanisation of field and light artillery began but progress was anything but fast.[30] By 1933 most of the Territorial Army Brigades had been mechanised but the first trials of the Dragon gun tower did not take place until 1935.[31] Eventually it was decided in 1938 to complete the mechanisation of the horse and field artillery and so the Regiment said farewell to the horse after more than two hundred years of faithful service.

Today the King's Troop of 13 pounders still provide a very welcome reminder of the past. The following describes the last medium battery that was horsed:

I also served with 18 Medium Battery at Larkhill which was equipped with 6 in. howitzers and was employed for calibration and trials of all sorts of 6 in. shells and fuzes. We sometimes fired as many as 300 rounds a day. No tactical wagon lines, the horses grazed with bits out behind the howitzers firing! It was the last Medium Battery RA to be mechanised so therefore we had posted to us the last four Command Show teams, each of eight beautiful heavy draught horses, each with two sets of show harness. What a sight! I shall never forget it. As a Second Lieutenant, I had the sixteen best Suffolk Punch heavy draughts in the world.[32]

Sad though it was that the horse had been replaced there was, however, another side to it.

In May 1940 when I was looking for a battery position, I came to a cross roads where a French horse-drawn battery had been caught either by shell fire or dive bombers. Every horse, of which there were about thirty-five, had been killed and lay in heaps along the road, some still hooked in to the limbers. I remember thinking how glad I was that we had been mechanized.[33]

Several changes took place in 1938 which were to have a considerable effect not only on the School but on the Regiment as a whole. The beginning of the year was marked by the introduction

of the 2pr anti-tank gun which was followed by the formation of
anti-tank regiments, each composed of four 12-gun batteries and
in the training of which the School took an active part. Later in
the year it was announced that horse field and medium artillery
brigades which were composed of four batteries each containing
six guns, were to be replaced by regiments composed of two batteries each consisting of three troops which contained four guns
apiece. At the same time the final mechanisation of horse and
field artillery was completed.

At the beginning of 1939 the government drew up plans for
compulsory military service and these were put into practice in
May 1939 with the formation of the Militia. At Larkhill, the more
immediate effect of this was the building of a temporary hutted
camp which was named Newcome Lines, in order to accommodate
the new intake. These lines occupied an area immediately to the
south of – and adjoining – Fargo Road, the eastern boundary of
which was the continuation of what is now Alanbrooke Road. The
western limit was a point some 210 metres beyond the intersection of Fargo Road and Willougby Road. During the first six
months of 1939, work at the School followed the usual pattern of
courses and practice camps but as the summer wore on it became
evident that war could not be far away. The arrival of Regular
Army reservists at Larkhill in the middle of August lent further
weight to this view and when, a fortnight later, war was declared,
anticipation gave way to realisation and the scene changed drama-
tically.

6. The Second World War

The first major impact that mobilisation had on the School was the tremendous increase in the demands on the School staff. This was not made any easier by the appointment of the commandant, Brigadier S.R. Wason, to be MGRA of the British Expeditionary Force and by two chief instructors, Colonel C.P.W. Perceval and Colonel R.H. Towell becoming CsRA.[1] In September five Gunner OCTUs were formed and to each of them an IG and three AIGs were posted.[2] On the embodiment of the Territorial Army it was necessary to teach the new regimental organisation and procedure to virtually all territorial artillery units.[3] This, in itself, was a considerable undertaking but in addition, during the winter of 1939–40, the artillery of each territorial division that was about to proceed overseas was set an exercise on Larkhill or West Down which lasted for three to four days. Some idea of the amount of work which was involved during the first few months of the war can be gained from the fact that between September 1939 and May 1940, over sixty post mobilisation courses – irrespective of rank – were provided by the School.[4] The expansion of the 1st Survey Battery into the 1st Survey Regiment in 1939 and the subsequent formation of 40th Survey Training Regiment RA created further staff problems.

In order to meet the increased demand for IGs and AIGs changes were introduced in the gunnery staff courses and from 8 November 1939 these were reduced in length from the pre-war period of twelve months. Officers' courses were renamed 'War Gunnery Staff Course Field' abbreviated to 'War GSC Field' and until 4 October 1941 each of these was of three months' duration. From that date until June 1946 when the last War GSC Field ended, the length of each course was extended to six months. However in August 1945 the Long GSC Field was re-introduced and until June 1946 it ran concurrently with the last two War GSCs Field. Courses for NCOs were at first designated Short Gunnery Staff Course Field – Short GSC Field – and the first started on 8 November 1939. To begin with these ran for periods of two and a half months but in April 1942 the length was increased to three months and at the same time they were renamed War Gunnery Staff Courses. At the end of June 1944 they were extended to four months; in February 1945 to six months and in 1946 to eight months while the Long GSC Field was restarted in May 1945.[5]

As the war continued, so the work of the School expanded.

Notwithstanding a shortening of the gunnery staff course, the scope of instruction increased during the war years. In addition to field and anti-tank gunnery, instruction covered observation of fire from the air by gunner pilots, co-operation with the R.A.F. and tactical handling of artillery units in the field.[6]

In March 1940, General Sir Edmund Ironside, Chief of the Imperial General Staff, visited Larkhill. As a result of this permission was granted for the Commandant (Brigadier F. FitzGibbon DSO) and the Chief Instructor Equipments (Colonel J. Penrose MC) to proceed to France and make a tour of the front. Their visit has been described as 'a very interesting experience if not very reassuring'.[7] In addition to the internal difficulties of readjustment and reorganisation with which the School was faced, there was a serious problem created by the lack of modern guns and equipment.

Not a single 25 pr had yet come off the production line; the makeshift 18/25 pr had reached few units outside the handful of Regulars; nearly all the medium pieces dated from 1914–18; and heavy artillery was almost non-existent. The only up-to-date weapon was the 2 pr anti-tank gun, and that was scarce enough; moreover it was only in 1938 that it had become an artillery weapon, and for demonstrations given at Larkhill in that year the gun detachments had to be provided by the infantry.[8]

Early in September 1939, No. 122 Officer Cadet Training Unit, generally referred to as 122 OCTU, was formed at Larkhill under the command of Lieutenant-Colonel J.V. Delahaye, DSO, MC. The unit occupied parts of 16 Camp which lay between Cator and Watson Roads and 17 Camp which was situated in the area between Watson and Ross Roads, the Packway forming the southern boundary in both cases. Each course lasted for five months and although the first two were composed of cadets from the Royal Military Academy at Woolwich, those who attended subsequent courses were, for the most part, cadets who had only recently left civilian life.[9] Unfortunately, little information is now available as regards 122 OCTU but it would appear that it was terminated in 1942 since it does not appear in the list of OCTUs published in an ACI of October 1942,[10] or in one issued early in 1943 which dealt with the reorganisation of OCTUs as a whole.[11]

Although range parties had been in existence since 1901, they were replaced by service batteries from 1926 until October 1939 when a Range Detachment was formed.[12] Further information on the ranges and those who looked after them will be found in Chapter 10. The winter of 1939 was an exceptionally hard one throughout the whole of Britain and much of Europe and conditions on the ranges became unusually difficult.

I first came to Larkhill in January 1940 on an Observation of Fire Course and the ice on the ranges was so thick that the guns would slide back five or six yards and the only way to alleviate the condition was to dig holes for the spades with pickaxes.[13]

However, as can be readily appreciated, it was not only the guns that were affected by such zero temperatures:

Transport was requisitioned for many tasks, and for taking courses to the ranges flatbed brick lorries with no sides at all, were used. To avoid frostbite *en route* standard dress from the inside outwards was underclothes (2 sets) pyjamas, Service dress, battle dress, great coat. For most people the final touch was a full flask in each pocket, and sometimes the standard of shooting suffered as a result.[14]

By the end of 1939 preliminary steps had been taken to form a school for heavy artillery on railway mountings and this was marked by the appointment of Major (afterwards Lieutenant-Colonel) S.M. Cleeve as IG in charge of super-heavy equipment. However, in the following spring it was decided to form a School of Super-heavy Railway Artillery at Catterick of which Lieutenant-Colonel Cleeve was appointed Commandant and Chief Instructor. During the period that the new School was in operation, a close connection was maintained with Larkhill.[15]

Towards the end of May 1940 the first survivors of the BEF began to arrive back in this country but by the beginning of June

PLATE 19: A battery of 9.2 in. howitzers firing on the Ranges, probably in 1939. The line of trees on the right, in the middle foreground is Down Barn Plantation with Prospect Clump on the centre horizon.

the trickle had become a torrent. The main problem was the provision of accommodation for a large number of men at a few hours' notice and among the locations that were available, Larkhill was high on the list.

> it became a concentration area for a large number of those who returned from the front – including a number of French and Belgians. They detrained at Amesbury and were met by buses and coaches. Most of the men – particularly the first arrivals – showed signs of the stress under which they had lived – many short of boots and clothing and few had any kind of equipment. A marked contrast was provided by a party of about a dozen Indians under a very smart Jemadar Sahib, who fell them in on the platform, inspected them closely, ticked off one or two for buttons undone, sent one back to the compartment for his respirator and then came up to me with a smart salute and reported his party all present and correct, before marching them out to the waiting coach.[16]

Altogether some five thousand men arrived over a period of about twenty-four hours and to ensure that they were reasonably comfortable and with a roof over their heads, officers and soldiers vacated their own hutted quarters and moved into tents. Lecture rooms were cleared so as to provide additional living quarters and when this proved insufficient, guns and vehicles were moved into the open so that the resulting covered space could be made available.[17] The disastrous end of the campaign on the Continent not only meant the evacuation of the Expeditionary Force and the advance of the German Forces to the channel ports but also the loss of practically all the artillery which had been shipped to France. This amounted to a total of no less than 1,954 guns ranging from 2 prs to 12 in howitzers.[18]

Although the first of the new 25 prs reached Larkhill later in June, it was found on arrival that there were defects in the recuperators. However, after working on them continuously for twenty-four hours or so, the School artificers were able to rectify the trouble. The immediate shortage of equipment was relieved to some extent by the arrival of several hundred 75 mm guns from the United States of America. For the most part these were the 1897 model of the well known 'French 75' but were augmented by a number of British 18 pdrs Mark 1 which had been converted to 75 mm together with some of a later American design.[19] With the issue of these guns, it was essential to provide first-class

instruction in their operation and maintenance and the School was
very fortunate in obtaining the services of Major C.P.F. Pierret. He
had served in the French Army during the First World War and
had subsequently become a partner in a firm of merchant bankers
in London. When war was declared in September 1939 he was
appointed an officer of the French Military Mission in this country
but after the fall of France he volunteered for the British Army
Emergency Reserve.

> He first came to Larkhill after the Dunkirk evacuation (his com-
> mission and promotion to the rank of Major were both dated
> 23rd July 1940) and his assignment was to teach the Regiment
> about the French 75. He remained as Instructor in Foreign
> Equipment in the Equipment Wing of the School until the end
> of April 1945 when he joined the staff of the Military Section
> of the Control Commission . . . His contribution to knowledge
> in the field of Foreign Artillery was of immense value and was
> appropriately recognised by the award, in 1948, of the Nevile
> Walford Medal.[20]

A further addition to the steadily increasing catalogue of new
equipment was the 5.5in gun for medium artillery which first
appeared at Larkhill during the autumn of 1940 although it was
not issued to regiments until the following year.[21]

In due course a conference for senior gunner officers who had
recently returned from France was convened by the MGRA,
Major-General O.M. Lund (afterwards Lieutenant-General Sir
Otto Lund, KCB, DSO). One of the results of this was the introduction of a new procedure for fire control, since it was agreed
that the existing method was too complicated. In recognition of
the fact that the 2 pr anti-tank gun was inadequate to deal with the
heavily armoured German tanks, a wooden model of the proposed
6 pr gun was demonstrated during the conference. While it met
with general approval there were some reservations as to whether
it was too heavy a gun for the task in hand, and it is interesting
to think what might have been said had it been known that the
17 pr anti-tank was already being considered.[22] In October 1940 a
major alteration in the organisation of horse, field and medium
regiments, which had been laid down in 1938, was approved. This
changed the structure of the Regiment from two batteries of three
troops each to three batteries of two troops. However life still
held some compensations. 'During 1940 we saw the ATS arrive

and take over the Church Hut (and the Squash Courts for those who were brave enough to take them on).'[23]

Larkhill was never specifically selected as a target by the German Air Force during the war, although damage was caused by bombs on three occasions which resulted in total casualties of fifteen killed and thirty-five wounded.

> The first bomb which fell in the camp went through the roof of the medium and heavy regiment's lecture and recreation hall, slid harmlessly across the dance floor and finally, brought up short by the wall, burnt itself through into the earth beneath and expired. The young soldiers and their ATS partners were in luck.[24]

When the School of Artillery was established in 1920, its responsibilities included training instructors, carrying out trials of new equipment, giving demonstrations and preparing training manuals,[25] and during the years of peacetime soldiering that followed, its original organisation was well able to satisfy these requirements. However, as the war developed, calls on the School increased very considerably and it soon became clear that in order to meet these expanding demands, some form of decentralisation was inevitable. The first step in this direction was taken in 1940 when a subdivision was formed to deal with the increased demands on the organisation and administration of the School and was known as Headquarters Wing. In March of that year, the Royal Artillery School of Survey was established and, at the same time, it absorbed the 40th Survey Training Regiment RA which had been formed in September 1939.[26] Further information on the history and development of the different wings will be found in Chapter 9.

The winter of 1940/41 was marked by the beginning of a period of close liaison with the Royal Navy when a party of Gunner Officers were attached to HMS *Excellent* on Whale Island in Portsmouth Harbour. The object was to provide instruction in the observation of naval gunfire by forward observation officers (FOOs) and in the duties of army liaison officers on board HM Ships. Subsequently, every gunnery staff course paid a visit to Whale Island and each naval gunnery staff course spent a week at Larkhill,[27] but a more detailed account of the Regiment's associations with the Royal Navy will be found in Chapter 13. In the early years of the war, one of the most valuable services performed by the School was the collection and assimilation of battle experiences and ideas through the medium of conferences, courses and personal communications. Although, at one time, there was a feeling that rather too much importance was being attached to the conditions which existed in the desert, since these would not apply in Europe, much valuable information was nevertheless obtained. The conferences which were instituted by the MGRA, Major-General Otto Lund, became a regular feature of Larkhill during this period of the war.

The Adjutant General, Sir Ronald Adam usually attended and gave very interesting information to the meeting. Most of the time was spent indoors over discussions of matters such as gunnery, employment of artillery and training but there was usually at least one demonstration on the ranges as well as visits to the gun park, when new equipment and modifications were seen and also captured weapons.

At a conference held in the winter of 1940–41, the MGRA ordered a discussion on methods of providing quick artillery support for an attack. As experience showed that ideas on this subject were few and any discussion likely to fade out after a few minutes it was decided that there must be a School solution to the problem prepared for use if necessary. As anticipated, hardly any suggestions came from the CsRA and others and the School solution was therefore put forward. It produced quite a sensation and letters poured into the School for sometime afterwards, offering amendments and improvements. So much interest was taken that it was decided that a demonstration be staged at some future date to test it out.

The trial duly took place before a large body of spectators which included the CIGS, Sir Alan Brooke. A Divisional Artillery commanded by Brigadier Eric Earle, with a regiment of mediums, did the shooting. The reconnaisance was done in view of the spectators and orders for a barrage were sent to the guns by signal message. For safety reasons it had been decided that one gun per troop was to fire a test round after all the guns had been reported ready, but no corrections were to be allowed. Fortune favoured us. The barrage was almost perfect. As the spectators included several General Officers including the CIGS (originally we had been warned that the Prime Minister might attend) and all were standing right in the line of fire, the CIGS and some others were requested to watch from inside a concrete OP. This he refused to do and the Staff heaved a considerable sigh of relief when the demonstration passed off without any casualties. The procedure was incorporated in the Training Manual, under the title of the 'Quick Barrage'.[28]

In 1941 further steps were taken to continue decentralisation within the School when the Anti-Tank, Air and Equipment Wings were formed. The Air Wing was concerned with the use of light unarmed aircraft, generally referred to as Air OPs which were normally flown by gunner personnel in order to observe and direct gun fire. When the new 6 pr anti-tank gun was issued to infantry battalions in 1941, the School provided a number of instructors who were attached to the Heavy Weapons Wing of the School of Infantry.[29]

In the spring of 1941 the School was honoured by a visit from Their Majesties, King George VI and Queen Elizabeth.

The first Royal visit to Larkhill took place on 3rd April 1941, when HM King George VI and Queen Elizabeth spent the forenoon going round the ranges, Gun Park and miniature

PLATE 20: Their Majesties King George VI and Queen Elizabeth at Larkhill, 3rd April 1941. From left to right: HM the Queen; HM the King; Col R. Hilton; Lt-Gen. The Hon. Harold Alexander; Brig. F. FitzGibbon; Brig. S. Collingwood, Gen. Alexander is pointing out the flight of a shell. (*Imperial War Museum*)

range. On the previous day much of the ranges had been under snow, but this had mostly thawed out during the night leaving the ground rather slippery for motor transport. It was considered safer to transfer Their Majesties to a staff car with chains on the wheels rather than run the risk of the Royal vehicle getting stuck in the mud. The day was fine and all went very well. Normal practice shoots were going on on the ranges and the 5.5 in gun, then on the secret list, was laid on for the occasion. Both the King and Queen possessed the wonderful power of making everyone think that this was the sort of day they were really enjoying. The King took a great interest in the manner of instruction by the IGs, both on the ranges and in the miniature range.[30]

In April 1942, the Prime Minister, Mr Winston Churchill paid a visit to the School, primarily to see the 6 pr anti-tank gun in action. He was accompanied by General George Marshall of the United States Army, General Sir Hastings Ismay (afterwards Lord Ismay), Deputy Secretary (Military) the War Cabinet, Lord Cherwell, personal assistant to the Prime Minister and Mr R.G. Casey, Minister of State in the Middle East. Every secretary of state for war paid a visit to the School during his term of office while General Sir Edmund Ironside (afterwards Field Marshal Lord Ironside, GCB, CMG, DSO) came on two occasions when he was CIGS. Lieutenant-General Sir Alan Brooke (afterwards Field Marshal Viscount Alanbrooke, GCB, OM, GCVO, DSO) when C-in-C Home Forces and later as CIGS and also Lieutenant-General Bernard Paget (afterwards General Sir Bernard Paget, KCB, DSO, MC) when C-in-C Home Forces, were both frequent visitors.[31]

When, in 1900, the question of moving the School of Gunnery for Horse and Field Artillery from Shoeburyness was under consideration, it was suggested that it should be transferred to Netheravon.[32] It was also proposed to take over Syrencot House (grid reference 159461) which had been bought by the War Department from G. Knowles, as part of a 2,000-acre estate, in 1898.[33] However, the intended move did not materialise and Syrencot subsequently became the official residence of the commandants of the School of Artillery, the last to live there being Brigadier S.R. Wason. When he left in 1939 his successor, Brigadier F. FitzGibbon, felt that it was inappropriate to live in such a large house during a national emergency and he accordingly decided to live at No. 12, Strangways.[34] During the war, Syrencot was closely connected with the Airborne Forces and a plaque which has been fixed to the wall adjoining the main entrance to the house, bears the following inscription.

Syrencot House
This house was used between November 1941 and
May 1943 as the headquarters of Major-General, later
Lieutenant-General F.M. (Boy) Browning, CB, DSO, the founder of
Airborne Forces. Much of the planning which lead to the
formation of the 1st and 6th Airborne Divisions was done in this house.
In May 1943, it became the headquarters of the
Sixth Airborne Division commanded by Major-General R.N. Gale, OBE, MC
later General Sir Richard Gale, GCB, KBE, DSO, MC.
The Airborne Assault by the 6th Airborne Division on the night of
5/6 June 1944, to secure the left flank of the Allied Invasion of
Europe – Operation Overlord was planned and mounted from this house.
AD UNUM OMNES

By the end of 1941 no less than twenty different types of courses were available at the School and these catered for the following:

Selected regimental commanders
Commanding officers and seconds-in-command
Anti-tank courses for regimental commanders
Mobile anti-aircraft (5 courses)
Majors and potential battery commanders
Troop commanders
Anti-tank troop commanders, warrant officers and sergeants
Adjutants and assistant adjutants
Command post officers
Counter battery officers' assistants
Gridded oblique photographs
77mm gun (French)
Counter battery clerks
Equipment courses
Unit fitters' refresher courses
Battery commanders' refresher courses.[35]

At the same time the war gunnery staff courses continued to be held and the 8th Course which began on 14 July 1941 was not without incident.

Day 2 when most students were still overawed by being there
at all. The IG, commissioned in 1919, doing the AIG's job and
trying to explain the difference between the rocking-bar and the
independent-line-of-sight systems, with much arm waving but
little success. Our horror when one student asked if he could
help which he did in two minutes flat and absolute clarity. The
IG's comment was 'Thank you – now we *all* know', but the
student later became CIG – Harold Taylor.[36]

Perhaps this was not altogether surprising in the light of subsequent events, for after his appointment as Chief Instructor in Field
in 1942, Lieutenant-Colonel H.M. Taylor's work was described in
the following terms. 'He combined the highest academic mathe-
matical honours with a severely practical common sense outlook.
His capacity for work was prodigious, his gunnery pamphlets are a
model of lucidity and will stand as examples for all time.'[37]

Later, during the same course, another problem arose which was
overcome by the usual resourcefulness displayed by members of
the Royal Regiment.

Before we had done our stint at the School of Survey two
students, I was one, were sent to the Survey School for two
days to learn about a special new idea – Gridded Oblique
Photos. [In case these have been forgotten, a grid was printed
over a series of oblique air photos. OP or Air OP officers read
off the grid reading from three adjacent photos and by plotting
these on the artillery board, one coud get target location]. The
day of the big demonstration with VIPs at the OP and two
students at the gun position. The most I of the VIPs selected
the target, the centre of three white craters but we were not to
know that. Our problem arose when the three bearings on the
artillery board gave a whopping great triangle of error, at least
1000 metres long, and at that stage of the course we had not
learnt how to correct for a t of e. Answer: stick a pin in the
middle, read data for guns, concentrate and correct for meteor
and behold – four rounds on the crater! We kept quiet, everyone said how wonderful were the ways of gridded oblique, and
they were adopted.[38]

On 5 October 1942, the School of Survey became a part of the
new Survey Wing[39] and this brought the number of instructional
wings to five; namely, the Air, Equipment, Gunnery, Survey and
Tactical Wings;[40] there was in addition the Headquarters Wing.

As the work of the School increased so did the production of training manuals, drill books, pamphlets and directives and, in order to meet the demand, a publication section was formed as part of the School headquarters in 1942.[41] By 1943 a new camp had been built between the Packway Mess and Fargo Ammunition Depot, in order to meet the demand for additional accommodation. Known as Fargo Hutted Camp, it covered an area of some 26 acres, the grid reference of the centre of the camp being 117442. In November 1944 it was converted to a prisoner-of-war camp.[42]

As the war continued the demands on the School increased: in 1940 provision had been made for the instruction, at any one time, of 220 officers and 144 soldiers;[43] by 1945 these figures had expanded to 260 and 160 respectively.[44] Similarly the total establishment of the School had risen from 370 in 1940,[45] to 2584 in 1943,[46] falling to 1261 in 1945.[47] In addition to its instructional role the School also undertook, through the medium of the Equipment Wing, a considerable amount of work connected with the trials of equipment and methods of operation on behalf of the War Office, the Board of Ordnance, and the Ministry of Supply.[48] A further innovation was the attachment to the School in 1943 of a group of scientists under Dr R.J. Whitney to advise on certain matters concerned with radar, gunnery and equipment and they soon became a valuable and integral part of the School.[49]

After the arrival of the Canadian Forces in this country in 1939, many members of the Royal Canadian Artillery attended courses at the School and this lead to an exceptionally close connection between Larkhill and Canadian gunners, so much so that 'so far as the School was concerned there were not two armies, British and Canadian, but one'.[50] When Major J.L. Etherington who had served in the Royal Canadian Artillery, visited the School in 1980, he recalled several incidents that had occurred whilst he was Canadian Liaison IG from July 1943 to May 1944.

We were very active at the School in training air OP pilots as well as Arty R procedures with Tactical Air Force types. One over zealous OP Gunner pilot flew the wrong pattern and was hit with a 5.5 HE shell at an altitude of about 1,000 feet and that was the end of him, poor chap.

The air force types rather resented having to sit in class for several days learning the procedures with miniature ranging, etc. – and so when they were actually able to fly sorties to practise, they were usually pretty exuberant at once getting again into the air, and the poor IG who had to fly with them

was subjected to various sickening forms of aerobatics after
each shoot. Then the next pilot would go up and try to outdo
the former. Naturally we learned to temper our critique of his
shoot while we were still in the passenger seat (Anson trainers
were used, supplied by Andover air base).[51]

However, as the demand for courses at Larkhill continued to
increase, it was felt that the pressure could be relieved to a large
extent by the formation of a Canadian artillery school. Authority
for this was given by the Canadian government in November 1942
and in December No. 1 Canadian School of Artillery (Overseas)
was established at Pinewood, Whitehill about one a half miles due
south of Bordon Camp on the Farnham – Petersfield Road (A325).
On 10 August 1943 the School moved to Seaford which lies
between Eastbourne and Brighton. The first courses began on
3 January 1943 and the School continued to operate until June
1945 [52] On 11 December 1942 the Master Gunner, Field Marshal
Lord Milne, GCB, GCMG, DSO, held a dinner in the RA Mess
which provided a welcome shaft of sunlight through the clouds of
war. To it, were invited twelve senior officers of the United States
Army together with representatives of the artilleries of the Domin-
ions. On the following day a demonstration of the fire power of
anti-aircraft, anti-tank, field and medium artillery was given on the
ranges.[53]
    From 1943 to 1945 Royal Marine personnel attended courses
at Larkhill in order to train in the use of the equipment with
which Landing Craft Gun (Medium) – LCG (M) – were armed.
These were comparable in size to Landing Craft Tank and were
equipped with two 25 prs or two 17 prs in armoured turrets which
were used in landing operations between the time that the preliminary naval bombardment ended and the Field Artillery dis-
embarked. The guns were manned by a Royal Marine detachment
under the command of a lieutenant who was also trained as an
FOO. Practice was subsequently carried out in the area of Poole
Harbour and on one unfortunate occasion when a correction of
30 minutes was ordered, the detachment inadvertently laid the
gun at 30 degrees. As a result a 25 pr shell landed on Brownsea
Island but happily its source was never discovered.[54]
    With the expansion of the war effort, the demand for artillery
publications increased still further, so that by the end of 1943
the average output amounted to one training pamphlet or gundrill
and one amendment per week. In order to compete with this,
the Publications Section which had been formed in the previous

year, was enlarged and became a part of the Commandant's headquarters.[55] As the war zones increased in number and the disposition of British troops became more widespread, so the difficulties of keeping in touch with Larkhill increased. Consequently a number of artillery schools were established in or near some of the theatres of operations and these included Almaza near Cairo; Deolali near Bombay; Chateaudun in Tunisia and Eboli near Salerno in Italy. Nevertheless they all maintained close contact with the School of Artillery at home and adhered to its precepts.[56] By 1943 the prospect that the invasion of Europe could not long be delayed, provided an additional stimulus to the activities of the School. In the autumn of 1943 an exercise was held by XII Corps on the Larkhill and Westdown ranges when some four hundred guns were deployed. In addition to field and medium artillery, a number of railway-mounted howitzers took part in the exercise. Several 9.2 in and 12 in howitzers occupied positions on the railway line between Bulford and Porton, while an 18in howitzer came into action on the Bulford branch,[57] a single round from which produced a shell crater 33 feet (10 metres) across and 12 feet (3.6 metres) deep.[58] The fact that this event passed off without mishap, was a great credit to those who were concerned with the safety aspect of the exercise and especially the Range Detachment.

As the first few months of 1944 passed, so the activities at School increased, and exercises and tutorials were held primarily to assist the artillery of 21st Army Group to anticipate the problems which they were likely to encounter in the invasion of Europe. As the time approached, many of the formations which were to take part in the Normandy landings, known by the code name 'Overlord', assembled in the Salisbury Plain area. This provided an excellent opportunity to hold three important exercises which were set and directed by the School, the first of which was an indoor exercise dealing with the anti-aircraft aspects of a beach landing and the establishment of a base port. The second, which was also held indoors, was concerned with the problems facing the artillery during a corps attack while the third consisted of a five-day outdoor exercise to practise artillery support during an attack by a corps. The work which the last of these exercises involved can be appreciated by the fact that its preparation required more than six weeks of continuous work by eight officers and, when it was held, a directing staff of sixty officers was needed. Until the war in north-west Europe came to an end, the School maintained close contact with artillery commanders in the field and Tactical Wing received the fire plans for all major attacks within a few days of the operation being carried out.[59]

In July 1944 authority was given for the formation of a Radar Wing while in the same year the Photographic Research Branch ceased to be a part of the Air Wing and, in 1945, became the Army Photographic Research Branch. For the whole of its existence the branch was under the command of Lieutenant-Colonel John Morton.[60] During 1944 the following new items of equipment arrived at the School.

> 25 pr on the Ram chassis known as the 'Sexton'.
> 99 mm. Self propelled howitzer.
> 17 pr Self propelled gun on a Valentine chassis.
> 7.2 in. howitzer on USA 155 mm/8 in. mounting.
> 155 mm. gun on a similar mounting
> 8 in. gun.
> 240 mm. howitzer.
> 3 in. 'Land Mattress' rocket.[61]

Not surprisingly the most eminent visitor to the School in 1944 was General Sir Bernard Montgomery (afterwards Field Marshal Viscount Montgomery KG, GCB, DSO) commander of the 21st Army Group.[62] Once again the Master Gunner, Field Marshal Lord Milne, held an impressive dinner in the RA Mess at which the Artilleries of the Empire were entertained and, as in 1942, the occasion was marked by the presence of the regimental band and much of the silver from the mess at Woolwich.[63]

On 8 May 1945 the war on the European Front came to an end with the unconditional surrender of Germany. At the School, victory in Europe which became known as VE Day, was marked by the firing of a 7.2in howitzer manned by the staff of Gunnery Wing.[64] To commemorate the occasion a plaque was fixed to the carriage which was inscribed as follows:

VICTORY IN EUROPE 1945
THIS EQUIPMENT FIRED THE
VICTORY SALUTE
AT
LARKHILL
ON THE NIGHT OF 7/8 MAY 1945

This howitzer has now found a permanent resting place in the Rotunda Museum at Woolwich. The capitulation of Japan on

14 August brought the hostilities in the Far East to an end and throughout Larkhill the occasion was greeted with unrestrained jubilation, and not the least in the RA Mess.

> The first postwar DRA's conference was held at Larkhill and VJ Day happened in the middle of it. Great celebrations, and memories include that night when the whole company was led in singing 'Alouette' by a Canadian brigadier, and the entry through the main door of a horse bearing three Generals with a fourth holding the horse's tail in one hand and a bottle of whisky in the other.[65]

The last of the dinner parties which were held by the Master Gunner in the mess, took place in 1945 when the British and Canadian artilleries were hosts to the American Army. And so, with the ending of the war, the School took stock of the position and began to organise itself for the post-war years which lay ahead.

7. The Changing Scene

Throughout the country the immediate post-war period brought the inevitable problems which were related to the change from war to peace. At the School these included the reorganisation of the Gunnery Staff Courses and a review of the demand for instructors although at the same time, it was necessary to try and envisage the extent of post-war requirements. Of immediate importance were the needs of the 'Interim Army' which consisted of those who wished to remain in the Service after the war, and those who had been too young to take part in the war but now wished to enlist.[1] To clarify the position it was laid down in May 1946 that

> the primary function of the School is to train *Instructors*; Long and Short Gunnery Courses and Long Observation courses are, therefore, the first priority. The length of these courses and the number of students attending them, determines the instructional staff and accommodation available to take such other courses as may be required by the Regiment, from time to time.[2]

Shortly afterwards, three additional functions were enumerated.

> To keep all RA Training Manuals under review, preparing new manuals and amending existing ones as necessary. To act as the DRA's agency for the preliminary examination of new projects. To carry out equipment trials as required by the DRD.[3]

An ACI containing instructions for those attending courses at the School which was published in June 1947 included a table setting out the organisation of the School at that time.[4] This shows five wings: air, equipment, gunnery, observation and tactical which were composed as follows. The Air Wing included two GSO 2s - one for 'air' and the other for 'photos' - with an IG at Larkhill and another at Andover who later moved to Wallop. The Equipment Wing consisted of two branches, 'trials' and 'instructional' while the Gunnery Wing was divided into field, medium and heavy on the one hand and anti-tank on the other. The Observation Wing was concerned with observation, location, sound ranging and radar, and the Tactical Wing with 'field' (which included medium, heavy, anti-tank and counter-battery), communications and anti-aircraft.

The end of hostilities also saw the initial closures of the schools of artillery which had been set up during the war. In Egypt, the Middle East School of Artillery at Almaza was terminated and moved to Acre in Palestine where it remained until 1948 while in that year the School of Deolali, near Bombay, came to an end. At home, two important demonstrations arranged by the School took place in 1946; the first was provided for senior officers attending the DRA's Conference and the second as part of an exercise for commanders and their staff officers.[5] These were the first of the many demonstrations that have been staged by the School since the Second World War. They have not only become an outstanding feature of Larkhill but have also increased the knowledge and appreciation of the Regiment amongst both the general public and other arms.

In 1945 a change took place in the designation of the Survey Wing which had been formed in 1942 in place of the School of Survey, when it was renamed the Observation Wing. Seven years later its title was to be changed once again to that of Counter Bombardment Wing. Another aspect of education at Larkhill was provided by 4th RA Training Regiment (Field) which had been formed in 1943 for the express purpose of producing potential NCOs and officers for the regiment. After completing a training period of thirty-two weeks, the 'young artillerymen' were posted to other Gunner units and the importance of this can be judged from the fact that between 1943 and 1946 more than 3,700 young men passed through this training regiment.[6] During the war Figeldean House had been used as 'B' Mess of the 6th Airborne Division but in November 1945 it was taken over as the official residence of the Commandant of the School and it has continued to be used for this purpose up to the present time. Another sign that life was gradually returning to normal was the holding of the first general meeting of the newly formed RA Saddle Club in February 1946.

In November of that year the first of a series of exercises was held at Larkhill under the designation of 'Exercise Ubique' and the subsequent report on it included the following comments:

It not only provided valuable instruction for a limited number of RA Commanders and staffs, but established the basic principles of handling artillery at corps and divisional levels . . .

It is proposed, therefore, to hold one exercise of the Ubique type at Larkhill every year. It will be regarded primarily as a means of crystalizing artillery tactical doctrine as it develops from year to year with the development of new weapons.[7]

When the Territorial Army was re-formed in January 1947, the situation regarding instructors required appropriate action and a succession of ten-week courses were arranged for those who had been selected as Permanent Staff Instructors in Territorial Gunner units. At the same time it was decided to produce a new series of Artillery Training pamphlets and of these, Volume III was to deal with field gunnery.[8] While the wartime overseas schools were in process of being closed, the establishment of a new School of Artillery which was to be formed within the British Army of the Rhine (BAOR) was announced in September 1947.

An event of world importance which also occurred in 1947 was the partition of India and Pakistan and the consequent demise of the Indian Army. This resulted in the transfer of some three hundred officers to the British Army and of these a large proportion elected to join the Regiment.[9] To meet this contingency, seven conversion courses were organised by Gunnery Wing and one of the sequels to these has been described as follows:

A Regimental Guest Night was held in the RA Mess, Larkhill, on Wednesday 17th March 1948 with the Master Gunner, Field Marshal The Viscount Alanbrooke in the chair.

The guests of the evening were the first batch of ex-Indian Army Officers (76) who have transferred to the Royal Regiment as Majors and Captains . . .

After dinner, speeches were made by the Master Gunner in proposing the Toast of the ex-Indian Army officers and welcoming them into the Regiment and Major E.C. Pickard replied.[10]

In April of the same year, Larkhill saw the formation of 192 Independent Survey Training Battery, RA. As indicated by its title, this was an independent unit which was responsible for training all surveyors for the Regiment, whether Regular or National Servicemen. On the completion of their course, they were posted as trained surveyors to locating regiments and batteries wherever they might be serving.[11] In 1961, after fourteen years' service, the

Battery was placed in suspended animation.[12] As a matter of interest the three artillery schools – the School of Artillery, the School of Anti-Aircraft Artillery and the Coast Artillery School – were all concerned during this period, with teaching various aspects of defence against air attacks. To avoid overlapping and duplication their respective responsibilities were defined in 1947.[13]

A number of senior officers visited the School during 1947 amongst whom were Lieutenant-General Sir John Harding (after-

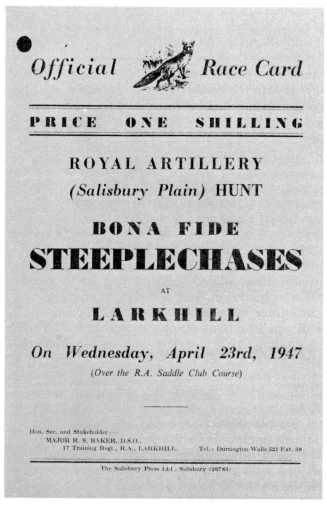

PLATE 21: Cover of the Race Card for the first point-to-point meeting on the Larkhill course, 1947.

wards Field Marshal Lord Harding of Petherton GCB, CBE, DSO, MC), General Sir William Bartholomew, GCB, CMG, DSO and Lieutenant-General Sir Wilfrid Lindsell, GBE, KCB, DSO, MC. Of more domestic importance, however, was the acquisition of Totterdown House by the War Department in 1947. 'One of the first houses . . . along the high road from Stonehenge Inn to Amesbury was 'Totterdown', built for a Gunner officer named Wood who, it was understood, had had the foresight to marry a rich wife.'[14] From 1947 to 1978 it was occupied by successive deputy commandants but in 1979 it was allocated to a Gunner officer on the staff of United Kingdom Land Forces (UKLF). He was followed for a short time by the then CIG at the School but in 1982 it became the residence of the CRA South whose headquarters are in Mason House, Tombs Road.

As far as sporting events are concerned, there are two good reasons why 1947 should be remembered. On 23 April the newly built point-to-point course which had been laid out to the northeast of Knighton Down was opened. The second which was a rather more mechanised occasion, was the holding of the first post-war Army motor cycle trial at Larkhill.[15] In August and November 1948 the first two post-war Young Officers Courses were held and, for the Territorial Army, correspondence courses prepared by the Gunnery Wing were introduced. These proved to be extremely popular and having been expanded in both scope and distribution over the past thirty-five years, are now available to all members of the Regiment.[16] Early in the year work began on the construction of buildings for the Royal Aircraft Establishment a little to the south of OP3 (grid reference 104483) and since then a number of buildings have been erected for the RAE on the ranges. Amongst those who visited the School in 1948, two were of especial eminence – Field Marshal Viscount Montgomery, KG, GCB, DSO and Mrs Odette Churchill, GC, MBE (now Mrs Odette Hallowes).

Although there had been close liaison between the School and the Royal Canadian Artillery during the Second World War, it was not until 1949 that a regular exchange of IGs began between the two countries. The success of this led to similar arrangements being made with the Americans in 1964 and the Australians in 1966. The period for which officers are attached to the School is normally from two to three years and the fact that this system of exchanges was still operating in 1983, was an indication of its undoubted success. In the case of students, these were now being drawn from an increasing number of nations.

During a recent period at the School of Artillery, Larkhill,
students from the following countries were attending courses:
    Australia, Canada, Malta, New Zealand, South Africa,
Pakistan, India, Eire, U.S.A., Egypt. Iraq, Syria, France,
Netherlands, Transjordan, Burma and Norway.
Is this a record?[17]

Unless one has a good knowledge of the language it is never
easy, when visiting a foreign country, to understand all that is
said but when much of it is concerned with a technical subject
such as gunnery, it can be very difficult:

> The Commandant had expressed concern that foreign students
> were attending courses at the School without sufficient know-
> ledge of the English language to understand the instruction. He
> therefore decided to visit the various courses with foreign stu-
> dents, in order to gain a first hand impression of the situation.
>   After sitting at the back of the classroom during a lecture to
> the Long Gunnery Staff Course NCOs, he approached two
> Iraquis during a break in the instruction and said to the first
> one:
>
> > 'Are you managing to cope all right with this course or is
> > the language difficulty making things tough for you?'
>
> The Iraqui stood rigidly to attention and replied:
>
> > 'I am speaking not very good English sir, but I am very
> > understanding'.
>
> Reasonably impressed by this reply, the Commandant turned
> to the second Iraqui and said:
>
> > 'And what about you? Are you managing all right?'
>
> The Iraqui snapped to attention, produced a guardsman-like
> salute and replied:
>
> > 'Baghdad sir'.[18]

The British element at Larkhill also increased in May 1949
due to the arrival of the first party of National Servicemen who
were to undergo their basic training with 'G' Battery (Mercer's
Troop) of 5th Regiment RHA which was then the Depot Regiment.[19]
By the summer of 1948 Gunners had taken over responsibility
for the development and manning of heavy mortars from the
infantry[20] and, on 1 January 1949, 4 Mortar Troop was formed
at Larkhill.[21] At very short notice it provided a troop which

joined 170 Light Battery RA and proceeded to Korea in September 1950.[22] However with the proposed reorganisation of the Regular Army and the introduction of guns normally able to fire in the upper register – that is, with the piece elevated at a high angle – the future of the 4 Mortar Troop became uncertain. In 1956 it was decided that it would remain at Larkhill 'to keep techniques alive for T.A. Training',[23] but on 1 April 1960 the Troop was finally placed in suspended animation.[24]

Although the Korean War made comparatively little impact on the School, an important change took place in its organisation during 1950. This was brought about by the closure of the All Arms Wing of the Royal Corps of Signals School at Catterick and, to replace it, a Signals Branch was established at Larkhill. This became an important part of the School and was advanced to the status of a wing in 1963. Another alteration which took place in 1950 was the renaming of Tactics Wing as Tactical Employment Wing, although it was to revert to its former title in 1969. In 1951 a new commission of Technical Instructor in Gunnery (TIG) was introduced, 'to produce a second career for the senior and long serving members of the Gunnery Staff and was to equate their terms of service with those of any other QM'.[25]

The first TIGs of the Field Branch were commissioned in September 1952 and as a result the number of IGs gradually decreased. By this time the pattern of equipment was gradually changing from towed to self-propelled guns and this transition was to continue over the coming years. In the meanwhile, not only was metrication being adopted but under a NATO agreement calibres were being standardised.

The death of HM King George VI, on 6 February 1952, shocked the whole nation and this great loss was deeply felt in the Royal Regiment. The happy occasion when Their Majesties visited the School in April 1941 was remembered with great pleasure and much affection. At the School, 1952 saw the Observation Wing renamed the Counter Bombardment Wing, and assume the additional responsibilities of radar and electronics, although ten years later its title was to be changed again – to Locating Wing. Another development during the year was the conversion of the RA Workshops into REME Workshops which paved the way to the establishment of a REME Wing in 1965.[26] It was indeed a changing scene.

During June 1952 the CIGS, Field Marshal Sir William Slim, GCB, GCMG, GCVO, GBE, DSO, MC, held his annual conference at Larkhill which proved to be an outstanding occasion attended

PLATE 22: Mr 'Taffy' Gould being presented to HM the Queen by Brig.
G.W.E. Heath when Her Majesty attended the United Services Point-to-
Point on 23rd February 1953. (*Salisbury Journal and Times*)

by all the Commonwealth generals.[27] A month earlier it was decided to stage 'Exercise Ambassador' although this was a demonstration rather than an exercise. It was felt that possibly more should be done to encourage cadets at Sandhurst to enter the Regiment when they were commissioned and with this in view a display of towed and self-propelled guns, anti-aircraft guns, airborne artillery and air OPs was held with the emphasis on a subaltern's command.[28] In 1957 'Exercise Ambassador' was replaced by 'Exercise Young Ambassador' which continued until 1962 when the first 'Larkhill Day' was held.

On 21 February 1953, HM the Queen and HRH the Duke of Edinburgh attended the United Services Point-to-Point which was held on the Larkhill Course. Her Majesty and Prince Philip were the guests of the Stewards and Committee at a buffet lunch which was held in the RA Mess before the meeting. The fact that this visit was made during the year of Her Majesty's coronation was especially appreciated and it was estimated that nearly 20,000 people were present, many of whom were serving and retired Gunners and their families.[29] Coronation celebrations included a parade service for all troops in Larkhill Garrison on Sunday, 31 May, which was followed by the planting of a copper beech by the Commandant, Brigadier C.H. Colquhoun (afterwards Major-General Sir Cyril Colquhoun, KCVO, CB, OBE), in the grounds of the Garrison Church. The wrought iron railings around the tree which incorporates the initials 'E II R' were made in the REME Workshops and the plaque which bears the following inscription is attached to the railings on the east side.

THIS TREE WAS PLANTED
BY
BRIGADIER C.H. COLQUHOUN OBE
TO MARK THE CORONATION OF
H.M. QUEEN ELIZABETH
JUNE 2, 1953

That night a firework display was arranged on the Stirling Sports Ground, on which the administrative buildings and the main instruction block, have since been built. In addition to the fireworks, dances, both indoor and outdoor, were held and a bar, refreshments and music were provided throughout the evening. At 2200 hours a bonfire which had been built by the Larkhill Boy Scout Troop was lit to provide a link with other fires on Beacon and Sidbury Hills.[30]

Early in the 1950s a new appointment was established with the title of Technical Advisor in Gunnery and Research (TAIGR), the acronym being pronounced 'Tiger'. The holder of this post works in conjunction with the Ordnance Board and the Royal Armaments Research and Development Establishment (RARDE) and is concerned with the technical aspects of gunnery and their practical application.[31] Construction of the new married quarters for officers in and around Wells Road began in 1954 and, in effect, this marked the beginning of the post-war development programme, although the major part was carried out during the 1960s. In April 1954 the Cookery Team from the Women's Royal Army Corps at Larkhill won the Unit Team Event in the Southern Command Cookery Competition and shortly afterwards the Deputy Director of the WRAC visited the School in order to congratulate the winners. On 11 May Field Marshal Sir John Harding, Chief of the Imperial General Staff, paid another visit to the School although it was his first as CIGS.[32]

Owing to the introduction of a considerable amount of new equipment and the consequent revision of drill and procedures, the output of new publications increased substantially. This meant that while in 1955 one IG was responsible for 'Publications and New Techniques',[33] in 1956 it was necessary to divide the work between two IGs who were responsible for 'Publications and Correspondence Courses' and 'Current and New Techniques' respectively.[34] During 1955, a Guided Weapons Wing was formed in order to train personnel in the operation of the 'Corporal' missile that had been obtained from America, while in the following year the American 155 mm SP gun, M44, arrived at Larkhill to undergo trials. As new developments took place in the world's armaments, so the School took the necessary steps to maintain its lead in such matters and in 1956 a Nuclear Warfare Branch was formed within Tactical Employment Wing. This was renamed Tactics Wing in 1969 and further information regarding its work will be found in Chapter 9.

Although 1957 was chiefly notable for the Suez crisis, there were a number of other events which had an important bearing on the work of the School. As a result of the adoption of Target Grid Procedure and the Field Branch Artillery (FBA) Plotter, the zero line was replaced by the centre of arc in January 1957 and to many Gunners it must have seemed like saying goodbye to an old friend. Another link with the past disappeared shortly afterwards when the teaching of panoramas was discontinued.[35] On the other hand, the first Corporal missile arrived at the School

PLATE 23: The demolition of the old huts in 1959 many of which dated
from the First World War. (*T.L. Fuller*)

during the year and, in anticipation of this, the instruction of
units in guided weapons began in January, the 47th Guided
Weapons Regiment RA being stationed at Larkhill for about six
months.[36]

Later in 1957 the Army Restructuring Programme was announced
and, as a result, eighteen regiments and five training regiments
were, with profound regret, terminated. In spite of this, efforts
were still being made to attract young men into the Regiment,
and 'Exercise Ambassador' – which had first been held in 1952 –
was superseded by 'Exercise Young Ambassador' which took the
form of both a training demonstration and a recruiting display.
Amongst the visitors to the School during 1957 were the Secretary
of State for War, Mr John Hare, PC, OBE (afterwards Viscount
Blakenham), who was accompanied by the DCIGS, General Sir
Richard Hull (afterwards Field Marshal Sir Richard Hull, GCB,
DSO), and later in the year, the Master Gunner, General Sir
Cameron Nicholson, GCB, KBE, DSO, MC.[37]

It was decided in 1958 that the study of electronic warfare
and instruction in the subject, other than communications, should
be the responsibility of the School and accordingly an electronic
warfare section was formed in the Counter Bombardment Wing.[38]

At the same time another change had become apparent as equipment, marked in mils instead of degrees, began to be issued.

On 8 January 1958 the School was honoured by a visit from HRH The Duke of Gloucester and on the following day by a visit from HRH The Princess Royal. Her Royal Highness who was inspecting units of the WRAC in Southern Command, lunched in the RA Mess and, after her visit, graciously presented a signed watercolour by Orlando Norrie entitled 'Field Artillery' which now hangs in the Baker Room.

Another notable event was the visit in June of His Majesty the Sultan of Muscat and Oman who was accompanied by his Chief of Staff. His Majesty had previously expressed a wish that he would prefer not to lunch in the Mess in order to spend as much time as possible on the ranges. To meet the situation, a tent was erected at Prospect Clump complete with carpets and other accoutrements, silver on the table and the Mess Staff on duty with their usual discreet efficiency. After lunch, the Commandant Brigadier A.J.C. Block (afterwards Major-General A.J.C. Block, CB, CBE, DSO) had arranged for a demonstration of anti-tank shooting with 25 prs. At the end of it, the Sultan took his seat as layer on one of the guns with his Chief of Staff laying on another, to see which of them would score the greatest number of hits, the result being a decisive victory for His Majesty.[39] The chief sporting success in 1958 was achieved by the School Hockey XI which won both the Army Cup and the Southern Command Cup.

By 1958 the Army Council had agreed that steps should be taken to find a replacement for the 75 mm pack howitzer and the 4.2 in mortar,[40] and in October of that year an Italian 105/14 pack howitzer was demonstrated by a detachment of the Italian Army at Larkhill.[41] In April 1959 two of these howitzers arrived at the School for trials and, after they had been put through a series of exhaustive tests, they were finally dropped on a pallet from an aircraft. Having survived this and other experiences, a sufficient number were acquired to equip several regiments and it subsequently came into general service in 1960.[42]

Two important events took place in 1959: first, the opening of the Royal Artillery Guided Weapons Range in the Hebrides, and second, the firing of four 'Corporal' missiles from the new range on 23 June. It was the first time that this missile had been fired by any army in Europe. At Larkhill, trials began on the prototype of a 5.5 in gun mounted on a Centurion MK.7 chassis but the project was abandoned before the trials were completed.[43] The 105 mm howitzer had now been accepted as the basic equipment for instruction at the School, while at the same time the metre had replaced the yard for all lineal measurements.[44]

During the previous twenty years the composition of brigades and regiments had been subject to a number of changes. In 1937 a field brigade consisted of four batteries each of six guns, giving a total of twenty-four guns and this overall figure remained constant until 31 March 1960. In 1938, when the brigade became a regiment, the organisation was changed to two batteries each of three troops of four guns – that is a 12-gun battery. However, in October 1940 another battery was added so that the regiment was then made up of three batteries each of two troops of four guns thus producing an 8-gun battery. In March 1960 the composition was changed once again and although the number of batteries in a regiment remained at three, the number of guns in a battery was reduced to six in peacetime and eight in war, which produced an 18- or 24-gun regiment. Under this arrangement, the troops were omitted from the chain of command but, although they no longer existed on the battery position, they were retained within the organisation of the battery for administrative purposes. In April 1982 another change occurred when, in the case of regiments which were equipped with Abbots and M109s, the 6-gun battery became an 8-gun battery once again. In other field regiments the 6-gun battery continued to operate.

The outstanding event of 1960 was the laying of the foundation stone of Alanbrooke Barracks by Field Marshal Viscount Alanbrooke on 27 September. It has been described as 'a day of great splendour'[45] and among the large number of distinguished guests were seven former commandants of the School, namely, General Sir Clement Armitage, KCB, CMG, DSO (1926–9), Brigadier Lord Malise Graham, CB, DSO, MC (1934–6), Lieutenant-General S.R. Wason, CB, MC (1938–9), Brigadier R.H. Towell, CBE, MC (1942–5), Major-General G.W.E. Heath, CB, CBE, DSO, MC (1945–7), Brigadier G.G. Mears, CBE, DSO, MC (1947–9) and Lieutenant-General Sir Edward Howard-Vyse, CB, KBE, MC (1953–6).[46] The foundation stone which is built into the front wall of the Soldiers Dining Hall, facing Brackenbury Road, carries the following inscription:

THIS FOUNDATION STONE WAS LAID BY
FIELD MARSHAL
THE VISCOUNT ALANBROOKE
KG GCB OM GCVO DSO
ON THE TWENTY SEVENTH OF SEPTEMBER
1960

PLATE 24: FM Lord Alanbrooke laying the foundation stone of the new buildings on 27th September 1960. On the left is Mr. Alfred Chivers representing the contractors, Messrs. W.E. Chivers & Sons. (*The Gunner*)

PLATE 25: The Foundation Stone seen as a white rectangle in the front wall of the Soldier's Dining Hall, 1983. (*RSA Reprographics*)

The ceremony was followed by a service, after which members of the staff of Messrs W.E. Chivers & Sons Ltd, the contractors, were presented to Lord Alanbrooke.[47] The occasion marked the commencement of the main rebuilding programme which was to replace the timber and corrugated iron huts in which the School had been housed since the First World War, with modern buildings.

At the beginning of 1961, under the authority of the War Office, the School was designated the 'School of Artillery, Larkhill' and the School of Anti-Aircraft Artillery became the 'School of Artillery, Manorbier'.[48] During the year, three notable changes occurred at Larkhill, the first being the closure of the Equipment Wing and the transfer of development and trials to individual wings. The second affected the Salisbury Plain Range Detachment which ceased to function as a separate establishment and became a part of Gunnery Wing being known as the Larkhill and Westdown range detachment. The third concerned the 192 Independent Survey Training Battery which, as previously mentioned, was disbanded. For some time the DRA and commanding officers had considered that the Officer's Long Gunnery Staff Course was too long and in 1960 and 1961 the course was reduced to ten months. A further curtailment to seven months took place in 1962 and, as a result, it was renamed the Gunnery Staff Course.[49]

On 7 November 1961, three days before the completion of their course, the students on No. 20 LGSC (Officers) were carrying out course shooting practice on the 155 mm howitzer, M.44. Despite the fact that stringent safety precautions are always taken, it is still possible for accidents to happen. On this occasion the staff of the Royal Aircraft Establishment, who were working at OP3, had, with one exception, fortunately retired to the canteen for their official tea break. The exception was the Establishment's safety officer, Mr 'Smudger' Smith, a retired AIG who had remained in the observation tower.

A few moments later the Range Liaison Officer's telephone rang and the order 'STOP' was received from the tower at OP3. This was followed by the information, given in a very casual voice, that 'there's a . . . . . great shell landed a few yards from my tower – and there goes another one'. The RLO subsequently remarked that 'it is difficult to paint the real picture but Smith dealt with it as calm as a nun on Good Friday'. The second round hit the canteen but by sheer good luck the only casualty was a man who was hit by a few splinters. Fortunately the last three rounds of '5 rounds gunfire' were stopped in time.[50]

In June 1961 the first Joint Services Demonstration was held at

Larkhill when formations and units of the Royal Navy, the Royal Marines, the Army and the Royal Air Force took part. A grand stand was built on Knighton Down by the Royal Engineers and since then this site has become the scene of many displays, including those given on 'Larkhill' and 'Artillery Days'. The next year, another Joint Services Demonstration took place and this followed a similar pattern but with the addition of a fire-power demonstration. The programme for the day contained an introduction which read:

> The aim of the demonstration is to show aircraft, weapons and equipment in service or in production for the Royal Navy and Royal Marines, Army and Royal Air Force and to demonstrate some of their capabilities in the move to battle and in battle. The demonstration is particularly designed to educate the young officer and cadet.[51]

Later in 1961, HMS *Excellent* kindly presented a gun tampion to the School and it was felt that this gift should be suitably reciprocated. However, it was then realised that the School did not have a badge or insignia of its own and steps were immediately taken to provide one. It was decided that the design should be based on the badge of rank as then worn by Warrant Officers Class 2 (AIG), that is to say, the crossed guns surmounted by a St Edward's Crown – sometimes referred to as 'The Queen's Crown'. This was adopted as the insignia of the School and, as such, it has remained in use up to the present time.[52]

A rather different emblem appeared in the Garrison Church in November when a new window was installed above the West Door. This portrays St Barbara, the Patron Saint of Artillerymen, and was dedicated by the Chaplain-General to the Forces, the Venerable Archdeacon I.D. Neill on 3 December 1961.[53]

By the end of the year the American 'Honest John' Free Flight Rocket and the 8 in howitzer had been issued, although the latter did not appear at the School for some time.[54]

During the course of 1962 a number of developments and changes took place in respect of equipment, and new examples soon appeared at the School. In February the Command Post vehicle (FV432) for an Abbot Battery arrived and, in March, this was followed by the first Abbot (105 mm SP Field Gun) both of which became the subject of extensive trials. At the same time the School returned its last 75 mm Pack howitzer to Ordnance which had been declared obsolete. Amongst the new instrumental equipment was the Elliott 803 Computer which was delivered in February and the No. 13 MK 1 Radar which reached the School in April.[55] Several changes were made in the length and designation of courses during the year and these included the renaming of the Royal Artillery Senior Officer's Course as the RA Lieutenant-Colonel's Course. This was run in alternate years and when it did not take place, a four-day Air Defence Convention was held at Manorbier.[56] By the end of 1962 the title of the Counter Bombardment Wing had changed once more when it was renamed the Locating Wing: ten years before it had been known as the Observation Wing.

The second Joint Services Demonstration took place in June 1962 while, at the end of July, the first 'Larkhill Day' was held. This had previously been known by the name of 'Exercise Young Ambassador' when it had taken the form of a display which was primarily for young officers and cadets. However, with a change of name, it was decided to open it to the general public and, largely due to the work of the Chief Instructor in Gunnery, Colonel J. Fairclough, this new departure proved to be an outstanding success.[57] The programme included a demonstration of artillery fire in support of an attack in which more than seventy guns took part, followed by the firing of an 'Honest John' rocket. It was just as well that the grandstand which had been built the year before had, in the meantime, been enlarged.

The School also distinguished itself in Rugby football by winning the MacIlwaine Cup, later in the year.

During 1962 it was announced that it had been decided to retain two separate Schools of Artillery, one at Larkhill and the other at Manorbier on the grounds that 'With the wide variety of Artillery weapons in service now and in the foreseeable future, it is impossible to find any one place or area which can meet all the training requirements.'[58] Six years later this decision was to be reversed.

The deaths occurred in 1963 of two leading figures who had been very closely connected with the School. The first (25 February) was that of Major-General H.W. Newcome who was the first commandant of the School from 1920 to 1922, having previously been commandant of Chappterton Down Artillery School. On 17 June the death occurred of Field Marshal Viscount Alanbrooke who had been commandant from 1929 to 1932. He made a very valuable contribution to the School during this period and his subsequent career, culminating in his promotion to field marshal, is too well known to be repeated here. Memorials to these two officers which had been placed in the Garrison Church, were unveiled on 28 April and 1 December respectively.

During 1962 it was decided that the time had come to introduce work-study into the Army and accordingly work-study teams were formed in January 1963. In the case of the Royal Regiment, the team, which initially consisted of an officer and a warrant officer, was known as the RA Army Work Study Group and was stationed at Larkhill. However in 1974 the title was changed to the RA Army Management Services Group (Work Study) but seven years later, owing to a reduction in manpower, all arms teams were withdrawn to a central headquarters at West Byfleet, Surrey.[59] On 1 October 1963, 160 (Middleton's Coy) Battery, RA and 22 (Gibraltar 1779–83) Battery, RA were amalgamated at Larkhill, the title adopted for the new unit being that of the second battery, but on 18 March 1964 this was changed to 22 (Gibraltar 1779–83) Locating Battery, RA.[60]

An unusual feature of Larkhill Day 1963 was the display given by an American Artillery unit. This was Battery 'A' of the 2nd Howitzer Battalion of the 2nd Artillery Regiment of the United States Army whose visit to the School from 29 July to 12 August created a great deal of interest.[61] On the other hand, visits were paid by the Commandant, Brigadier W.D.E. Brown (afterwards Major-General W.D.E. Brown, CB, CBE, DSO) during the year to the Canadian School of Artillery at Shilo, the American School at Fort Sill, the West German School at Idar Oberstein and the French School at Chalons-sur-Marne.[62] Visits of this kind have also been made by other commandants and their value cannot be overestimated.

A massive programme for the redevelopment and rebuilding of Larkhill had been planned to take place during the 1960s, and one of the first results of this was the opening of the new married quarters, on 4 May 1962, by the Secretary of State for War, the Rt. Hon. John Profumo, PC, OBE.[63] This was followed by a new building for the Navy, Army and Air Force Institutes Canteen which was named 'The Wagon Lines Club' and was opened by Lieutenant-General Sir Robert Bray, KCB, CBE, DSO, GOC-in-C, Southern Command on 6 December 1962.[64]

The main building programme, however, was divided into four phases each of which covered clearly defined projects that were to be undertaken in accordance with a pre-arranged time schedule. Roberts Barracks which comprised Phase I were completed and handed over in 1964 while in April 1966, the Headquarters Block,

Instructional Block and Newcome Hall were taken over by the
School. By July 1966 most of the buildings between Glover Road
and the eastern camp boundary had been finished and were
occupied.[65]

With the completion of what may be described as the 'heart'
of the School, it was decided that the new buildings should be
officially opened and this was performed by the Master Gunner,
General Sir Robert Mansergh, GCB, KBE, MC on 6 October 1966.
A guard of honour was provided by 22 (Gibraltar 1779-83)
Locating Battery, RA and a commemorative plaque was unveiled
by the Master Gunner.[66] This is fixed on the right hand side of
the main entrance to the School headquarters in Bell Road and
bears the following inscription:

> THIS PLAQUE
> WAS UNVEILED ON 6 OCTOBER 1966 BY
> GENERAL SIR ROBERT MANSERGH GCB KBE MC
> MASTER GUNNER ST JAMES' PARK
> TO MARK THE OPENING OF THE NEW
> HEADQUARTERS SCHOOL OF ARTILLERY

A copy of *Artillery Training*, Volume II and a nominal role of
the officers on the staff of the School were placed in a sealed
recess behind the plaque.[67] To mark the site of the old headquarters, the base and iron retaining clamps of the flagstaff which
stood outside the headquarters were left in position,[68] and were
still in existence in 1983 (grid reference 13714435). During 1967,
the Young Officers quarters, the Warrant Officers and Sergeants
Mess Annexe, the WRAC quarters, the NAAFI shop, the medical
inspection room and the dental centre were completed.[69]

By April 1968, the messing office and ration store, the telephone exchange and two sports pavilions had been handed over
and in September the new Roman Catholic Church had been
finished. Finally, with the completion of the REME and MT lines
in October 1968, it could be said that the rebuilding of Larkhill
had been brought to a most successful conclusion.[70] The greater
part of the work had been carried out by Messrs W.E. Chivers &
Sons of Devizes whose connection with Larkhill had begun before
the First World War.

In August 1967 it was necessary to carry out structural alterations to the RA Mess and all feeding arrangements were transferred to the old 'A' Mess. By the following August the work had
been finished and the RA Mess became fully operative once again

PLATE 26: 'A' Mess. Built in 1915 and demolished in 1968. (*T.L. Fuller*)

while at the same time 'A' Mess was finally closed. Since it had been built in 1915, it had been used by many generations of Gunner officers and its demolition in December 1968, after more than fifty years of 'faithful service', marked the end of an era. By 1982, the only buildings which had been erected at Larkhill before or during the First World War, and which were still in existence, were the two hangars constructed by the Bristol and Colonial Aircraft Company in Wood Road in 1910, the balloon hangars at Rollestone erected in 1916 and the stables adjoining Glover and Brind Roads built in 1917 or thereabouts.

Since the Corporal guided missile was being phased out and, as its intended successor – 'Blue Water' – was not after all to enter service, the future of the Guided Weapons Wing itself became uncertain and in July 1965 the Wing was closed. On the other hand in November a new wing was formed which was to be concerned with the work of the Royal Corps of Electrical and Mechanical Engineers and was accordingly named the 'REME Wing'.[71] During this year it was also decided to introduce 'career courses' for young officers, gun position officers, troop commanders and battery commanders, the last being mandatory for all BCs before taking command of a battery.[72]

In the field of new equipment, 1965 became an important milestone with the arrival at the School of the Abbot 105 mm SP gun, the M107 175 mm SP gun, the first M109 155 mm SP howitzer and the American SP 80 155 mm SP howitzer.[73] Although the first Abbots were issued to regiments in January 1966, the SP medium and heavy equipment were not distributed until a year later.[74]

In sporting activities, the School surpassed itself during 1966 when it won all the leading awards in respect of Rugby football, cricket and tug-of-war competitions. In the Army and RA Hunter Trials the School was responsible for the organisation of the trials which were held over the Knighton Down Course.[75] On such occasions and when point-to-points were held over this course, young officers were expected to tread-in loose turves near the jumps but this was not always popular.

On the YOs course which was on during the Point-to-Point Season in 1966, some bright sparks tried to put an advertisement in *The Times*, announcing that the Larkhill Racecourse was for sale. This was in revenge for being made to 'tread' jumps during the races. Fortunately a lady sub-editor thought it a bit odd and 'phoned up to check. If it had appeared, I suspect several of the old and bold would have burst.[76]

Although a great deal of work had been carried out on testing and assessing heavy equipment, much time and effort had also been spent on the development of new instruments. Of these, one of the most important was the Field Artillery Computer Equipment (FACE), the trials of which began in 1967.

The Field Artillery Computer Equipment is a digital computer designed to produce gun data in field branch artillery. In addition to this the computer can carry out survey computations and store target records. Needless to say it does all this with more speed and greater accuracy than the old manual methods. The core of the system is the Elliott 920B stored programme computer and a control console. The system also includes a teleprinter for the passage of data between command posts.[77]

At the same time steps were taken to provide a 'manual' alternative should FACE not be available. Known as Graphical Control Instruments (GCIs), these consisted of firing tables, wind and displacement graphs, gun rules and so on, but in 1976 a simpler system known as Field Artillery Manual Equipment (FAME) was introduced. The need to improve the accuracy of orientation and fixation had been appreciated for some time and in 1967 the Precision Indicator of the Meridian (PIM) came into service and proved to be of the greatest value.[78] Since then a much improved form known as the Position and Azimuth Determining System (PADS) has become available.

On 12 January 1967 the foundation stone of the new Roman Catholic Church of St Barbara and St Anthony was laid by the Right Reverend G.W. Tickle, Roman Catholic Bishop-in-Ordinary to the Forces. After its return from Germany in 1966, the Royal Artillery Portsmouth Band was stationed at Larkhill and in the following year was renamed the Royal Artillery (Larkhill) Band, although in 1971 a further change was made in its title when it became the Royal Artillery Alanbrooke Band.

In spite of the decision which had been reached in 1962 that two separate schools of artillery should be retained at Larkhill and Manorbier respectively,[80] it was announced on 10 April 1968 that the Army Board had decided that the two schools should be amalgamated at Larkhill by 31 December 1970.[81] In another sphere of activity, trials and firing of the 105 mm light gun had begun in 1968 while the assessment of FACE continued. Investigations and tests were also carried out to find the most suitable tractors for the light gun and the FH 70 as and when they were issued to regiments. In March 1968, No. 9 Company WRAC, which was stationed at Larkhill, was disbanded and a new WRAC Battery was formed in its place, as an integral part of the School.[82] By 1969 trials of FACE had been completed and during the year, three of these computers arrived at Larkhill. Instruction on a large number of different types of equipment which was taught by the School has been summarised by Lieutenant-Colonel J.R. Guy who recorded that in 1969 teaching was being given on the following:[83]

25 pr gun howitzer
5.5 in gun
105 mm Pack howitzer
Abbot 105 mm gun
M109 155 mm SP howitzer
M1 8 in howitzer
M110 8in SP howitzer
M107 175 mm SP gun
Honest John free flight rocket

Field Artillery Computer Equipment (FACE)
Graphical Control Instruments (GCIs)
Ground surveillance radar (ZB298)
Director L1A1
Precision Indicator of the Meridian (PIM)
Theodolite

When the School celebrated its 50th Anniversary in 1970, the occasion marked an event that was of far greater importance than simply the elapse of fifty years. Established shortly after the end of one World War, the School was to be faced with another nineteen years later and with all the expansion and development in artillery matters that such conflicts inevitably produce. However, it was between 1950 and 1970 that the greatest changes occurred with the development of rocket-propelled missiles, the introduction of guns and howitzers of fundamentally new designs, the employment of electronics through the medium of the computer and the implications of nuclear warfare. Consequently the School's Anniversary may be regarded as one of the most significant landmarks in its history.

Numerous events contributed to the year's celebrations which began with an Anniversary Dinner on 10 April. Amongst those present were the Master Gunner, General Sir Robert Mansergh, Lieutenant-General Sir Denis O'Connor, the Director Royal Artillery, Major-General H.C. Tuzo, thirteen previous commandants at Larkhill and seven previous commandants at Manorbier.[84] This was followed on 5 June by 'Past v. Present' golf and cricket matches with a dinner in the evening while on 16 July an open-air concert was given by the massed bands of the Regiment and the WRAC in front of the RA Mess. In the meantime a well-illustrated brochure had been published which provided a concise history of the School and an account of its work since 1920. However, it is probable that the displays and demonstrations which were held on 17 and 18 July, will be remembered as the outstanding event in the Anniversary year. Known as 'Larkhill Day' since 1962 it was renamed 'Artillery Day' for this occasion, a title which has since been retained for other similar events. The main display which was held in the afternoon was opened by Major-General H.C. Tuzo, Director Royal Artillery (afterwards General Sir Harry Tuzo) on 17 July and by the Chief of the General Staff, General Sir Geoffrey Baker (afterwards Field Marshal Sir Geoffrey Baker) on the following day. On each afternoon the display began with what may be described as 'Gunners in the Air' which demonstrated parachuting,

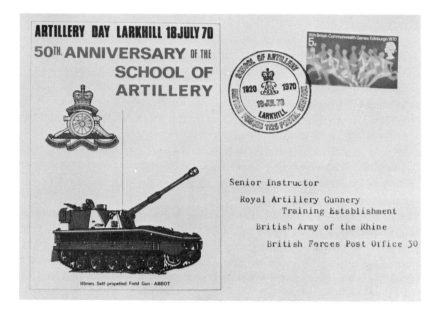

PLATE 27: The 'First Day Cover' issued to commemorate the 50th Anniversary of the School.

an Auster Light Aircraft formerly used as an 'Air OP', helicopters and gliding. This was followed by numerous examples of the use and effect of various types of artillery support that can be provided by different kinds of equipment, ending with the firing of the Honest John Free-Flight Rocket.[85] One of the most impressive displays was the drive past of 2nd Field Regiment RA in their Abbots and Stalwart high-mobility load carriers.

The occasion proved to be an outstanding success and it is estimated that approximately 30,000 people visited Larkhill during these two days. To mark the occasion a Special Commemorative Philatelic Cover, more commonly known as a 'First Day Cover' (Plate XX, see page 000), was issued and these were postmarked with a specially designed RA handstamp bearing the date and posted in the arena area. The proceeds of the sales of this cover were given to Service Charities.

On 24 July an Anniversary Ball was held in the RA Mess and this was followed, a week later, by a similar occasion in the Warrant Officers and Sergeants Mess while a School Reunion Dinner took place on 23 October. It was felt that such an outstanding year ought to be commemorated in some tangible form and it was decided that there could be no better way than by planting a wood.

A topographical reminder of the School's 50th Anniversary was established on Larkhill ranges on 19th November when our affiliated Colonel Commandant, Lieutenant-General Sir Denis O'Connor planted the first of 50 golden sycamore trees. These will form a golden grove at one corner of a training woodland, consisting of sycamore, beech, Norway maple and Scots pine which is being planted on Alton Down on the east side of Larkhill Racecourse. This woodland has been named Anniversary Plantation and is in the shape of the Roman numeral L.[86]

The plantation consists of five separate sections, three sections and a part of the fourth forming the vertical portion of the 'L' and one section and the balance of the fourth forming the horizontal arm. The grid reference of the centre of the vertical portion is 133468. As the year drew to a close, a special service was held in the Garrison Church.

Our celebration of the 50th Anniversary of the establishment of the School of Artillery at Larkhill, culminated in a special Commemoration Service on St Barbara's Sunday, 6th December. This service was conducted by the Rev. J.S. Westmuckett, Garrison Chaplain, and the address was given by the Chaplain General, the Venerable Archdeacon J.R. Youens, Chaplain to the Queen. Augmented by the Garrison Choral Society, the choir led the hymn singing and sang a special anthem, accompanied on the organ by Major D.J. Harris. The RA (Larkhill) Band, under the direction of Captain A.R. Pinkney provided the accompaniment to the hymns. The lesson was read by the Commandant, Brigadier G de E. Collin. The congregation of 400 included several visitors having a close association with the

PLATE 28: The second painting by Miss Joan Wanklyn for 50th Anniversary covering the years 1945-70 and portrays, from the top left corner, the following scenes. The Gun Park with 175 mm SP gun; 8 in. howitzer; 'Abbots' and 'Honest John'; Lt.-Col. F.B. Edmeades with the RA Hunt passing a 'Green Archer'. Survey training near Stone henge; the Newcome Hall and School Headquarters with the Commandant, Brig. G. de E. Collin on 'Ministrel'; the School RSM, WO1 G.E. Slim; the pack howitzers of 27 (Dragon) Battery, 49th Field Regiment RA, and instruction in the FACE room. Inside the Newcome Hall; the Point-to-Point Course; 'A' Vehicle Workshops, REME Wing, with 155 mm SP gun, M109 and 25 pr.

School over a number of years, as well as members of the Garrison and their families. Past Commandants of the School were headed by the Representative Colonel Commandant, Major-General J.M. McNeil (1959–60) who was joined by Major-General P.J. Glover (1960–62) and Brigadier G.G. Mears (1947–49). We were also pleased to welcome the BRA Army Strategic Command, Brigadier J.G. Bagnall and Major John Newcome, son of the first commandant, the late Major-General H.W. Newcome.[87]

Very appropriately, the School was particularly successful during the year in its sporting activities, winning the Gillet Cup for hockey, the Broken Wheel Cup for rifle shooting and the Crane Mills Cup for sailing. In cricket the School won the Army Championship and were runners-up in the Army Golf Championship.[88]

Among the other events which took place in 1970 was the transfer of the Air Defence Wing from Manorbier in accordance with the decision to amalgamate the two Schools after 31 December. In order to deal with the increasing demand for the services of the Support Regiment, for equipment, instruments and ammunition, a new School Booking Centre (SBC) was set up.[89] Finally, as the Anniversary Year came to an end, the Commandant announced that Her Majesty the Queen had been pleased to confer on the School the title of 'The Royal School of Artillery'. The first fifty years had received the royal accolade.

8. The Latter Years

With the amalgamation of Larkhill and Manorbier successfully concluded and encouraged by the prestige of its new royal title, the School could look forward to the beginning of a new era in its history. One immediate result of the incorporation of the two Schools was the establishment of an Air Defence Wing at Larkhill so that in 1971 the School comprised seven wings, namely, Gunnery, Air Defence, Tactics, Locating, Signals, Administrative and REME.[1] As trials of the 105 mm light gun continued, another equipment of a very different kind was introduced – the AN/USD 501 or Unmanned Surveillance Drone which 22 (Gibraltar 1779–83) Locating Battery flew successfully on the RA Range in the Hebrides. A further innovation was the production of a booklet containing information on current technical developments and procedures both at the School and throughout the Regiment which, it was hoped, would also provide a channel for an exchange of ideas. Entitled *Plain Talk – The Royal School of Artillery Liaison Notes*, the first number appeared in May 1971 and the Commandant, Brigadier G. de E. Collin (afterwards Major-General G. de E. Collin, CB, MC) writing in the foreword made the following comments:

Despite the continuous contact maintained by the Gunnery Staff, and especially those at commands, I have felt for some time that the link between the School and its various wings, and individual regiments and batteries is not as strong or as effective as it should be. In some cases, the reasons for certain decisions, policies, drills or techniques emanating from the School are not easily understood by those who have to put them into practice and use them. At the same time, I am sure that there are many ideas, views and suggestions at the user level which would be of great assistance both to the School and to other users, but which for one reason or another do not get beyond the level of the battery or regiment concerned. I hope that this publication will help to bridge this gap in communications, with benefit to the Regiment as a whole.

However the anticipated support was not forthcoming and, after appearing in 1972, 1973 and 1974, the fifth and last number was published in 1976. It seems unfortunate that such an admirable idea did not succeed.

On 6 May 1971 HRH The Duchess of Kent, as Controller Commandant of the Women's Royal Army Corps, paid a visit to the School and the WRAC Battery. After being welcomed by the Commandant and the Battery Commander, Major C.G. Parsons, Her Royal Highness visited different parts of the School in which members of the Battery were working. After lunch in the RA Mess she watched a game of rounders and called at the stables where members of the Battery were receiving riding instruction. Before leaving Larkhill, the Duchess had tea in the Newcome Hall with the officers and seniors NCOs of the Battery.[2] Other visitors during the year included the Australian Minister of Defence, the Rt Hon. John Gorton, the GOC-in-C Southern Command, General Sir Basil Eugster, KCB, KCVO, CBE, DSO, MC and Mr G.J. Smith, MP, Under-Secretary of State for Defence (Army).[3]

To mark the 50th Anniversary, the Wiltshire County Council honoured the School by granting it the privilege of using the County's badge. Depicting a bustard against a green and silver background, the heraldic description of the badge (see Plate XX, page 000) is as follows:

> On a roundel barry of eight argent and
> vert a bustard wings addorsed proper.

A roundel is the heraldic name for a circle and in this case it is shown with the same field or background as occurs on the County's coat of arms, that is to say, eight alternate horizontal bars of silver and green. The bustard is the same as that which forms a crest to the coat of arms and is shown with its wings raised and in its true or proper colours.

It was also felt that the School should have its own flag and this first came into use on 22 April 1971. The design incorporates the County badge and the crown and crossed guns on a dark blue background (see Plate 29, page 119). The amalgamation of the two Schools was finally recorded in a unique manner when 150 silver wine goblets of the King Charles II pattern were presented to the RA Mess. Of these, sixty-six were provided from the combined silver funds of the two Officer's Messes, twenty-one were given by past commandants and other officers who had served at

PLATE 29: The County Badge which, in 1971, the Wiltshire County Council
granted the School the privilege of using.

the School, while the remaining sixty-four were presented by
Gunner headquarters and regiments.[5]

On 6 January 1972 a new Heavy Air Defence Compound which
housed the Thunderbird 2 Guided Missile System was opened by
Mrs Peter Foster, wife of the Commandant. Covering some 40
acres it adjoins the western end of Brackenbury Road and includes
the site of the old Hamilton Battery.[6] When it was known that
Thunderbird was to be withdrawn in 1977 the enclosure was renamed the Anti-Tank Compound on 29 July 1976 and this name
was still in use in 1983. Having satisfactorily completed the necessary trials, the light gun was accepted for service in 1972 and at
the same time it was decided to approve the 3½ litre Rover 1
tonne vehicle as a gun tower, light ammunition limber and so on.
During this year the first two Rapier air-defence guided weapons
arrived at the School although they were early models and not
representative of the type which was subsequently issued for service.[7]

In October 1972, the WRAC Battery was visited by the Director of the United States Women's Army Corps, Brigadier-General Mildred C. Bailey, who was only the second officer in the Corps who had attained such rank. She was met by Major C.G. Parsons, the Battery Commander and Lieutenant-Colonel Pat Norman, Assistant Director WRAC. After meeting the Commandant, Brigadier P.B. Foster, she was shown the work that members of the Battery were doing in the course of their duties, in various parts of the School.[8]

On 3 April 1973, the School was greatly honoured by a visit of Her Majesty the Queen, Captain General of the Royal Regiment. The day was bright and sunny and on her arrival she was greeted with a fanfare sounded by the Herald Trumpeters of the Royal Artillery Mounted Band. Her Majesty was welcomed by the Lord Lieutenant of Wiltshire, Lord Margadale, and the Master Gunner, Field Marshal Sir Geoffrey Baker, and, after a number of presentations, the Queen entered the Newcome Hall where the Commandant gave a short account of the work and aims of the School. Her Majesty then walked to the Gun Park, stopping on several occasions to speak to members of the Permanent Staff and the Garrison who, with their families, lined the route. After inspecting some of the equipment and meeting the Chief Instructors and their staffs, the Queen visited the Electronics Workshop of REME Wing before proceeding to the RA Mess for lunch where she presented a silver goblet to the Commandant, to mark the occasion of her visit. After lunch, Her Majesty attended the Royal Artillery Hunt Point-to-Point and when, later in the afternoon, her visit came to an end, one of the happiest and most memorable days in the history of Larkhill was brought to a close.[9]

Shortly afterwards the following telegram was sent to the assistant private secretary.

> From Commandant to Assistant Private Secretary to Her Majesty the Queen. I would be grateful if you would convey my humble duty to Her Majesty the Queen and inform her that All Ranks of the Royal School of Artillery and members of the Royal Artillery Hunt deeply appreciate the honour paid to them by Her Majesty as their Captain General by visiting Larkhill. Would you convey to Her Majesty the thanks of her officers for her gracious gift of a silver goblet, which will be a treasured possession of the Officers' Mess.

To this, the Master Gunner received the following reply:

PLATE 30: Visit of HM the Queen to Larkhill, 3rd April 1973. On Her Majesty's right is the Commandant, Brig. P.B. Foster and on her left, the Master Gunner, FM Sir Geoffrey Baker. (*RSA Reprographics*)

The Queen greatly appreciated the telegram received yesterday from the Commandant of the Royal School of Artillery, Larkhill. Her Majesty has instructed me to write to you to say how tremendously she enjoyed her visit on Saturday. It was undoubtedly a highly successful occasion and Her Majesty particularly appreciated the way in which the visit had been organised to enable her to meet as many Gunners and their families as possible.

The visit to the Royal School had been devised with much originality and your Captain General was delighted by the way in which officers, NCOs and other ranks, families and equipments were all given a part in the programme.

At the end of the morning the excellent lunch made a perfect climax to the Royal School and The Queen much enjoyed the spirited rendering of the post horn gallop and the regimental marches.

It was a most happy thought to invite Her Majesty to join you at the Royal Artillery Point to Point in the afternoon. I think you will have seen how much pleasure this gave Her Majesty and she was indebted to Colonel Webb and Lieutenant Colonel Heaton-Ellis for organising the occasion so efficiently and yet with a welcome informality.

I should be grateful, if you would convey The Queen's warm congratulations and appreciation to Brigadier Peter Foster and his staff for everything they did to make the visit of their Captain General such a happy one. They really did an outstanding job.

Finally, may I thank you on behalf of the Members of the Household for your very kind hospitality. We enjoyed ourselves hugely.[10]

In conclusion, Miss Joan Wanklyn recorded the occasion of her Majesty's visit in a painting which now hangs in the RA Mess.

Following further reorganisation of the School which took place in September 1973, Locating and Gunnery Wings were amalgamated. During the year the first preproduction 1 tonne Rovers arrived at the School for towing trials with the light gun and the Rapier launcher while the new Artillery Meteorological System (AMETS) was accepted into service. A meteor balloon is still a vital part of this system, the necessary information being obtained by tracking the balloon with radar and passing the results through a computer to the guns. Throughout this period defence sales were becoming increasingly important and staff and members of the School carried out demonstrations and gave presentations of equipment both overseas and at Larkhill. The first Technical Gunnery Conference was organised by the Deputy Chief Instructor in Gunnery during 1974 and although these were held annually at first, they now take place twice a year, in March and October. They are attended by representatives of other instructional wings, the United Kingdom Land Forces (UKLF) Gunnery Staff and the RA Gunnery Training Establishment (RAGTE) from BAOR.[11]

During 1969 the Commandant, Brigadier G. de E. Collin was asked to examine the possibility of constructing a 'close OP' on the ranges. The object was to enable a number of spectators to observe the effect of an artillery concentration when only a short distance from the point of impact but, at the same time, in complete safety. Work on this OP began during the summer of 1973 and was finished in 1974 and it is now possible for up to a hundred people to watch the effect of shell fire at close quarters without any of the inconveniences which are usually associated with such an experience.[12] In January 1969 a Training Evaluation Section had been set up at the School but during the middle of 1973 it had been renamed the Training Development Team RA (TDTRA) and further information on the Team's work will be found in Chapter 13.

The mortar locating radar known as 'Green Archer', which had been in service since 1962, was finally replaced in 1974 by a much improved system named 'Cymbeline' which was still in service in 1983. Although early models of 'Rapier' had reached the School in 1972, a 'Pilot Battery' composed of Army and Royal Air Force personnel was formed in Lincolnshire during 1973 in order to carry out operational trials with the new equipment, but the Battery later moved to Larkhill.[13] Units that were to be converted to Rapier were stationed at Rollestone Camp where various improvements were carried out to the living accommodation while the two balloon hangars were modernised so as to provide a workshop and a garage for vehicles.[14] In 1976 the 'Honest John' free flight rocket was withdrawn and replaced by the 'Lance' missile while the need for a short-range guided weapon for defence against low-level air attack was met by the introduction of 'Blowpipe' in 1975. By this time, the Light gun and the 1 tonne gun towing vehicle had become the basic teaching equipment at the School.[15]

After the Wagon Lines Club had opened in December 1962, the building which had previously been the NAAFI Canteen was put to various uses. However in 1975 it was taken over by the Administrative Wing as a social centre and is available, at the request of members of the School and the Garrison, for meetings, dances, displays and so on. Now known as 'The Gun Club', much of the initial work in organising this scheme was carried out by WO1 W.A. Buckley who was the School Regimental Sergeant-Major from 1972-1976. By 1976 the idea of a Unit Training Officer (UTO) had emerged and to a large extent this was due to the work which AIGs had done during their tour of regimental duty. To meet the requests of commanding officers for continued assistance in training, it was decided that the appointment of Regimental

Signals Officer (RSO) should be filled by a TIG who, as a Unit
Training Officer, would cover a wider field than had previously
been the case.[16]

The year 1977 marked the completion of the first twenty-five
years of the reign of Her Majesty the Queen and, to commemorate
this event, a group of Norway maple was planted on the edge of
the cricket field some 225 metres to the south-east of the RA Mess.
A stone bearing the following inscription has been erected on the
site, the grid reference of which is 133445 or thereabouts.

> THIS COPSE OF NORWEGIAN MAPLE
> IN THE DESIGN OF E II R WAS PLANTED
> TO COMMEMORATE THE SILVER JUBILEE OF
> HER MAJESTY QUEEN ELIZABETH II
> CAPTAIN GENERAL ROYAL ARTILLERY.

Amongst the new instruments which were now being tested at
the School was the Position and Azimuth Determining System
(PADS) which, when fitted to a vehicle, supplied the grid reference of any point at which the vehicle stopped. As regards heavy
equipment, a major event was the arrival of the 155 mm howitzer
(FH 70) at Larkhill.[17]

At the end of November, an Allied Command Europe Mobile
Force (AMF) exercise was held on the Salisbury Plain Training
Area under the title of 'Exercise Avon Express' in which units
from Belgium, Germany, Italy, the United Kingdom and the
United States of America took part. Its purpose was to practise
the deployment of the AMF and to employ the Force in its
deterrent and combat roles. After the exercise a dinner was held
in the RA Mess to which all senior officers and representatives of
NATO were invited.

> I sat next to H.E. Rolfs F. Pauls who was the NATO Ambas-
> sador for West Germany and who had served in the German
> Army during the Second World War. During dinner, I told him
> that I had heard that if an invasion of England by Germany had
> been successful, Larkhill was to be the Headquarters of the
> German Army. He then remarked, with a twinkle in his eye,
> 'So, we have now arrived'.[18]

A new model of the M109, 155 mm SP howitzer which was
equipped with a longer barrel and designated the M1091A, entered

service in 1978 while at the same time changes were taking place on the ranges. Following the decision to rebuild the anti-tank range at Lavington Folly, work began on this formidable task in 1976 and after much effort and expenditure, the range was re-opened in 1978. Unfortunately difficulties soon arose over the question of noise which affected parts of the Avon Valley and although every effort was made to overcome the problem, it eventually became necessary to restrict firing on this range under certain weather conditions.[19] On 25 May 1979 the School was honoured by another Royal Visit when HRH The Prince of Wales arrived at Larkhill in order to see the Battle Group Commander's Course at work. After joining the members of the course who were studying tactical problems on the ground in the Wylye Valley, His Royal Highness piloted a helicopter of the Queen's Flight back to the RA Mess where he joined the staff and students for lunch.[20]

For many years practice at conducting shoots from the OP had been carried out on what were generally referred to as 'miniature ranges'. In their simplest form these often consisted of an army blanket spread over a table, the 'contours' being provided by books placed under the blanket with pebbles, matchsticks or chalk lines representing the target. The 'fall of shot' would be indicated by the instructor's touching the blanket with a stick at the appropriate point. It was not difficult to improve on this primitive arrangement and artistic representations of the countryside, complete with houses, roads, woods and so on, soon appeared. At the same time the ranges were built at a sufficient height to enable an operator to walk beneath it. On the Nutt range bursts of shrapnel were represented by a small piece of cottonwool descending on a string from an overhead framework while on the Raikes range, ground bursts were indicated by puffs of smoke-producing chemicals (or sometimes from cigarettes), ascending from below. Although the Nutt range went out of use in 1936 when shrapnel was withdrawn, the Raikes which developed into the Perspective Miniature Range, remained in use at the School until 1979.[21] However, in May 1975 the SAAB OP Trainer was installed at the School and by 1977 it had become 'the most used trainer that the Royal Regiment ever possessed'.[22] During the latter part of 1978 another design, known as the 'Master Gunner' was tested and this was followed by trials of a trainer named 'Invertron' which proved to be so successful that it was adopted by the School and installed in July 1979. It provides an extremely realistic representation of shooting from an OP even to the extent of the sound of the shells passing overhead and is a very long way removed from the blanket on the table.

May 1979 was marked by the arrival at Larkhill of the Battle-field Artillery Target Engagement System (BATES) military team. The object was to provide a focus, within the Regiment, for the introduction of BATES during the following decade and further information on this will be found in Chapter 13. In October of the same year the appointment of Assistant Instructor in Gunnery (AIG) which had been in use since 6 January 1860, was replaced by that of Sergeant-Major Instructor in Gunnery (SMIG). This was brought about by the fact that the Armed Forces Pay Review Body considered that the word 'assistant' did not adequately describe the work that AIGs were required to carry out in order to be paid at the appropriate rate. Consequently, to meet the requirements of the Board, it was agreed that this appointment should be renamed.[23]

9. The Wings

It was not until the Second World War that steps were taken to decentralize the work of the School by creating divisions known as 'wings'. In this chapter the sections dealing with the respective wings are arranged in the chronological order of their formation while at the end of the chapter an alphabetical list is provided. In order to appreciate the position of the wings in relation to the School as a whole, see Figure 9.1, which shows the organisation of the School as at 31 January 1983. Charts are also provided later in this chapter for those wings which were in operation at that date. From these it will be seen that a wing may divided into branches, sections or other specialised divisions while a branch may also be subdivided into sections.

The names of the senior officers who have served in the various wings will be found under the appropriate section except in the case of Headquarters Wing and Anti-Tank Wing for which no records can be found. Unfortunately, in the case of senior warrant officers, the necessary information is only available for Air Defence, Guided Weapons, Gunnery, Signals and Tactics Wings and for the Young Officers' Wing and Branches.

Headquarters Wing, 1940–4
Presumably in order to deal with the rapid expansion of the School's activities, following the declaration of war a Headquarters Wing was formed in 1940. Excluding any instructional staff the establishment provided for six officers at Headquarters, namely, the commandant, the officer in charge of Headquarters Wing, a staff captain, an administrative staff officer, an equipment officer and a quartermaster.[1] Although the Wing was still operating in 1943 it had apparently ceased to be a wing two years later since the entry in the establishment for 1945 shows it simply as 'Headquarters'.[2]

Anti-Tank Wing, 1941–2
The Home War Establishment for the School dated 3 July 1941 contains details of three wings – Headquarters, Tactical and Anti-

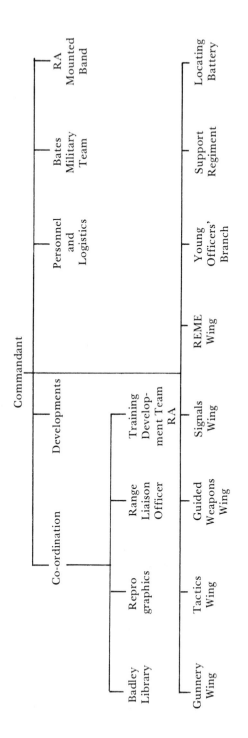

Figure 9.1 Royal School of Artillery, 1983

Tank – but, apart from this, little if any information is available in respect of the Anti-Tank Wing and there is no further reference to it in any subsequent establishments. It would appear that all matters relating to anti-tank instruction were transferred to Gunnery Wing since, in the Establishments of 1946[3] and 1948[4] two Senior Instructors are shown, one for 'Field' and the other for 'Anti-Tank'. The following establishment of 1949[5] shows an 'Anti-Tank and Mortar Branch' under a Senior Instructor as part of Gunnery Wing, and although this information was included in the 1950 Establishment it was the last occasion when any reference was made to anti-tank instruction. The staff of the original Anti-Tank Wing of 1941 included a Chief Instructor in Gunnery, an adjutant, an IG and 3 AIGs.

Air Wing, 1941–50

In February 1940 a small unit of light aircraft, D Flight RAF, was formed and was later stationed in France with the intention of using it for observation of fire and artillery reconnaisance. However the flight did not take part in the operations with the BEF, and Major H.C. Bazeley, a Gunner officer who had been seconded to the RAF, brought it back to Larkhill where it occupied an area near the air strip on Knighton Down. Although there was a proposal to terminate the flight, this was successfully resisted by Colonel R. Hilton, MC, DFC and Major Bazeley with the support of Lieutenant-General Sir Alan Brooke, C-in-C Home Forces. The flight later became 1424 Flight and led to the formation of the Air OP and ultimately the Army Air Corps.

Despite initial difficulties, an Air Wing based on this unit was formed in 1941 and the School Establishment[6] for that year shows, under the Instructional Section of Headquarters Wing, a chief instructor in air co-operation (colonel). The 1942 establishment[7] gives full details of the wing under a Chief Instructor whose rank was now lieutenant-colonel.

A close liaison was established between the Royal Air Force and the School, the former teaching Gunners to fly and the latter teaching pilots to observe . . . The Air Wing trained 12 air OP pilots in 1941; in 1943 it trained 324 air OP pilots and 80 RAF pilots.[8]

The Wing was divided into two parts, the Air Co-operation Branch and the Photographic Research Branch. The latter 'had by 1944 become the best informed centre on air photography for the field army. It then became the Army Photographic Research Branch and extended its activities to all three services.'[9]

By 1943, the Wing had three main responsibilities:

Training subalterns from Coast Defence and AA, in field gunnery with a view to them becoming Air OP pilots.
Disseminating the gospel of Army/Air support to every kind of course.
Running a photographic department.[10]

With a large number of young officers undergoing training, unscheduled events were bound to happen from time to time.

A trainee Air OP pilot who was doing his cross-country landing test, got out to relieve himself. While so engaged he left the engine ticking over when a gust of wind caused the flaps to move and the control stick to knock open the throttle. The plane took off by itself in spite of his efforts to hold on to the tail. Fortunately it only flew about 100 yards before crashing.[11]

During 1946 the Intercommunication Section that had been attached to Headquarters, moved to Air Wing which was accordingly renamed Air and Communications Wing. By 1948 the Section had moved once again, this time to Tactical Wing which then became Tactical and Communications Wing while Air Wing had its title reinstated.

In 1950 the wing was amalgamated with Tactical Employment Wing in which an Air and Anti-Aircraft Branch was then formed.[12] However the Branch was disbanded in the following year and with it the last remnants of Air Wing finally disappeared.

Chief Instructors
1941   Colonel J.S.L. Norris, MC
1943   Lieutenant-Colonel A.B. Davies
1944   Lieutenant-Colonel G.N.C. Smith
1945   Colonel W.G. Stirling, DSO
1947   Lieutenant-Colonel P.R. Henderson, DSO
1949   Lieutenant-Colonel C.E. Peck, DSO

Equipment Wing, 1941–61
Although there was a serious shortage of modern equipment at the beginning of the war which was made worse by the losses of the

BEF in the summer of 1940, by 1941 new equipment had begun to arrive at the School for examination and testing. As the war progressed, artillery equipment from other countries, some of which had been captured also found its way to Larkhill and it was accordingly decided to establish a new wing to be known as Equipment Wing. It is not entirely clear when it was formed and although it was known to be in operation in 1941, it is possible that the Wing was established during the previous year. However since the Establishments which are dated September 1940 and July 1941 contain no reference to the Wing it would seem that this was not the case and consequently 1941 has been accepted as the correct year.

During the war several well known members of the Regiment served in the wing among whom were Colonel E.E. Gee, CBE, DSO, MC who was Chief Instructor from 1941 to 1945, his personal assistant, Lieutenant-Colonel W.A. Owens, TD, Captain W.A. Hicks, DCM and Major C.P.F. Pierret to whom reference has already been made in Chapter 6. The wing was affectionately known as 'The Plumbers' and its members were trained to turn their hands to many tasks and to deal with a variety of equipment.

During this period we acquired the 'Experimental Detachment' – two AIGs (BSM (IG) Cashmore and BSM (IG) Burroughs), two senior NCOs and some 30 gunners. In the critical years 1943 to 1945 they manned 2 pr, 6 pr, 17 pr, 25 pr, 4.5 in. and 5.5 in. guns, 25 pr Valentines, US 3 in. M10, 25 pr RAM, 40 mm and 3.7 in. AA guns, 7.2 in. howitzers, the American 155 mm gun and 8 in. howitzers on field carriages and the 95 mm recoilless gun in its original experimental form.[13]

In 1945 the name of the Wing was changed to Equipment and Trials Wing[14] but in the following year it reverted to Equipment Wing.

It was not only on the ranges that the Wing earned a reputation for being able to solve unusual problems.

The Merchant Navy had complained that the Army was using too many merchant ships to send stores to the Middle and Far East and that the main source of wastage was the large number of 25 prs which occupied too much storage space, so could we please do something about it and release ships for the Atlantic and Russian convoys. We stripped a 25 pr. into its main component parts and stowed them on either side and on top of the trail. A REME Captain was sent along from Command Workshops to design a crate in which to stow and secure it. We then wrote a pamphlet on how to strip, pack and reassemble the gun including photographs and a copy was nailed inside each crate. We found that we could stow four crated 25 prs. in the space previously occupied by one. The Merchant Navy was delighted.[15]

Although the Wing continued for some years after the war, it was subsequently decided that each wing should be responsible for carrying out the trials and development of the equipment with which it was concerned. As a result of this decision Equipment Wing was disbanded in 1961.

Chief Instructors
1940   Colonel W.H.F. Crowe, MC
1940   Colonel E.R.G. Wilmer, DSO
1941   Colonel E.E. Gee, DSO, MC
1945   Colonel A.G. Cole, OBE
1948   Colonel E.F.S. Brodie
1952   Colonel K.D.I. Duncan
1954   Colonel E.F.H. Key, DSO
1957   Colonel J.M. Northen, MBE
1958   Colonel P.R. Gold

Gunnery Wing, 1942–
The first four wings to be formed at the School were Headquarter, Anti-Tank, Air and Equipment but by August 1943, three more had appeared in the Establishment,[16] namely, Gunnery, Tactical and Survey although Anti-Tank had closed in the meantime. The reason why Gunnery Wing was not one of the first to be established may have been based on the opinion that since the whole School was concerned with gunnery, in one form or another, there was no point in creating a wing to deal with it. However as the war proceeded and the work of the School expanded, it was soon covering a far wider field than it had in pre-war days. In order to meet this situation, wings were formed and by 1942 it may have been felt that the time had come to apply the policy of decentralisation to gunnery as well.

In 1949 the Wing was divided into three branches, Field, Anti-Tank and Mortar, and Anti-Aircraft.[17] The Field Branch remained

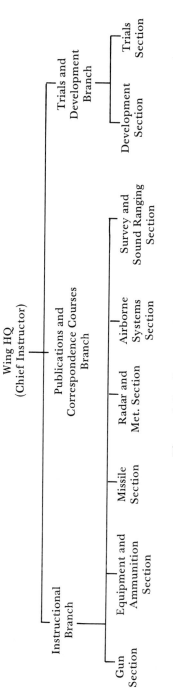

Figure 9.2 Gunnery Wing, 1983

in operation until 1955 but in the following year it was replaced by the Instructional Branch which still formed part of the Wing in 1983. The Anti-Tank and Mortar Branch only functioned for two years and although a Mortar Branch was set up in 1952,[18] no further reference is made to it in later establishments. In 1950, the Anti-Aircraft Branch was superseded by the Anti-Aircraft, Heavy and Super-heavy Branch,[19] but this closed after 1955. Although the establishment for 1952 included an Equipment Branch, this does not appear in the Establishment again until 1961 when Equipment Wing was terminated. In the same year a Development Branch and a Trials Section were formed in Gunnery Wing and these were amalgamated in 1969 to become the Trials and Development Branch of the Wing. A slight alteration was made in its designation during the 1960s when it was shown in the Establishment of April 1961[20] as 'Field Gunnery Wing' and it was not until September 1969[21] that it reverted to 'Gunnery Wing'.

When the first Guided Weapons Wing was disbanded in 1965, the Free Flight Rocket Branch which was concerned with 'Honest John', was transferred to Gunnery Wing in 1966. During 1973 Locating Wing which had its origins in the Survey Wing of 1942, became a part of Gunnery Wing. In the course of its history the wing has been closely concerned with the training of young officers (see page 000). The full story of the Wing has been admirably told by Lieutenant-Colonel J.R. Guy in *A History of Gunnery Wing – Royal School of Artillery* which was published by the Wing in 1981. A chart of the Wing in 1983 is shown in Figure 9.2.

Chief Instructors
1920   Colonel P. Suther, CMG, DSO
1924   Colonel O.C.L. Oldfield, CB, CMG, DSO, ADC
1925   Colonel C.C. Armitage, CMG, DSO
1926   Colonel O.S. Cameron, DSO
1930   Colonel R.C. Prance, DSO
1934   Colonel P.M. Medill, DSO
1936   Colonel F.L.M. Crossman, DSO, MC
1938   Colonel C.P.W. Perceval, DSO
1939   Colonel R.H. Towell, MC
1939   Colonel C.M. Christie, MC
1940   Colonel H.M. Stanford, MC
1940   Colonel J.D. Shapland, MC
1941   Colonel C. Neville, MC
1945   Colonel W.E.G. Hemming, CBE

1947 Colonel R.H.L. Wheeler, OBE
1949 Colonel J.F.S. Rendall, DSO
1951 Colonel J.W. Wainwright
1953 Colonel J.H. Slade-Powell, DSO, OBE
1956 Colonel H.R.L. Hodges
1957 Colonel F.G. MacMullen, DSO
1959 Colonel J. Fairclough, OBE
1962 Colonel H.A. Hardy, MBE, MC
1964 Colonel A.W. Mathew
1967 Colonel E.D.V. Prendergast, MBE, DFC
1970 Colonel G.C.K. Rowe
1973 Colonel B.G. Simpson, MBE
1976 Lieutenant-Colonel J.M. Browell, MBE, RA
1977 Colonel W.M. Weighill
1980 Colonel D. Gray Newton
1983 Colonel J.S. Bennett, OBE

Warrant Officers
1936 WO1 (SMIG) W. Hicks
1939 WO1 (SMIG) H. Smith
1942 WO1 (SMIG) F. Heggie
1951 WO1 (SMIG) J. Pitt
1952 WO1 (SMIG) A. Scott
1953 WO1 (SMIG) E. Beauchamp
1956 WO1 (SMIG) J.J. McMenemy
1962 WO1 (SMIG) T. Laing
1962 WO1 (SMIG) D.W. Firmager
1963 WO1 (MG) D.W. Firmager
1964 WO1 (MG) N.F. Anderson
1965 WO1 (MG) H. Inkster
1966 WO1 (MG) F.P. Riordan
1966 WO1 (MG) S.W. Smee
1968 WO1 (MG) D. Tupper
1971 WO1 (MG) W.D. Keay
1972 WO1 (MG) C.C. Clegg
1974 WO1 (MG) D.G. Rawson
1974 WO1 (MG) K. Hennessey
1976 WO1 (MG) D.J.N. Lodge
1977 WO1 (MG) B.W. Tandy
1978 WO1 (MG) B.W. Collis
1980 WO1 (MG) D.A. Claridge
1981 WO1 (MG) D.W. Cobley

Tactics Wing, 1942–

The Wing had its origin in a Tactics Branch which was formed at the beginning of the war under Lieutenant-Colonel H. Thicknesse, RA. In 1941 it was decided to form a Tactical Wing and its Establishment which was published during that year, provided for a Chief Instructor, three GSOs 2 and one GSO 3.[22] However the Wing did not come into being until October 1942[23] when Colonel H.B. Latham was appointed as the first Chief Instructor. It was subsequently divided into two branches, Tactics and Anti-Aircraft, each under a lieutenant-colonel and the position remained virtually unchanged until 1946 when instruction in anti-aircraft tactics was transferred to the School of Anti-Aircraft Artillery at Manorbier.

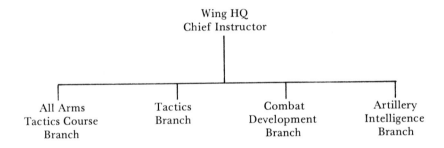

Figure 9.3   Tactics Wing, 1983

In 1946 the Signals Section of the School Headquarters was transferred to Air Wing which was accordingly renamed Air and Communications Wing.[24] This arrangement did not last long however, for in 1948 the Signals Section moved to Tactical Wing which for a short time was known as Tactical and Communications Wing.[25] To complete the picture, in 1950 Air Wing was amalgamated with what had now become Tactical Employment Wing and an Air and Anti-Aircraft Branch was formed within that Wing.[26] The Establishment for 1950[27] shows a Signal Wing but this apparently had a short life as the 1953 Establishment omits the new Wing and once again includes a Signals Branch as part of Tactical Employment Wing. It was not until 1963 that the present Signals Wing was formed.

After the war against Japan had ended the staff of Tactics Wing was gradually reduced but when the Korean War started in 1950 it became deeply involved in courses for battery commanders, troop commanders and counter-battery staff.[28] With the advent of nuclear warfare, instruction in basic nuclear target analysis was at first undertaken by Gunnery Wing but in October 1959 it was transferred to Tactics. This was followed by the holding of a Senior Officers All Arms Nuclear Course which was revised in 1966 and renamed the All Arms Nuclear and Tactics Course, while two years later it became the All Arms Tactics Course. During the summer of 1965 the Wing began a series of courses for battery commanders which all officers who were appointed to command a battery were required to attend before taking up their appointment.[29] In 1976 the Artillery Intelligence Section was transferred from Gunnery Wing to Tactics.[30] The composition of the Wing in 1983 is shown in Figure 9.3. The Establishments for the School show that since 1941 the name of the Wing has changed as follows:

1942-7	Tactical Wing
1948	Tactical and Communications Wing
1949	Tactics Wing
1950-68	Tactical Employment Wing
1969	Tactics Wing

Chief Instructors

1942	Colonel H.B. Latham
1943	Colonel H.M. Stanford, MC
1945	Colonel C.H. Norton, CBE, DSO
1947	Colonel G.D. Fanshawe, DSO, OBE
1949	Colonel G.A. Thomas, OBE
1951	Colonel D.S.S. O'Connor, CBE
1953	Colonel R.C. Symonds, DSO
1956	Colonel G.W. Goschen, DSO
1958	Colonel R.L.T. Burges, DSO
1958	Colonel R.G.S. Bidwell, OBE
1959	Colonel R.D.B. Taylor, OBE, MC
1962	Colonel T.D.H. McMeekin, OBE
1964	Colonel P.A. Lowe
1967	Colonel J.S. Fielding, MBE
1970	Colonel C.M.F. Webb
1973	Colonel B.R.W. Barber
1976	Colonel J.B. Bettridge
1976	Colonel B.G. Crowe, OBE
1979	Colonel T.D.G. Quayle
1981	Colonel J.M. Jones

1981   Colonel R.S. Mountford, OBE
1982   Colonel P. Jones, MBE

Warrant Officers

Artillery Intelligence Branch
1976   WO2 (AIG) D.K. Rose
1978   WO2 (SMIG) F. Westmoreland
1979   WO2 (SMIG) R.J. Mitchell
1982   WO2 (SMIG) D.F. Richmond
1983   WO2 (SMIG) C.J. Eady

Warrant Officers Artillery Intelligence
1981   WO1 (RSMI) J. Bailey
1982   WO1 (RSMI) G. McEleny

Survey Wing, 1942–5
Prior to the formation of the Survey Wing in October 1942, training in survey was provided by the following units which were stationed at Larkhill:

1921   The Survey Company RA
1922   1st Survey Company RA
1938   1st Survey Battery RA
1939   1st Survey Regiment RA

On 3 September 1939, the 40th Survey Training Regiment RA was formed but it became a part of the School of Survey when that School was established on 6 March 1940.[31] Shortly afterwards an ACI was published which contained the following paragraph:

> The School incorporates the 40th Survey Training Regiment, RA and takes over the training of officer cadets and surveyors as reinforcements for survey regiments, RA, to replace wastage in the field. It also holds courses . . . in advanced survey, flash-spotting and sound-ranging . . .[32]

By 1941 the School had been formed into two wings: a courses wing for officers, WOs, NCOs and specialists of survey regiments and a training wing for training surveyors RA.[33] It was emphasised that 'The RA School of Survey although stationed at Larkhill, is an entirely separate establishment and is not quartered at the School of Artillery.'[34]

However this state of affairs did not continue for very much longer and on 5 October 1942, the School of Survey became the Survey Wing of the School of Artillery. An ACI of 1945[35] shows that the new wing was divided into four branches, flash spotting, sound ranging, survey and wireless (survey) and these were still in operation in 1944.

In 1945 the name of the Wing was changed to Observation Wing although in 1946 it appears in the School's War Establishment as Survey and Locating Wing but in the 1948 Establishment, which was the next to be issued, it had again become Observation Wing. Changes in its name continued and in 1952 it was designated Counter Bombardment Wing and in 1963 Locating Wing finally being amalgamated with Gunnery Wing in 1973.

Officers Commanding, Commanding Officers and Chief Instructors

1921   Major J.N. Biggs Davidson, RA
1922   Major (Bt Lieutenant-Colonel) H.P. Garwood, DSO, RA
1925   Major F.P. Wye, MC, RA
1926   Major T.E. Durie, DSO, MC, RA
1930   Major (Bt Lieutenant-Colonel) A.F.V. Jarrett, MC, RA
1933   Major G.L. Kaye, MC, RA
1936   Major H. Greene, MC, RA
1939   Lieutenant-Colonel C.T. Beckett, MC, RA
1939   Lieutenant-Colonel Sir Henry Imbert Terry, Bart, DSO, MC, RA
1940   Colonel H. Greene, MC
1940   Colonel J.A. Keigh, MC
1944   Colonel K.S. Bellamy, OBE

Radar Wing, 1944–6

On 28 July 1944 a Radar Wing was established at the School under the command of Lieutenant-Colonel G.P. Chapman, DSO.

I came home from North Africa in 1943 to the School as Senior Instructor Light A.A. in the Tactical Wing. On an ill-omened day I met Ambrose Pratt as we walked up to lunch. He said 'We are forming a Radar Branch here and I want you to run it'. I replied at once 'I know nothing of radar,' to which he replied 'You'll have a bunch of chaps under you who know all about radar and all you have to do is to keep their eyes firmly on the ball. The object being radar as an aid to gunnery.' In 1944 I moved from the Tactical Wing as SI Radar.[36]

In the initial stages the Wing was only concerned with trials of equipment but these presented considerable problems.

Difficulties were experienced at once as the sets had all been designed for location of large objects such as aircraft or ships at sea. No set had been designed primarily for use in a field role and methods had to be devised and tried out whereby the existing sets could carry out an efficient job for the Field Army.

It is of credit to Radar Wing that methods were devised whereby a set which was designed to locate a ship of at least 2000 tons, was used successfully to locate the position in space of a mortar bomb weighing 10 lbs.[37]

It was now clear that radar could be of the greatest assistance in locating enemy mortars, and radar operating units were formed which then joined existing counter-mortar batteries. In July 1945 the Wing was separated into two parts, the trials element and the instructional element. Although the Wing is shown in the War Establishment for 1945,[38] it does not appear in any subsequent Establishments. In July 1946 it was decided that the Wing should be divided between the Observation Wing and the Equipment Wing, the instructional element joining the former and the trials element, the latter.[39] Further changes took place in February 1947.

The Commandant of the School ordered that trials were to be the responsibility of the SI Radar and not the CIE. Further he ordered that Radar although nominally a branch of Observation Wing would henceforth be regarded as a separate Wing with direct access to the Commandant . . . At some future date we hope the Radar Wing will have a war establishment of its own.[40]

In fact Radar Wing was not officially formed again and consequently its span of life only extended from 1944 to 1946.

Senior Instructor
1944   Lieutenant-Colonel G.P. Chapman, DSO

Observation Wing, 1945-52

In 1945 Survey Wing was renamed Observation Wing and at that time it comprised two sections – survey and flash-spotting. However the Establishment for the following year shows that the title had been changed to Survey and Locating Wing,[41] and in 1948 it was altered once more to Observation Wing.[42] When Radar Wing was terminated in 1946, its instructional section was transferred to Survey and Locating Wing, by which name the Observation Wing was known during 1946 and 1947. The Establishment for 1946 shows that the Wing was divided into two branches: the Survey Branch which consisted of a Survey Section and Observation Section and the Location Branch which comprised a Radar Section and a Sound Ranging Section. These sections were upgraded to branches in 1949 although during the next year the Observation Branch had been renamed the Flash Spotting Branch. In 1952 the name of the Wing was changed to Counter–Bombardment Wing (see page 143).

Chief Instructors
1945   Colonel K.S. Bellamy, OBE
1948   Colonel R.C. Longfield
1952   Colonel R.J.F. Anderson

Administrative Wing, 1950–83
Reference has already been made to Headquarters Wing which was formed in 1940 but had ceased to be a wing by 1945. From then until 1950 successive Establishments only showed 'Headquarters' but in that year the designation was altered to Administrative Regiment Headquarters.[43] When the next Establishment was published in 1952 it was shown as Administrative Wing Headquarters but as the headquarters personnel were, with one exception, identical and the two organisations very similar, 1950 has been adopted as the initial year. From 1950 to 1956 the Wing was composed of five constituent parts: Headquarters, the Depot Battery, the Mechanical Transport (MT) Branch, the Equipment Officers Branch, the Quartermaster's Branch and the Workshops of the Corps of Royal Electrical and Mechanical Engineers (REME).

In 1961 all the REME detachments at Larkhill were placed under a central command and consequently the REME workshops ceased to be a part of the Wing. In 1963 the MT Branch became the MT Troop of the Depot Battery but in 1969 it was formed into an MT Battery. The Equipment Officers' Branch consisted of three sub-branches in 1963: field artillery and signals, surface-to-surface guided weapons and locating. When in 1967 the name of the branch was changed to Central Accounting Organisation, it was divided into five sections, namely, headquarters, field gunnery section, locating section, signals section and the Fargo Ammunition Depot. This rather unusual title was discarded in 1969 and the name reverted to Equipment Officer's Branch although the sections retained their designations.

After 1963 several changes were made in the organisation of the Wing which had become responsible for a number of matters including the messes, the WRAC Battery, Fargo Ammunition Depot and the Support Battery which took the title of 1st Battery RA (The Blazers) in November 1975. In 1981 the Wing consisted of Headquarters, Headquarters Battery commanded by a major of the WRAC, Support Battery, MT Battery, Equipment Branch and Quartermaster Branch. During 1981 the Morgan Report[44] was published and in the light of some of the recommendations which it contained, the Support Regiment, Royal School of Artillery and the Administrative Wing were merged with effect from 10 January 1983. On that date the commanding officer moved from Roberts Barracks to Stirling Barracks and assumed responsibility for the work of the Administrative Wing which then ceased to exist.

Further information regarding the Support Regiment and its new role will be found in Chapter 13.

Commanding Officers
1950   Lieutenant-Colonel P. de N. Ramus, OBE, RA
1953   Lieutenant-Colonel J. Longden, RA
1955   Lieutenant-Colonel J. Poe, OBE, RA
1958   Lieutenant-Colonel E.G. Poole, RA
1961   Lieutenant-Colonel F.B. Edmeades, MC, RA
1965   Lieutenant-Colonel F.C. Dudley-Jones, RA
1967   Lieutenant-Colonel A.G. Hogg, OBE, RA
1968   Lieutenant-Colonel D.B.W. Jarvis, DFC, RA
1971   Lieutenant-Colonel P.R. Heaton-Ellis, OBE, RA
1973   Lieutenant-Colonel D. St. D. McCulloch, RA
1974   Lieutenant-Colonel K.R.H. Eve, RA
1978   Lieutenant-Colonel R.D. Upton, OBE, RA
1979   Lieutenant-Colonel J.M. Jago, RA
1981   Lieutenant-Colonel C.W. Blandy, RA

Regimental Sergeant Majors, Royal School of Artillery
1950   WO1 (RSM) T.E. Dunne
1952   WO1 (RSM) T. Marsh
1954   WO1 (RSM) S. Scogins
1957   WO1 (RSM) H. Flowers, MM

1958   WO1 (RDM) F.W. Fields
1959   WO1 (RSM) C. Cullem
1961   WO1 (RSM) G.W. Blavins, MBE
1963   WO1 (RSM) J.P. McDonald
1966   WO1 (RSM) K. Stanford
1968   WO1 (RSM) G.E. Slim
1971   WO1 (RSM) G.F. Knowles
1972   WO1 (RSM) W.A. Buckley
1976   WO1 (RSM) B. Armitage
1977   WO1 (RSM) R.E. Miller
1980   WO1 (RSM) L. Dare
1981   WO1 (RSM) J.A. Green
1983   WO1 (RSM) P.R. Collins

Counter-Bombardment Wing, 1952–62
When the Observation Wing was given the new title of Counter-Bombardment Wing in 1952 the only immediate change in its organisation was the addition of a Counter-Bombardment Branch to the other four existing branches.[45] The structure of the Wing remained virtually unchanged until 1956 when the Counter-Bombardment Branch became the Counter-Bombardment and Co-ordination Branch and the Survey and Flash Spotting Branches were amalgamated.[46] Two years later a new branch was formed for the study and instruction of electronic warfare[47] while in 1959 the Wing took over the training of meteorologists.[48]

A major reorganisation of the Wing was carried out in 1961 when it was reconstituted with two branches – the Locating Branch and the Developments Branch. The first was divided into five sections: locating radar, meteorological, sound ranging, survey and surveillance while the Developments Branch was divided into four: electronic warfare, publications, staff duties and trials.[49] In May 1962 an ACI was published which laid down that the term 'counter-bombardment' was to be replaced by the new term 'locating' and, more specifically, that 'Counter-Bombardment Wing (School of Artillery) Larkhill' would in future be known as 'Locating Wing'[50] (see page 150).

Chief Instructors
1952   Colonel R.J.F. Anderson
1955   Colonel G.E. Drought
1958   Colonel E.H. Cox, MC
1961   Colonel R.C. Winfield, OBE

Young Officers' Wing and Branches, 1952–
From its earliest days, Larkhill has been associated with the train-
ing of young officers and in 1901 the section of the Annual
Gunnery Report which was concerned with 'Salisbury Plain' –
that is Larkhill – contained the following paragraph headed
'Young Officers':

> Considering the large number of young officers (many of whom
> had not been educated at the Royal Military Academy) and
> men who were present at practice for the first time, the fire
> discipline and drill of the batteries was most creditable.[51]

Five years later the comments were not so reassuring: 'I do not
recommend the practice of the R.M.A. Cadets at this camp being
continued on present lines. I think the cadets would obtain more
real insight by watching service batteries at practice.' To this
the Conference of Camp Commandants added the comment,
'We are of opinion that the practice by Cadets as carried out at
present, is useless.'[52] In spite of this, two batteries manned by
cadets from Woolwich carried out practice at Larkhill during the
following year.

Owing, no doubt, to the First World War, no further developments took place as regards the training of young officers at Larkhill until 1926 when the first of a long series of young officers
courses was held in February of that year.

I was a member of the first entry of Gentlemen Cadets to the
Royal Military Academy at Woolwich ('The Shop') when the

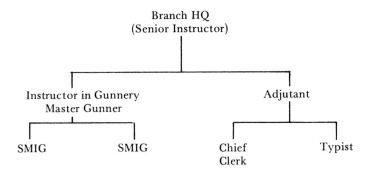

Figure 9.4   Young Officers' Branch, 1983

2 year course was shortened to 18 months before commissioning as second lieutenants. This was to be followed by 6 months at Larkhill on a new practical course to be called the Young Officer's Course (YOs Course).

Instead of the former rather restricted drill orders on Woolwich Common, the first YO's course had the advantage of space on the ranges and equipment and horses from the School of Artillery and the Field and Medium Brigades stationed at Larkhill and Bulford. We were exercised (including 'live' shoots) with 18 pounders, 4.5 in. howitzers, 60 pounders, 6 in. howitzers, 3.7 in. howitzers, 9.2 in. howitzers and Observation Balloons (Rollestone).

The Course assembled at the School of Artillery on 2nd February 1926. It was under the command of Major Wyndham Greene, DSO, MC assisted by Major Ambrose Pratt, MC.[53]

Two courses were run every year until 1939 except in 1932 when only one course was held, but the first course of 1933 made up for this in one respect. In addition to the forty young officers, the course photograph includes no less than sixteen dogs of various shapes and sizes which must be one of the highest dog–student ratios on record. In 1935 the headquarters for the courses were located in three huts adjoining the old Stirling Barracks cricket pitch which is now the site of the administrative buildings. The Young Officers used the old 'A' Mess and lived in a collection of huts opposite the mess which were known as 'The Spider' while their instruction was in the hands of a major supported by three captains.[54] The course held in August 1939 was reduced from six months to three months and thereafter Young Officers' courses were suspended for the duration of the war. In September 1939, No. 122 OCTU was formed at Larkhill and information on this unit will be found in Chapter 6.

In 1948 it was decided to form a Young Officers Branch as a part of Gunnery Wing and the first post-war YOs Course, No. 29, assembled at Larkhill in August. It consisted of eighty-seven young officers who, unlike their predecessors, had attended Sandhurst and not Woolwich and consequently many of them had little, if any, knowledge of gunnery. The course entailed ten weeks at Larkhill, ten weeks at Manorbier studying anti-aircraft gunnery and two weeks at Plymouth on coast defence artillery.

The next four years proved to be a period of change and reappraisal throughout the Armed Forces and it became clear that alterations were necessary in the training of young officers.

However by 1967 it was felt that perhaps there had been too many changes and steps were taken to stabilise the position.[55] The headquarters of the Branch were situated close to what is now the Badley Library and the first Establishment which was published in 1950 shows that it was divided into four troops, two of which were field and two anti-aircraft. Although in 1948 the Branch was a part of Gunnery Wing, it became an independent branch in 1950[56] and a Wing in 1952.[57] In 1960 the Young Officers once again became a Branch of Gunnery Wing[58] but by 1969 it had been transferred to Headquarters.[59] During the whole of this latter period when the YOs Branch was shown in Gunnery Wing establishment, they remained under the control of the Deputy Commandant. Figure 9.4 shows the Branch as it was in 1983.

Two events of importance took place in 1967: the first was the move of the Branch into new headquarters in Stirling Barracks which it was still occupying in 1983, and the second was the preparation of a new syllabus. Between 2 February 1926 when the first course assembled and 31 December 1982, 108 courses have been held which have been attended by 4,298 young officers. Excluding 1939, the highest number on any one course was ninety-four on Course No. 31 in 1949 while the lowest was nine on Course No. 105 in 1981. In 1982 the prizes which could be awarded to young officers were reorganised and the following are now offered:

Spring Term:	The Ambrose Pratt Memorial Prize instituted in memory of Major-General F.W.H. (Ambrose) Pratt, CB, CBE, DSO, MC
Summer Term:	The Earl Roberts Memorial Prize, instituted in memory of Field Marshal Earl Roberts, VC, KG, KP, etc.
Winter Term:	The Royal Artillery Association Prize

Each prize is a Royal Artillery Sword engraved with the winner's name and is awarded to the officer who, during the course, shows himself most deserving in general efficiency and character while his interest in sport and his sense of humour are also taken into account. In 1972 the Tombs Prize (in memory of Major-General Sir Henry Tombs, VC, KCB) and the Benson Prize (in memory of Lieutenant-Colonel G.E. Benson, RFA) were combined and is now awarded three times a year to the Young Gunner Officer who passes out highest in order of merit at Sandhurst after his Regular Career Course.[60]

Chief Instructors

1926 Major W.W. Green, DSO, MC
1927 Major F.L.M. Crossman, DSO, MC
1928 Major W.W. Green, DSO, MC
1929 Major A.R. Roney-Dougal, DSO, MC
1930 Major E.W.G. Wilson, MC
1931 Bt. Lieutenant-Colonel A.R. Roney-Dougal, DSO, MC
1932 Major C.P.W. Perceval, DSO
1934 Major M.A.B. Johnson, MC
1935 Major W.T.H. Peppi, MC
1936 Major W.H.F. Crowe, MC
1937 Major E.A. Lee
1938 Major B.C. Trappes-Lomax, MC
1939 Major G.R. Mockler
1939 Major J.S.L. Norris, MC
1948 Lieutenant-Colonel J.E.F. Linton, DSO
1949 Major L.P. Cocks
1949 Major F.R. Lucas, MC
1950 Major H.C.R. Gillman, MBE
1951 Major J.D. Oliver
1953 Major R.A. Norman-Walker, MBE, MC
1955 Major A.B. Howard, MC
1957 Major G.M. Glendining, MC
1958 Major D.P.H. Dyson
1959 Major D.A. Imlay
1960 Major J.H. Peyton-Jones, MBE
1961 Major J.A. Fraser, MC
1962 Major F.D. Lloyd
1963 Major P.R.R. de Burgh
1965 Major A.J.B. Stagg, MBE
1967 Major D.A. Lloyd
1969 Major D. St. J.M. Gore
1972 Major J.G. Williams
1974 Major C.N.R. Bateman
1976 Major C.W. Payne
1978 Major N.J. Bird
1980 Major P.A.J. d'Apice
1982 Major W.J. Easterbrook

Warrant Officers

1948 WO1 (SMIG) E.C.G. Bird
1949 WO1 (SMIG) S.J. Timmins (Field)
1949 WO1 (SMIG) P.J. Meany (AA)

1950   WO1 (SMIG) S.J. Timmins (Field)
1950   WO1 (SMIG) S.G. Hounsell (AA)
1951   WO1 (SMIG) J.S.N. Poole
1952   WO1 (SMIG) J.S.N. Poole (Field)
        WO1 (SMIG) C.W. McKinder (AA)
1953   WO1 (SMIG) J.J. McMenemy
1953   WO1 (SMIG) P.J. Barclay (AA)
1955   WO1 (SMIG) R.J. Cooper
1956   WO1 (SMIG) V. Bloomfield
1959   WO1 (SMIG) G. Norton
1962   WO1 (SMIG) B.A. Cook
1963   WO1 (SMIG) R.A. Brown
1963   WO1 (SMIG/MG) D. Gibbs
1964   WO1 (MG) R. Myford
1966   WO1 (MG) F.P. Riordan
1966   WO1 (MG) E. Garfield
1967   WO1 (MG) R. Cook
1968   WO2 (AIG) R. Lees
1970   WO1 (MG) R. Lees
1971   WO1 (MG) K. Hennessey
1972   WO1 (MG) J. Nicholls
1974   WO1 (MG) B. Tandy
1976   WO1 (MG) R.C. Coleman
1976   WO1 (MG) M. Marsh
1978   WO1 (MG) E. Johnson
1979   WO1 (MG) A.L. Jackson
1980   WO1 (MG) A.A. Mitchell
1981   WO1 (MG) B.I. Wetherell
1983   WO1 (MG) N.J. Hills

First Guided Weapons Wing, 1955–65
Since 1955 two Guided Weapon Wings have been formed at Larkhill: the first was in operation from 1955 to 1965 and the second
from 1976 to the present time. This section is concerned with the
first Wing and information regarding the second will be found later
in this chapter.

As a result of purchasing the 'Corporal' surface-to-surface missile
from the United States, in accordance with the requirements of
the North Atlantic Treaty Organisation, it was decided to form a
guided weapons training establishment and that this should be a
Wing of the School of Artillery. This led to the formation on
1 June 1955, of Guided Weapons Wing and in September, selected

personnel assembled at the School for preliminary instruction, before leaving for America in December.[61] During 1956 a Survey Section was formed in the Wing in order to teach the new trade of Surveyor RA (SSGW), that is, surface-to-surface guided weapons, but in 1960 the section was transferred to Counter-Bombardment Wing. Instruction in guided weapons started in January 1957[62] and in March 1958 the first Long Gunnery Staff Course (SSGW) began at Manorbier.[63] The main purpose of this was to provide an appreciation and understanding of basic electronics and the course returned to Larkhill in October.[64]

The new Royal Artillery Guided Weapons Range on South Uist in the Outer Hebrides was opened in 1959 when the staff of the Wing arranged and superintended the first Hebrides Practice Camp and on 23 June the first 'Corporal' missile was fired. The vehicles and other equipment that were needed for this undertaking travelled by road to Poole and from there to the Hebrides in five landing craft of No. 76 Squadron RASC (LCT).[65] During the same year a party of officers and warrant officers spent several weeks with the United States Army at Grafenwohr in Germany training on the 'Honest John' free flight rocket. Those concerned became members of the Free Flight Rocket Branch which was formed in the Wing in 1960.[66] On 1 May of that year the Basic Science Section of the School of Anti-Aircraft Artillery at Manorbier moved to Larkhill so that the teaching of that subject in the Regiment could be concentrated at one centre.[67]

During 1961 a small trials team was formed within the Wing in anticipation of the introduction of the 'Blue Water' system. However this was not to be and as a result of its cancellation and the withdrawal of 'Corporal', the Long Gunnery Staff Course (SSGW) was discontinued in 1963 and the Wing reduced in strength. The appointments of Chief Instructor and Senior Instructor were terminated and the Basic Electronics Branch transferred to Locating Wing.[68] The days of the Wing were now numbered and it eventually came to an end in July 1965.

Chief Instructors
1955   Colonel J.P. MacD. Haslam
1958   Colonel P.C. Worthington, MC
1961   Colonel H.J. de Waller, MBE, MC
1961   Colonel L.H. Edwards, MBE
1963   Lieutenant-Colonel A.J. Nicholson, DFC
1964   Lieutenant-Colonel J.A. Fraser, MC

Warrant Officers
1955   WO1 (SMIG) C.F. Sandison
1960   WO1 (SMIG) H.R. Drummond
1961   WO1 (SMIG) R.B. Lockhart
1964   WO1 (SMIG) J.A. Webb

Locating Wing, 1962-73

When the 'Green Archer' mortar-locating radar came into service in 1962, the title of Counter-Bombardment Wing was changed to Locating Wing in accordance with ACI 164 of that year. The Establishment for 1963 showed that the Wing was divided into two branches, a Locating Branch which comprised three sections – radar and meteorology, airborne systems and basic electronics – and a Development Branch which included a trials section.[69] In 1965, when the first Guided Weapons Wing was terminated, all basic science teaching was transferred to Locating Wing but by 1973 it had been decided that the Wing should be merged with Gunnery Wing and it ceased to exist in September 1973.

Chief Instructors
1962   Colonel R.C. Winfield, OBE
1964   Colonel K.A.M. Bennet, MC
1966   Colonel J.A. Fraser, MC
1968   Colonel A.J.W. Harvey
1971   Colonel P.F.G. Barry

Signals Wing, 1963-

It was not until the end of the Boer War that the importance of indirect fire began to be appreciated and the normal practice of engaging the enemy over open sights was called into question. The chief limiting factor in this new technique was the difficulty in transmitting orders from the OP to the guns and several ways of overcoming this were tried. However megaphones could only be used over short distances; the passing of orders by word of mouth, from one man to another, was unreliable; and signallers had been withdrawn from horse and field artillery in 1899.[70] In 1902 Colonel L.W. Parsons, who was Camp Commandant for Larkhill, expressed the view that 'The reintroduction of signallers to field artillery is now a necessity . . . These signallers should be thoroughly trained in flag, semaphore and heliograph signalling and should receive extra pay.'[71] By 1906 telephones were being used between brigades and in the following year they were issued to batteries.

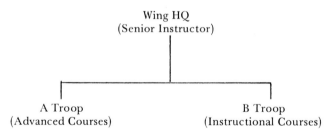

Figure 9.5   Signals Wing, 1983

Although the importance of artillery communications was apparent from the early years of the century, the first School Establishment which recorded a unit concerned with the subject appeared in 1943 when a wireless section was shown as part of Survey Wing.[72] The next development was the formation in 1945 of an Intercommunication Section as part of Headquarters which was composed of two staff sergeants RA and five Royal Corps of Signals personnel including one officer.[73] During the next year the section was transferred to Air Wing which was then renamed Air and Communications Wing but in 1948 the signals personnel moved again to become a part of Tactical Wing which was designated Tactical and Communications Wing.[74]

In 1950 with the closure of the All Arms Wing at the School of Signals, Catterick, a Signal Wing was formed at Larkhill[75] which was commanded by a Senior Instructor who was a lieutenant-colonel of the Royal Corps of Signals. This Wing was short-lived and the 1952 Establishment shows it as a Signals Branch in Tactical Employment Wing although the personnel remained the same as in 1950 and was still commanded by a lieutenant-colonel.[76] This arrangement continued for some years but the Establishment for 1961 records it as an independent Signals Branch which was no longer part of Tactical Employment. Two years later, in 1963, the Branch was once again raised to the status of a Wing. Since 1950, the Senior Instructor who is an officer of the Royal Corps of Signals has been supported by a Deputy Senior Instructor of the Royal Artillery. The present composition of the Wing is shown in Figure 9.5

Senior Instructors — Royal Corps of Signals
1950   Lieutenant-Colonel G. Mellor
1953   Lieutenant-Colonel P.C. Williams, OBE
1955   Lieutenant-Colonel E.G. Day, OBE, TD

1956   Lieutenant-Colonel Sir Evan Nepean, Bart
1957   Lieutenant-Colonel E.G. Day, OBE, TD
1959   Lieutenant-Colonel C.E.J. Booth-Jones
1961   Lieutenant-Colonel R.S. King, TD
1962   Lieutenant-Colonel A. Lamb, MBE
1965   Lieutenant-Colonel M.H. Broadway
1970   Lieutenant-Colonel J.F. Blake
1972   Lieutenant-Colonel D. Hall
1974   Lieutenant-Colonel D.D. Ranft
1975   Lieutenant-Colonel A.V. Swindale
1978   Lieutenant-Colonel W.D.A. Poole
1981   Lieutenant-Colonel I.J. Hamilton

Deputy Senior Instructors — Royal Artillery
1950   Major G.R. Brocklebank, DSO, MC
1951   Major F.G. Dixon-Didier
1952   Major E.G.W. Davidson
1955   Captain G.S. Carter
1957   Captain T.H. Pares
1958   Captain J.G. Gutteridge
1960   Major S.W. Satchell
1962   Major M. Maynard
1964   Major I.N. Crichton
1965   Major R.E. Ward-Best
1968   Major N.J. Cavell
1971   Major J.E.T. Hoare, DFC
1973   Major P.C. Phipps
1974   Major D.M. Barnard
1976   Major D.J. May
1979   Major R.C. Chamberlain
1979   Major P.J. Lucas
1982   Major C.H.P. Inness

Regimental Sergeant Major Instructors — Royal Artillery
1956   WO1 C.R. White
1962   WO1 V. Jones
1965   WO1 M.P. Fitzpatrick
1966   WO1 G.D. Gibson
1968   WO1 J.H. Angell
1970   WO1 A. Easton
1972   WO1 W.G. Cracknell
1975   WO1 J.R. Spedding
1977   WO1 J.F. Miles

1980   WO1 T.J. Styles
1983   WO1 B. Elliott

Foremen of Signals — Royal Corps of Signals
1972   WO1 (F of S) J. Edgington
1975   WO1 (F of S) R.B. Kelby
1978   WO1 (F of S) B. Hassall
1981   WO1 (F of S) A.G.A. Brittenden
1983   WO1 (F of S) L. Nicholas, BEM

REME Wing, 1965–
When, during the period from 1948 to 1958, the Corps of Royal Electrical and Mechanical Engineers, more usually referred to as REME, was at Larkhill, it was divided into a number of small detached groups each working in its own particular sphere and having little contact with the remainder. There were, in addition, specialist advisers who covered the various aspects of the work undertaken by the School, as well as advisers in Gunnery Wing, Equipment Wing and Observation Wing. As the work of the School expanded after the war it was decided that the RA Workshop should be taken over by REME and in 1952 the Small Vehicle and General Workshop, which was part of Administrative Wing, was transferred to the Corps. During 1956 a REME Guided Weapons Workshop was established in order to provide the technical service required in connection with the 'Corporal' SSGW System.[77]

Towards the end of 1958 the Commandant of the School, Brigadier A.J.C. Block suggested to the Deputy Director of Electrical and Mechanical Engineering, Brigadier M.F. Scott, that the various REME operations at the School should be brought together under one command. This suggestion was accepted and on 1 April 1961 all REME activities at Larkhill were, with one exception, combined to form the School of Artillery, Larkhill, Workshop, REME. The exception was the Light Aid Detachment (LAD) of the Support Regiment. This new constitution was an independent command under a lieutenant-colonel who was directly responsible to the Commandant, but some seven years later, on 1 September 1965, the workshop became a Wing of the School.[78]

When the two Schools of Artillery merged in 1971, their respective REME Wings were amalgamated and became a colonel's command. Finally, on 23 August 1982, the LAD of the Support Regiment, which had not become a part of the REME Workshop in April 1961, joined the Wing. Figure 9.6 shows the Wing in 1983.

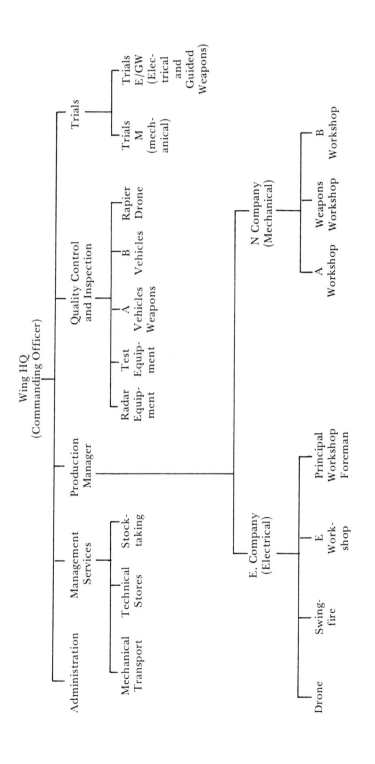

Figure 9.6 REME Wing, 1983

Commanding Officers

1961	Lieutenant-Colonel A.W. Reading, OBE, MC, TD, REME
1963	Lieutenant-Colonel R.C. Miller, REME
1966	Lieutenant-Colonel P. Andrews, REME
1968	Lieutenant-Colonel W.D.J. Redmond, REME
1971	Colonel J.H.T. Reynolds
1974	Colonel A.J. Alborough
1977	Colonel G.W.A. Pearce
1979	Colonel D.S. Brown, MBE
1983	Colonel B.G. Keast

Air Defence Wing, 1971-6

The Air Defence Wing was established as a result of the amalgamation of the School of Artillery at Larkhill and the School of Artillery at Manorbier which took place on 1 January 1971. The new Establishment which came into effect on the same day shows that the Wing was divided into three branches: Light Air Defence, Heavy Air Defence and Trials and Development, together with a Publications and Correspondence Section.[79] The Light Wing from Manorbier was merged into the Light Air Defence Branch in the spring of 1971 and the Heavy Air Wing of the Manorbier School became the Heavy Air Defence Branch in December.[80] By September 1973, a Basic Science and Technology Branch had been added while the Publications and Correspondence Section had become a Publications Branch so that the Wing now comprised five branches.[81]

A few months after the formation of the new Wing, it was involved in what was fortunately a unique experience.

It was the afternoon of 1st July 1971, a fine summer's afternoon. I had taken over as Commandant of the Royal School of Artillery that morning. My predecessor's parting words had been 'Inevitably, you will have some sort of incident with rounds falling outside the range area. Play it as it comes.' The telephone rang: an old friend, the CRA 3rd Division, was on the line. 'I surrender, stop shelling us'. In answer to my horrified query, he told me that rounds were falling in Bulford and that for the first time in years he was wearing a steel helmet. Frenzied activity resulted among the staff to discover the culprit. The Range Liaison Officer professed ignorance, nobody using the range could possibly be firing into Bulford. Then a distraught Chief Instructor Air Defence burst into my room. Air Defence Wing was to blame.

The Wing had recently received a consignment of new type break up shot: this was excellent for drill purposes, as not only could loading be practised but the mechanism of the L40/70 Bofors Light Air Defence Gun was activated. One, or maybe two, guns under control of the Air Defence Gunnery Staff were testing this new training ammunition from their gun park with the guns facing in the direction of Bulford Camp. Break-up shot was, of course, totally safe; it disintegrated a few yards in front of the barrel and could safely be used on a gun park – it had often been so used at Manorbier.

But this occasion was different. It was not break-up shot at all, but solid shot. The catalogue markings for the new break-up coincided with solid shot and 30–40 rounds of solid had gone winging their way into Bulford Camp. Rounds landed all over the place – in the NAAFI, in the car park, in a children's school, through the roof of a cottage where an old lady was in bed – the noise of their coming scared CRA 3 Division and the pekes belonging to the C-in-C's wife disappeared beneath her bed and refused to emerge for 24 hours. Mercifully, of course, being solid shot there was no explosive content and even more mercifully, not one single person was hurt.

The Public Relations and Claims side of Headquarters Strategic Command were superb, they were on the ground explaining what had happened and assessing the damage that afternoon: damage was promptly repaired and claims were paid in full and quickly. The resultant Court of Inquiry exonerated those of Air Defence Wing, although I dare say the IG in charge has examined ammunition markings very carefully ever since. I never did hear what happened to the culprits, presumably in Ordnance, who marked the boxes wrongly. It was astonishing, when one considers what tragedies could have resulted, how little fuss there was. A mild murmur from an MP, a brief paragraph in the local Press, a hope expressed by the old lady that the 'poor boy who made the mistake wouldn't get into trouble'. But I didn't get invited to the Commander-in-Chief's house for dinner for over a year and the CRA 3 Division claimed an inordinate amount of gin off me.

The moral to this tale is: if you sin, go in big and make it worthwhile, and, if you're going to be found out anyway, get your confession and apologies in first. I must confess I enjoyed telling my predecessor, still in the throes of packing up, that my incident was bigger and better than any of his, though I wasn't quite sure at that point that I might not hold the record for the shortest tenure of appointment as Commandant.[82]

Work on the Rapier surface-to-air guided weapon system was started in Air Defence Wing in 1971. In 1976, with the introduction of the 'Swingfire' Anti-Tank guided missile system into the Wing, Air Defence was renamed Guided Weapons Wing (see below).

Chief Instructors
1971 Colonel D.C. Cooke
1973 Colonel H.M. Garnett

Warrant Officers
1971 WO1 (MG) H.A. Smith
1971 WO1 (MG) G.J. Booker
1972 WO1 (MG) J. Shorlin
1973 WO1 (MG) B.P. Concannon
1975 WO1 (MG) A.D.D. Green

Second Guided Weapons Wing, 1976–
When the Royal Artillery took over the 'Swingfire' system from the Royal Armoured Corps in 1976, Air Defence Wing was renamed Guided Weapons Wing. The Establishment of 1977 shows that it was composed of an Instructional Branch, a Trials and Development Branch and a Basic Science and Technology Branch.[83] The Instructional Branch was subdivided into three sections, Rapier and Gun, Blowpipe and Anti-Tank while there was also an Independent Publications Section. This organisation is very similar to that which was in operation in 1983 and is shown in Figure 9.7.

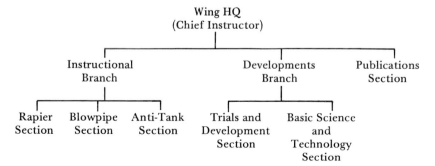

Figure 9.7 Guided Weapons Wing, 1983

Chief Instructors
1976   Colonel D.M. Jones
1978   Colonel L.M. Halfpenny
1980   Colonel P.F.J. Painter
1983   Colonel M.F.L. Shellard

Warrant Officers
1976   WO1 (MG) A.D.D. Green
1976   WO1 (MG) T.L. Towers
1981   WO1 (MG) J.D. Beeton
1982   WO1 (MG) I.S.R. Eaton

Wings of the Royal School of Artillery, 1940–83
Administrative Wing: 1950–83
Air Defence Wing: 1971–6
Air Wing: 1941–50
Anti-Tank Wing: 1941–2
Counter-Bombardment Wing: 1952–62
Equipment Wing: 1941–61
Guided Weapons Wings:
    1st: 1955–65
    2nd: 1976–
Gunnery Wing: 1942–
Headquarters Wing: 1940–4
Locating Wing: 1962–73
Observation Wing: 1945–52
Radar Wing: 1944–6
REME Wing: 1965–
Signals Wing: 1963–
Survey Wing: 1942–5
Tactics Wing: 1942–
Young Officers' Wing and Branches: 1952–

10. The Ranges

The acquisition of Larkhill and West Down ranges, their extent and their boundaries, are described in Chapter 2, and a list of farms which were extinguished when the ranges were established is given in Appendix XV. Although the length of the old Salisbury–Devizes road which runs between the Bustard and Redhorn Hill has always formed the dividing line between the two ranges, the following directive was published in 1948: 'Owing to the increase in range of modern weapons and various new safety regulations, it is no longer possible to regard Westdown and Larkhill as separate ranges. They will in future be regarded as one range.'[1] However the two ranges are still shown separately on the range maps and for convenience of identification are referred to individually in this chapter. Each range is divided into two parts: the impact area in which rounds fall and the deployment area in which gun positions are located. Although during the 1960s there were three impact areas – West Down, Larkhill and Northern,[2] the last named was subsequently merged into the other two.

Land belonging to the Ministry of Defence which is not in regular use as part of the ranges was originally divided into three categories: Schedule I, Schedule II and Schedule III. Today Schedule I land is that which is let on a full agricultural tenancy but over which training rights are reserved. When an exercise is to be held on any part of the land, the tenant is given notice of the fact by the Defence Land Agent, Property Services Agency, and compensation is paid for any damage which may occur. On the other hand, Schedule III land is only let on licence, frequently to those who are tenants of Schedule I land, since its main use is for training rather than agriculture.

In some areas a limited amount of ploughing is permitted but if the licensee wishes to erect any fencing, its extent is strictly controlled and it must be removed within three weeks. The only exception to this is in the case of enclosures known as 'permanent pennings' around which the fencing can remain in position. Under no circumstances however, is compensation payable in respect of

any damage which may occur to Schedule III land. Schedule II
referred to arable land which the War Department wished to lay
down to grass and for which it was prepared to provide the necessary seed, subject to the tenant's agreeing to maintain the area as
grassland. However, this scheme is no longer in operation.[3] A
commanding officer is said to have remarked, 'It is popularly
supposed that you can shoot farmers in a Schedule III area whilst
in a Schedule I area, they can shoot you.'

The Larkhill deployment area which lies to the south of the
track running from Wexland Farm, through Well Bottom and
Honeydown Bottom, has provided space for a number of activities. In about 1922, a polo ground was laid out, the northern end
of which lay immediately to the east of, and adjoining, Round
Covert (grid reference 128472). This is shown on the 1926 edition
of the Ordnance Survey 6in map of Wiltshire, sheet LIV.NE, complete with a pavilion and what appears to be a practice area to the
north of the covert. Apparently the ground was mainly used by
cavalry regiments from Netheravon. During the same period a golf
course was built in the area of Alton Gorse, some 1,000 metres to
the south of the polo ground, but this fell into disuse during the
Second World War. As mentioned in Chapter 5, it was on this
course that a round, inadvertently fired from the gun park, exploded
just as the Commandant, Lord Malise Graham, was about to drive
off. After the war another course, designed by Mr Percy Alliss,
was built in front of the RA Mess and for a short period in 1953 it
comprised eighteen holes. Unfortunately the cost of upkeep
proved to be excessive and in 1965 part of it was replaced by the
present cricket ground, only leaving two fairways on the south
side of the Packway as a practice area.[4]

In 1930-1 a Hunter Trial Course was laid out on Alton Down
by Lieutenant-Colonel W.R.E. Harrison, DSO, MC, the fences
being built by Mr John ('Taffy') Gould. During the 1970s it was
extended to the eastern edge of Robin Hood Ball. In 1946 and the
early part of 1947, largely due to the work of Lieutenant-Colonel
R.S. Baker, DSO, and the encouragement of Major-General G.W.E
Heath who was then Commandant, a point-to-point course was
built between Round Covert and Knighton Long Barrow.[5] There
can be few better places in which to exercise a horse than the area
that lies between the point-to-point course and Blackball Firs and
few people would expect it to hold any unforeseen hazards. However, on a dull winter's afternoon in January 1961, the CRA, 3rd
Division, Brigadier Peter Gillett (afterwards Major-General Sir
Peter Gillett, KCVO, CB, OBE) accompanied by his dog, Brandy,

was exercising a polo pony which he had been lent, not far from the course.

While cantering home at about half past three the pony collapsed, dying almost immediately and in falling pinned the Brigadier to the ground so that he was unable to move. Later on, the men who had been repairing the fences on the course, went past on a tractor but when the Brigadier waved to them, they simply waved back and drove on. Next day, when they were asked why they had not taken any action, the driver replied, 'Gawd, it was you, Sir - I thought it was a gunner having fun with his girl.' Although search parties were organised by both the School and units of the 3rd Division, it was not until ten o'clock that night that he was eventually found with his dog sitting beside him.[6]

The operation and use of the ranges today have developed considerably over the past thirty years. Datum points have been set up which greatly assist in the fixation of positions; in some parts tracks have been improved and roads built; OPs have been reconstructed; buildings have been erected and an underground cable installed for the telephones. Previously it was necessary to lay telephone cable when an exercise was about to take place, apart from that which was needed by the units taking part. A certain number of these lines were inevitably discarded and in course of time they became both an eyesore and a hazard, and in 1954 the CIG, very rightly, decided to take steps to tidy up parts of the deployment area. One Saturday morning when exercising his horse, he noticed yet another length of cable apparently left lying on the ground, and on his return, he gave orders for it to be recovered and this received immediate attention. Unfortunately he was not aware that the offending cable was, in fact, a 3,000 yard locating base that had been laid on the previous day for an exercise which was due to start on the following Monday morning.[7]

One feature of Larkhill that has never changed is the weather that each season brings:

A Staff College Demonstration was held in the depth of winter, in 1940 at which General Sir Robert Haining, GOC-in-C, Western Command was present. There was an icy blast blowing straight from the North Pole via Siberia, directly into the teeth of the spectators. The General turned to the Commandant, Brigadier FitzGibbon and remarked 'Now I know why all Gunners are hatchet faced'.[8]

As tanks began to occupy an increasingly important place on

the battlefield, steps were taken to provide facilities for training field batteries in an anti-tank role. Between the wars, moving targets took the form of large black balls constructed of a wooden frame covered with canvas which were towed by a six-horse team at the end of a long cable operating through a system of pulley blocks. A gun detachment that was lucky enough to occupy a position near a pulley could often obtain 'early warning' of the start of a 'run' from the squeak of the pulley wheels as they began to turn.[9] 'Anti-tank shooting necessitated the construction of mile upon mile of anti-tank runs so that the famous 'black balls' appeared at various positions.'[10]

This was very hard work for the teams but by the end of 1936 mechanisation had replaced them. It has sometimes been suggested that Blackball Firs took its name from these targets but this is not the case since Black Ball is marked on a map of the area dated 1773 and this is mentioned again later in this chapter.

> Instruction in anti-tank shooting suffered from the lack of suitable target material. The usual 'jinking' target towed by wire cable laid on the ground surface which had been in use since 1918, was never satisfactory owing to the delays through cut or broken cable and the necessity for towing the targets back to the starting point. Various forms of anti-tank ranges were put up in Commands in 1940–41 and sanction was obtained for the expenditure required for an installation of a range near Blackball Firs. Eventually two were constructed: one a simple crossing target on rails and the other a towed target range with cable below ground level allowing for engagement of targets at ranges up to 1,000 yards.[11]

The range at Blackball Firs consisted of a narrow-gauge railway track laid below the level of the surrounding ground, on which trucks carrying the outline of a tank, were hauled by a small petrol-driven locomotive on the side of which was a projecting arm. When this came into contact with a succession of ramps fixed to the side of the track, the engine would accelerate, slow down, reverse and stop. The track ran southwards from a point (reference 090484) to the north-west of Shrewton Folly and after following a course somewhat similar to the letter 'Z', it passed Little Folly and continued as far as 097475. At Little Folly it crossed a shorter independent line which was cable-operated and ran from a shed at 097476 in Blackball Firs to reference 091476. Each end of the main track was laid in a noose-shaped loop which enabled the engine and truck to turn round on their own. The lay-out of the track is shown very clearly on the Ordnance Survey map in the 1:25,000 First Series Sheet SU 04 of 1958, and the line of the track could still be seen on the ground in 1983. As well as presenting more realistic targets, the establishment of this range enabled anti-tank practice to be carried out in a clearly defined area with fixed safety limits.

Later an anti-tank range was built at Redhorn Hill[12] while another range on which the targets ran on light railway track was constructed some 230 metres to the north-west of Newcome's Gorse. In 1976 it was replaced by a new range known as the Lavington Folly Range which incorporated the old range and again adopted the principal of targets moving on narrow-gauge track but in this case a cable to which the trucks are attached provides the motive power. The layout of the track which runs for about 1,830 metres from grid reference 119501 follows the shape of the letter 'Z'.

Although the ranges are primarily concerned with providing facilities for course shooting, practice and exercises, they are also used for a number of other purposes. Before electronic equip-ment was used in calibration other methods were employed and in 1919 the following procedure was adopted:

I soon discovered that 878 Battery was employed on Screen Calibration. Working under the Gunnery Staff of the School of Artillery, our task was to fire series of rounds at progres-sively increasing gun elevations. The rounds were fired through two wire screens, sited exactly 75 ft and 225 ft in front of the gun position; the actual screen for each gun being about 6ft high by 3ft wide. An electrical circuit was broken as the shell passed through each screen and the time taken for the shell to traverse the distance between the two screens was then accur-ately measured on a special recording apparatus. The muzzle velocity of the gun being fired was calculated as the mean of a series of 12 rounds. At the same time the jump and droop effect was measured as a combined angle for each piece being calibrated.

The gun position was located north of Tilshead, just off the West Lavington road and firing took place across Chapperton Down. The position provided prepared platforms, with trail pits, for a six gun battery. The screen frames were constructed from 1½ inch diameter iron pipe, having counterweighted mechanism to raise and lower the actual screen. The near screen frame stood 25 ft high and the far frame 50 ft but both frames appeared higher as the ground sloped upwards away from the guns. They were monstrous erections. Guns had to be in action by 8.30 am and firing would usually continue until about 4 pm. By then, on an average day, each of the guns might have fired perhaps 40 rounds. The fortnight with Richards seems to pass in a flash; then suddenly I realised that I was out on my own. Richards' final words to me were, 'Whatever you do, mind you put your bullets through the slots. The Larkhill Rangers are apt to get into a bit of a tizzy if you knock down one of their perishing gantries!' Mental panic stations almost ensued as the Gunner rule of thumb concerning inches, minutes and a hundred yards raced through my brain. All at once those wretched slots seemed mighty small![13]

At the beginning of the Second World War, in anticipation of an increased demand for calibration, No. 1 Calibration Troop, the first of five, was formed and accompanied the BEF to France in 1939. It returned to Europe in 1944 and was finally disbanded in BAOR in January 1947. No. 2 Troop was established at Greenlands Farm in December 1941 and in the following July sailed for the Middle East where it remained until disbanded in March 1947. No. 3 Troop which was constituted at Woolwich at the end of 1943 subsequently moved to Market Lavington before being posted to India in 1944 where disbandment took place in September 1946. The 4th Troop came into being at Market Lavington in January 1944 and left for Italy exactly a year later but returned to Tilshead in the middle of 1945. It was then transferred to the Middle East where disbandment took place in February 1948. No. 5 Calibration Troop which was formed at West Lavington in August 1944 was based on Larkhill for the whole of its service although it also carried out calibrations at Otterburn and Sennybridge. In 1959 and 1960 it visited Höhne, Germany, but was finally disbanded at Larkhill on 31 March 1961.[14]

For many years trials of guns, vehicles, instruments and other equipment have been carried out on the ranges and these are conducted under the direction of the Gunnery Staff who are experts in such matters as well as on safety aspects. So that they can be readily recognised, all warrant officers belonging to the Staff wear white covers to their peaked hats.

In the middle of the 1960s the Airborne Systems staff of Gunnery Wing were concerned with instruction on the operation of

MQM Drones which were often flown on Larkhill ranges. However, since the Naval Pilotless Target Aircraft Squadron of the Royal Navy at Portland had more experience in operating drones, an informal relationship was soon built up between the Squadron and the Gunnery Staff. After a course from the School had visited Portland, the Squadron was invited to fly their drones at Larkhill.

After the Naval party had arrived wearing their usual white topped hats it soon became clear that the sailors had had little experience of map reading. To the consternation of the Gunnery Staff, the lines on the range map showing the safe area in which drones could fly were continually being disregarded although no harm was done. Later on a drone developed trouble and came down 500 metres inside the range impact area. However, since the red line marking the area on the map did not appear on the ground, the sailors drove off in a vehicle to pick up their drone, before they could be stopped.

An IG in one of the OPs had seen the drone land but as it did not interfere with his shooting he carried on. Fifteen minutes later he was amazed to see a vehicle drive into the impact area, disgorge five men with white hats who unhurriedly recovered the drone. He immediately rang control and reported to the RLO that as far as he could see the AIGs from Locating Wing had gone completely mad and were swarming all over the impact area without any regard for safety rules. All units that were firing that day and were stopped for a good two hours, are still convinced, I'm sure, that it was the AIGs who had stopped their activities because no one told them it was the Navy.[15]

The ranges at Larkhill have formed an ideal setting for exercises, displays and demonstrations on many occasions, especially since 1939. These have included XII Corps Exercise in 1943, the Joint Services Demonstrations of 1961 and 1962, Larkhill Days which were held from 1962 to 1969, Artillery Days which began in 1970, Exercise Avon Express in 1971 as well as numerous demonstrations for courses and other arms.

The first School Demonstration that my course (1 LGCS 1945-6) saw was at Knighton Down and took place at night! We had artificial moonlight and watched enemy troops coming towards us and saw defensive fire tasks fired with ground and air bursts to their flank. It was breath taking and most realistic.[16]

Artificial moonlight was obtained by directing searchlight beams on to low clouds which caused the light to be diffused. On some occasions unintended demonstrations of fire power took place as that which was provided by the HAC in 1934.

> We took up a gun position behind the butts of a rifle range with the guns spaced to fire between the target number boards which were wooden and about three feet square. The AIG looked up the barrel of one gun to see if it would clear the crest and gave his blessing. First shot OK then a 10 degree switch was given and the guns fired hitting the target boards, and filling the air with firewood. Everybody cheered loudly except the AIG.[17]

There have also been times when, for some particular reason, guns have fired from positions outside the range boundaries. During the exercise held by XII Corps in 1943 railway-mounted howitzers were fired from the Bulford branch line and from near Porton, on to the ranges. In 1943 there was 'a piece of land near Druids Lodge which we 'owned' and from which we fired longer range guns 'over the top' of various roads and houses'.[18] It was apparently used by 8 in guns and 240 mm howitzers, both of which came into service in 1943 but this was discontinued in about 1954.[19]

The efficient operation of two ranges which cover so large an area as Larkhill and West Down obviously needs considerable organisation and administration and over the years this has been achieved by successive range parties and detachments. In 1901 the first range parties were based on Newfoundland Farm[20] which occupied the present site of Newfoundland Farm Wood but by the end of the First World War they were established at Greenlands Farm (reference 067472) where they occupied the old farm buildings. By 1924 the administration of the Range Party had become the responsibility of the Adjutant of the School, Major R.B. Purey-Cust, DSO, MC, while the personnel were under the command of Captain A.V. Brown who was assisted by four Range Officers. In December 1924 Lieutenant H.S. Crane joined the unit and was made responsible for the Larkhill ranges. Affectionately known in later years as 'Daddy' Crane, he carried out the duties of Range Officer until he retired as a major in 1936 when he was appointed Secretary of the RA Mess. He was awarded the MBE in 1933. In the following year another well-known Gunner officer, Lieutenant T.F. Horton, DSO, MC, DCM, joined the unit and took over the West Down ranges. Universally known as 'Tom Horton',

PLATE 31: Greenlands Farm in 1975. The buildings to the left of the central clump of trees were the dining hall, cookhouse and NAAFI with barrack blocks on either side. To the right of the trees was the Sergeants' Mess with the married quarters at the top of the photograph. (*RSA Reprographics*)

he remained as Range Officer for the next twenty-three years until he retired in 1949. He was promoted to brevet major in 1934.[21]

Life at Greenlands in the early 1930s was not very sophisticated and officers who served there are unlikely to have put on much surplus weight, since in 1932 'M.W.W. Selby-Lowndes, captain of 96 Battery fed the Officers Mess on rabbits, Camp Coffee and bread thereby cutting the cost of messing to 6d (2½p.) per day.'[22]

Until 1925 all the work on the ranges which was hard and very demanding was carried out by horses but in that year a limited amount of mechanised transport was made available by the School, although complete mechanisation did not take place until 1936. In 1926 the Range Party was replaced by a succession of serving batteries drawn from different field brigades and it is believed that the following batteries were stationed at Greenlands:

1926	74 Field Battery RA (6th Field Brigade RA)
1927	39 Field Battery RA (19th Field Brigade RA)
1930	96 Field Battery RA (19th Field Brigade RA)
1932	22 (Residency) Field Battery RA (24th Field Brigade RA)
1934	50 (Dragon) Field Battery RA (24th Field Brigade RA)
1936-9	6 Field Battery RA (12th Field Brigade RA)

In order that their knowledge and experience of the ranges could be retained Lieutenants Crane and Horton were posted from one battery to the next as batteries were relieved, Crane always in charge of Larkhill and Horton of West Down.[23] Up to 1930 Greenlands Farm consisted of a collection of huts and farm buildings but in that year work began on converting them into a permanent camp of brick buildings. Barrack rooms were completed in 1931, Regimental Institutes in 1934 and the Sergeants' Mess and married quarters in 1936 although the Officers' Mess and the clerks offices remained as part of the original farm buildings.

Greenlands was always considered to be rather remote even in the 1930s and consequently somewhat beyond the direct influence of the School – and not without good reason.

On my return from India in 1938 I was posted to the Range Battery at Greenlands Farm. In December when I joined this was a happy but unmilitary little outfit responsible only for running the ranges. We posted vedettes, lit fires in the OPs, collected and destroyed unexploded shells and so forth. The Battery Commander who had long put aside all military ambitions, lived near Newbury where he kept pigs and came in on pay days to open the safe and when called in to deal with prisoners and so forth. Our soldiers supplemented their pay by selling rabbits and mushrooms in Salisbury.[24]

Nevertheless, the time that officers spent with the Range Detachment before the Second World War would not appear to have been wasted since the following were among those who served at Greenland Farm as young officers: Brigadier T.W.R. Hill, OBE; Brigadier M.W.W. Selby-Lowndes, DSO; Brigadier D.D.C. Tulloch, CB, DSO, MC; Colonel G.E. Drought, and Lieutenant-Colonel P. de N. Ramus, OBE.

By the end of 1938 there were unmistakable signs that changes were not far distant and the old way of life began to alter. Consequently it was felt advisable to erect a flagstaff at the approach to Knighton Down so that a red flag could be flown when firing was in progress. Sited behind the present POL Point at approximately grid reference 127449, it was known as Drought's Flagstaff, after Captain (later Colonel) G.E. Drought.

> Throughout 1939 the tempo of activity on the ranges increased, anti-tank runs sprang up in unexpected places and the new flagstaff was put up in an attempt to stop men and vehicles drifting on to the ranges between Knighton Down and the Packway. I remember Tom Horton, jokingly saying that my name would go down to posterity because of naming that flagstaff but to tell the truth this is the first mention I have heard of it for forty years.[25]

When mobilisation took place in 1939, 6 Field Battery rejoined 12th Field Regiment and in its place a range detachment was formed from those who were not proceeding with the Regiment and this detachment was to remain in existence until 1961.[26] On 1 April 1940 No. 1 RA Practice Camp Battery was established for duty on the West Down ranges, but it was subsequently disbanded on 17 September 1946 when it was merged with the Range Detachment to form the Salisbury Plain Range Detachment. On 1 August 1940 No. 7 Practice Camp Battery was formed and was allocated to the Larkhill ranges but in the following year, it was amalgamated with the Range Detachment on 29 October. It was redesignated the Range Detachment Larkhill with effect from 21 October 1942.[27]

During the war No. 1 Practice Camp had been established at Tilshead and was responsible for the West Down ranges. These were used by the Canadian and United States armies and the Range Detachment was only concerned with Larkhill. However, when No. 1 Practice Camp was disbanded, the Salisbury Plain Range Detachment took over the West Down ranges. In June 1946 the area for which the Range Detachment was responsible was extended to

PLATE 32: The last inspection of the Salisbury Plain Range Detachment by the Garrison Commander, Col. B. Cocks on 26th October 1960. On the right is Maj. H.G. Bennett, the Commanding Officer. (*RSA Reprographics*)

include the Imber ranges, and a sub-unit to cover this new commit-
ment was formed at Tilshead. This was in addition to the detachment which was already there and operated on West Down. After
twenty-three years of outstanding service on the ranges including
the whole of the Second World War, Major Tom Horton retired
in September 1948. He was succeeded by Major J.W. Kennedy,
MC, but in March 1949 Major H.G. Bennett took over command.
During 1949 the unit was relieved of its responsibility for the
Imber ranges and the Tilshead detachment returned to Greenlands.
The total strength was now 133.[28] Safety on the ranges was always
of paramount importance but occasionally the unforeseeable
occurred.

> During a shoot conducted from an Air OP in 1947 which
> involved two troops, one made a gross error and landed a
> round of gunfire near the Amesbury–Upavon road. The second
> troop hit the target and the Air OP ordered 'Repeat'. Meanwhile
> a retired admiral was being driven past by his daughter.
> 'Stop the car my girl, I'll go and have a look'.
> 'Won't that be dangerous daddy?'
> 'Nonsense, they won't do it twice.'
> But they did.[29]

In spite of its limited strength, the detachment was very active
in the sports field and in 1952 was successful in football, cricket
and tug-of-war competitions. Great interest was also taken in
gardening and, in addition to winning many awards at local
horticultural shows, it was awarded the Mitchell Hill Trophy for
the most outstanding unit gardens in the United Kingdom. During
1950 a small livestock farm was started.[30]

In 1961 the Salisbury Plain Range Detachment ceased to exist
as a separate unit and became a part of Gunnery Wing with the
new designation of Larkhill/Westdown Range Detachment, and so
after forty years there was no longer a range party at Greenlands
Farm. The last inspection by the Garrison Commander, Colonel
Brian Cocks, GM, TD, took place on 26 October 1960 (see Plate
32, page 170). The unit's final strength was seven officers, 110
soldiers and four civilians amongst whom was Mr F. Chilcott who
had been pay sergeant to the Range Party in 1921 and was still
employed at Greenlands as a civilian storeman in 1961.[31] The
location was always considered to be very remote: 'I spent some
time at Razmak on the Afghan border but I have never known
such isolation as this. However, they seemed to thrive on it – including the NAAFI manager!'[32]

In spite of the fact that it was '5 miles from Larkhill, 2 miles from Tilshead (by range roads) and 2 miles from Shrewton (by a very indifferent track)' Major Bennett referred to the closing of Greenlands Farm in the following words:

> It is understandable that considerable regret has been felt that this step has become inevitable. Greenlands Farm has been occupied by soldiers for about 40 years. When such a long attachment exists, ties with local villages become strong and this is most certainly the case here. The remoteness of the camp whilst being somewhat unpopular, has been the main reason for the high morale which has existed over the years. This fact has been commented upon by Senior Officers carrying out Annual Administrative Inspections. Personnel have always been heavily worked and in consequence, spare time has been spent within the unit lines thus creating a closer unit bond than is generally found.[33]

On vacating Greenlands, the Range Detachment moved to a hut (grid reference 127449) which stood opposite the present POL Point but has since been demolished. In 1965 it transferred to Hut 66 (now Hut 19) at refernece 130449, but in 1979 it moved to the buildings in the Anti-Tank Compound where it remained until February 1983 when it moved once more, to Hut 18 which is next to its 1965 location. In 1969 a further change in title appeared in the Establishment for that year when the words 'Larkhill/Westdown' were omitted.[34] In 1977 the Detachment was transferred from Gunnery to Administrative Wing.[35] Finally on 1 October 1982, the Range Detachment was renamed the Range Troop and is now a part of the Support Regiment with which the Administrative Wing was amalgamated on 10 January 1983.

In the School Establishment for 1943[36] a 'Range Liaison Officer (subaltern)' is shown under Gunnery Wing for the first time, but in the next Establishment the rank appears as captain. This entry did not change until 1950[37] when a major and captain are shown under 'Range Liaison Officers (instructors-in-gunnery)' but in 1952 these officers appear as 'technical instructors in gunnery'. By 1956 a 'Range Liaison Office' had been set up manned by three TIGs[38] who in 1972 were described as an RLO and two Assistant RLOs, and this was still in operation in 1980.[39] In 1983 the Range Liaison Officer was responsible for all Range Bookings which are made through Headquarters Salisbury Plain Training Area. He is also responsible for safety which is directed and controlled by means of instructions known as Range Details and also through the Range Troop. Although the Troop is now a part of the Support Regiment, its deployment is controlled by the RLO.

Although the principal user of the ranges is the Royal School of Artillery and, by virtue of it, the various Gunner units which come to Larkhill and West Down for practice, there are many other formations and establishments that have an interest in the area. The Proof and Experimental Establishment has a range and battery at Gore Cross near West Lavington, the Royal Aircraft Establishment occupies two main sites – at Larkhill and near the Bustard – and several OPs while the RA Target Operation Group has a depot at Rollestone Camp. Further information on these three establishments will be found in Chapter 13. The ranges are also used by the Royal Engineers for demolition training, the Royal Army Ordnance Corps for bomb disposal, the School of Infantry and Infantry Battalions for live firing in various forms, the Royal Air Force for bombing and the Royal Armaments Research and Development Establishment for trials. Training which does not involve live ammunition is also carried out by many formations, from time to time.

While there are strict rules regarding access to the ranges, the public are normally allowed entry when the red danger flags are not flying. However, there have been occasions when members of the public have made unexpected and sometimes unusual appearances on the ranges.

PLATE 33: Greenlands Farm in 1983. (*RSA Reprographics*)

Acting (as usual) as horse holder, I cantered off with the BC's party to direct fire on to a target which was a trench in front of a wood. The BC having done his sums and got a line through to the gun position, was about to order 'Fire!' when the BCA shouted 'Hold hard, sir, there's an Austin 7 on the target' and a family emerged shaking blankets and washing up breakfast. Evidently the Depot Battery 'gallopers' who used to scour sectors of the ranges and report in from various 'phone points, had missed that little lot who were, I believe, fined by the Salisbury magistrates.[40]

Some forty-four years later, on 27 October 1977, Major P.M. Gell who was a member of the Larkhill Shoot was paying an evening visit to Robin Hood Ball to see if the pheasants, which the shoot had reared, were all right. He walked down the main ride and, as he reached the end of it, something on the edge of a group of trees caught his eye and he walked over to investigate. He was more than surprised to find a bed, wardrobe, chair and bedside table, complete with a portable television set, and when he called out to find if anyone was in the vicinity, a woman's head appeared from amongst the bed clothes. She had apparently, had a difference of opinion with her husband and had hired a van into which her bedroom furniture was loaded with the intention of staying with a friend in Chitterne. However, on arrival, the friend was unable to take her in, so in desperation the van driver deposited her and her furniture at Robin Hood Ball and drove off. In due course the police arrived and 'moved her on' which was just as well, as a live firing exercise was due to start in the area early next morning.[41]

The ranges extend over an area of undulating ground which is roughly rectangular in shape and incorporates three main valleys. The first runs due north from Tilshead village, past West Down Camp and Candown Copse to a tumulus at grid reference 042533. Branches run roughly east and west towards New Copse, Can Down, Warren Down and Little Hill with the floor of the valley rising from 350 feet at Tilshead to about 440 feet at the northern tumulus. The second valley begins at Wexland Farm (grid reference 139485) and runs westward to Wexland Hanging, then north through Well Bottom bearing west again to Honeydown Bottom. The last of the three valleys originates at Compton (132520) and continues westward through Water Dean Bottom to a point some 340 metres south-west of Fox Covert (084541). On the south side of the valley, branches run into Compton, Thornham and Charlton Downs.

Three features dominate the ranges: Knighton Long Barrow in the south with a height of 482 feet above sea level, Ell Barrow in the centre of the ranges, 610 feet, and Urchfont Hill on the northern boundary rising to 704 feet. These three points are almost in a straight line running north-westwards from the Long Barrow on Knighton Down. In his history of South Wiltshire which was published in 1812, Sir Richard Hoare describes his visit to part of this area.[42]

Starting once more from my headquarters at Amesbury, I direct my course towards Knighton Long Barrow which from its elevated situation on a high ridge of land, rivals, if not surpasses Ell Barrow in pre-eminence of prospect. The first object of our attention, near a clump of trees called Robin Hood Ball is one of the ancient circles which I have before mentioned . . .

Returning to the ridge, I continue my ride to another clump of trees called Black Ball; and it is interesting on this spot to remark the actual progress of nature in creating woods and forests; for on every side, except the south-west, we see an interesting growth of young fir trees, raised from the cones of their parents which have been dispersed by the winds.

This down (Elston Down) leads us to the great road from Salisbury to Devizes which once most probably was a British track-way. Crossing it near the twelfth mile stone, and continuing upon it as far as the fourteenth, I then deviate to the right and approach a large *tumulus*, called most appropriately Ell Barrow, and still reserving its ancient British title of *Ell* which signifies *conspicuous*; a title which it most justly deserves, for I know of no single object in this wild district which so generally attracts the eye at a distance.

The only feature of the range area that John Speed, the seventeenth-century map-maker, showed on his map of the county in 1610, was 'Blacke Heathe'.[43] This is the area immediately to the south-west of Ell Barrow, but in 1773 a map published by John Andrews and Andrew Dury[44] showed Black Heath well to the north although it included Ell Barrow, Slay Barrow, Black Ball and Robin Wood [*sic*] Ball. In 1801 a map drawn by John Cary[45] showed the last named as Robin Hood Ball while the 1968-9 revision of the Ordnance Survey 1:50,000 map in the First Series marks it as Robin Hood's Ball. Hoare has defined a 'ball' as 'a landmark of earth set up as a boundary mark'[46] and this is undoubtedly correct in the case of Black Ball and Robin Hood Ball. The parish boundary passes through the actual ball or mound in each feature while the 1:25,000 Ordnance Survey map marks other 'boundary mounds' which are situated on the boundary line.

It would also seem very probable that Robin Wood is the correct name as Andrews and Dury's map marks the ball with a group of trees while Hoare refers to 'a clump of trees called Robin Hood Ball'. Over the course of years the spelling of other names in the area have changed of which Tyleshead, Shrawton Virgo (Shrewton), Nether Haven and Ambersbury are examples while Wexland was originally Waxland.[47] One of the most recent transitions is Larkhill which, until about 1920, was usually written Lark Hill and it appears in this form on maps of the ranges up to 1914. The letter heading of 1916 (see Plate 15, page 49), also shows it as two words. At the present time the name of West Down is beginning to enter a period of consolidation and although maps of the area still show it as two words, it is now frequently written as one.

A landmark recalling the days when the use of the road from the Bustard to Redhorn Hill was unrestricted was still to be seen on the ranges in 1983. This was a signpost standing about a mile beyond Honeydown Copse at the point where the old road to Market Lavington bears away to the north-west across Grove Down at grid reference 070495. It is said to have been here that, in 1785, Jarvis Matchan saw an apparition which, with subsequent visions, had such an effect on him that he confessed to the murder of Drummer Benjamin Jones of the 49th Regiment of Foot, which he had committed five years earlier. Matchan had joined the Royal Navy as a young man and after taking part in an action against the French in 1778, he deserted and returned to England where he was immediately seized by a press gang and returned to the Navy. However, he escaped shortly afterwards and enlisted in the 19th Regiment of Foot only to desert again at an early opportunity but, having little or no money, he re-enlisted in the 49th Foot which was then in Huntingdon.

On 19 August 1780, he and Drummer Jones were detailed to draw subsistence money from the recruiting officer at Diddington, some six miles from Huntingdon. On the way back Matchan got drunk, murdered the drummer and, after robbing him, rejoined the Navy in which he served for a further five years before being finally paid off at Plymouth. From there, he and a shipmate, John Shepherd, set out to walk to London and in the course of their journey took the road to Devizes. At about three o'clock in the afternoon as they approached the fork where the Market

Lavington branches off, Shepherd drew Matchan's attention to something about one hundred yards to their right, that was moving backwards and forwards. On approaching it, Matchan saw the upper half of a woman's body, much deformed, that seemed to shake its head at him. He returned to where he had left Shepherd and together they went back to the object which behaved as it had previously but shortly afterwards disappeared leaving only 'something in the form of a milestone in its place'. Continuing their journey, they noticed that some of the stones in the road turned over towards the side on which Matchan was walking. Later when they reached an inn, Matchan imagined that he saw Our Lord on the one hand and the murdered drummer on the other, both visions quickly turning to ashes.

The effect on Matchan was such that he immediately confessed to the murder and, after being tried at Huntingdon, he was convicted and executed on 2 August 1786. This account is based on the information contained in a pamphlet which was published at the time[48] but the Rev. R.H.D. Barham who wrote under the pseudonym of Thomas Ingoldsby, included a poem entitled 'The Dead Drummer' in his *Ingoldsby Legends*.[49]

There are, on the ranges and in the Garrison area, a large number of trees, small woods and plantations that have been planted over a period of many years. The oldest plantations were already in existence when the land was acquired by the War Office at the end of the last century and a list of those which were growing on the ranges in 1903 will be found in Appendix XIV. Eight of these are situated in the present impact areas and, understandably, no new planting has been carried out in those localities. It would seem that little planting was done between 1900 and 1939 but exceptions were Newcome's Gorse, Bunty's Folly, Candown Copse and the trees on either side of the Packway at Larkhill. The majority of the planting has been carried out since the end of the Second World War and in many cases the new plantations and shelter belts have been named either after a person who has been closely connected with the School or the ranges or to commemorate a special occasion. Thirty-four of these named plantations are given in Appendix XIII with a note as to the origin of each name and the grid reference of their location.

Unfortunately it has not been possible to discover the origin of the name of one of the best-known plantations on the ranges – Bunty's Folly. This was located some 620 metres to the west of Enford Penning at reference 103493 and formed a very obvious feature when seen from OP 3. It is said that before 1939 any

officer who dropped a round into Bunty's was fined £5 and even
if this cannot be substantiated there is no doubt that such a
practice was very unpopular. 'It was revered as a plantation for a
long time and I remember as a youngster on a course in 1931,
someone being given a terrible rocket for letting a ranging round
drop in the Folly.'[50]

During the Second World War the situation changed and by the
end of 1945 the plantation had ceased to exist. Later New Bunty's
Folly was planted on the south slope of Wexland Ridge at grid
reference 120485 – outside the target area!

All forestry work on land belonging to the Ministry of Defence
on Salisbury Plain is carried out by the Forestry Section of the
Property Services Agency under the direction of the Chief Forester
who is a member of the Defence Land Agent's Staff at Durrington.
The woodlands can be divided into three categories : those used
specifically for military training, those that form the usual woodlands on a large estate and amenity woodlands which are designed
to improve the local environment. On the Larkhill portion of the
Ministry's estate these three categories of woodland cover an area
of 342 hectares or 845 acres. On the newly planted sites the species have largely consisted of beech, sycamore, Scots pine, a certain amount of Lawson cypress and more recently, whitebeam.[51]

> The basic policy in Larkhill is that training features must be
> provided for the Gunners. The original suggestions for the siting
> of the new plantations are proposed by the Royal School of
> Artillery. The Forestry Section then assess the viability of these
> proposals and after discussion a compromise is always reached
> on the siting and species selection. The species selection is of
> necessity to give adequate cover as early as possible and in an
> area like Larkhill, with its own very particular micro-climate,
> this has posed all sorts of problems. However, over the years,
> by devising our own method of establishment, particularly by
> using our own thinning method, we have managed a fair estab-
> lishment . . . The object is to produce a final crop of beech.[52]

Since the end of the Second World War, farming methods have
changed to a very great extent. In order to attain higher production farmers have made extensive use of chemical sprays to control
weeds, insect and fungi; large areas are ploughed at frequent inter-
vals; pieces of previously unproductive land have been brought
under cultivation and hedgerows have been grubbed up. Although
this may result in the production of more food, it unfortunately

has an adverse effect on wild life and here the words 'wild life' are used in their broadest sense. At the same time the tremendous increase in car ownership has enabled large numbers of people to spend a day or a weekend in the country and places which, until recently, were considered to be too remote or inaccessible can now be visited without difficulty. Admirable though this may be for those concerned, the influx of numbers of people into a quiet rural environment can have an unfortunate effect on the natural habitat.

On the other hand, land to which public access is restricted, and where modern farming methods are not practised, can provide conditions which will encourage wild life to thrive and such a state of affairs exists on much of the land that the Ministry of Defence owns or occupies. The importance which the Ministry attaches to this, is evident from the fact that it has appointed a conservation officer in its Lands Department which is more correctly known as Defence Lands 3. In addition, Military Conservation Groups have been formed at almost every Ministry of Defence establishment.[53] Three groups have been formed for Salisbury Plain namely, Larkhill/West Down, Imber and Salisbury Plain Training Area (East). The ranges now form one of the most valuable nature reserves in the south of England and in this respect they are considered to be comparable to the New Forest.[54] Odd though it may seem, gunfire appears to have little effect on wild life, and roe deer – which have now colonised the Plain – can often be seen grazing. In September 1982, during a demonstration of the effect of gunfire that was being observed from the close or bombard OP, a hare moved slowly past the OP after a number of rounds had fallen and was clearly in no hurry to avoid the shelling. It may well be a case of familiarity breeding contempt.[55]

The work of the Group includes the recording of all wildlife, historical buildings, ancient monuments and subjects of scientific interest; the preparation of a habitat register and maps; protecting areas of importance; the issue of passes and liaison with national and local conservation societies. All information is recorded and passed to the MOD Conservation Officer. By 1982, members of the group had identified many varieties of shrubs, flowers, fungi, birds, butterflies and moths. These included several rare specimens which have survived or flourished on land that has not been subjected to cultivation since the beginning of this century. An archaeological sub-group has also been formed to record, survey and examine the undisturbed and often unique prehistoric and Roman sites on the Ranges.[56]

No account of the natural history of Larkhill would be complete without some reference to the Great Bustard, since it has always had a special association with Wiltshire, appearing in the county's coat of arms and on the School's flag (see Plate 29, page 119 and the illustrations facing page 224). It has also given its name to the Bustard Inn, known to countless generations of Gunners, that stands on the southern boundary of the ranges adjoining the old Salisbury–Devizes road. With a wing span of 6 feet and a height of 3½ feet, this magnificent bird fought a losing battle to survive, from 1545 when Henry VIII passed an Act for its protection, until about 1820 when it became extinct. Migrant birds were subsequently seen at Shrewton in 1852 and near Chippenham in 1872 which were some of the rare occasions when bustards have reached this country from Europe. This has generally happened when the Continent has been struck by heavy storms or exceptionally hard weather.

In June 1970, a hen was found on Fair Isle in the Shetlands which in due course arrived at Porton where a small flock of penned and pinioned birds has been formed.[57] It is also of interest that in January 1982, *The Times* reported that three great bustards had been seen on Romney Marsh.[58] In 1983 an exhibit showing a cock and three hens was on display in the Salisbury and South Wiltshire Museum, The King's House, 65 The Close, Salisbury.

11. Larkhill and the Territorial Army

Although the name 'Territorial Army' was not adopted until 1920, it is used in the title of this chapter to include all categories of volunteer units from the beginning of this century. One of the first references to volunteer artillery at Larkhill occurs in the School of Gunnery Report for 1902. This records that three batteries of the Lancashire Field Artillery (Militia) 'practised here and did creditably considering the very short training the men had' and that 'two horse batteries of the Honourable Artillery Company also practised here and shot most creditably'.[1] Both these units were on the ranges again in 1906 and 1907 and since no other volunteer batteries are mentioned in the Reports, it may be assumed that they were the only ones that practised at Larkhill during this period.

When the Territorial and Reserve Forces Act was passed in 1907, the character and standing of the volunteer forces underwent a complete change. This was part of the reorganisation of the British Army which was brought about by the ability and foresight of Lord Haldane who was Secretary of State for War. Under the Act a new Territorial Force was created in 1908 which replaced the earlier volunteers while the militia were re-formed as the Special Reserve. Some idea of the effect of this new legislation can be gained from the fact that in 1909, as compared with the attendances of 1906 and 1907, no less than 29 Territorial batteries practised at Okehampton and an unspecified number of brigades visited Trawsfynydd although none attended Larkhill.[2] The Report of 1908 also took note of this change and contained the following remarks:

The Honourable Artillery Company (2 batteries Horse Artillery) and the 4th London (2 howitzer batteries) practised during the season. In view of the present creation of a large number of these territorial batteries, their coming was of much interest. As the practice was conducted (in the case of these batteries) by the Colonel Commanding the Royal Artillery of the Territorial Division . . . the aspects of the practice do not

PLATE 34: Territorials with 15 pr BL field gun. *c* 1909. (*Mrs M.H. Fallon*)

come into the scope of this report, other than for me to say,
that the Honourable Artillery Company batteries came to camp
fully horsed and trained, displaying the same high efficiency as
in previous years. The 4th London made good practice from a
fixed position, they were not horsed, and were as yet untrained
in any mounted work.[3]

After 1909 the Annual Reports contain an increasing number of
references relating to Territorial units and the 1910 Report, when
stressing the need for 'an Artillery School . . . in the vicinity of the
new Salisbury Ranges near Tilshead', expresses the opinion that
'The advantage to the Territorial Artillery, could such a school be
established, would be incalculable, and the money spent on it
would be well spent'.[4]

By 1911 more Territorial units were carrying out their annual
training at established practice camps but as they were being
issued with 15 pr BLC guns and 5 in. BL howitzers which had
been discarded by regular batteries, it was felt that they were
worthy of better equipment.[5] In spite of this, it was noted in
1913 that the Territorial artillery had 'undoubtedly made progress
and some batteries are very well drilled and trained'.[6] Some
Territorial brigades were now practising regularly each year as for
example the 4th South Midland Howitzer Brigade which attended

Salisbury Plain (Larkhill) in 1910, Okehampton in 1911, Pembrey (Carmarthenshire) in 1912, Larkhill again in 1913 and Lydd in 1914.[7] However some practice camps had their disadvantages

> in very few places was space available for both manoeuvre and practice, and so, since the first essential for a gunner was ability to shoot, many batteries had to go to Lydd and Shoeburyness where no manoeuvre was possible. The need was, however, recognized, and in 1911 a large amount of additional ground was made available on Salisbury Plain (part of Westdown Range) while the following year saw the opening of a new range at 'Ad Fines' (Redesdale) on the Cheviots. The situation was relieved in the meantime by the adoption of biennial practice, which gave opportunities also for the Territorial artillery to join their infantry in camp on alternate years, and get some combined training.[8]

There were also difficulties in hiring suitable horses for practice camps and unit training. Some brigades solved the problem by purchasing horses with the grant that was allocated for hiring them and then letting them out to tradesmen, known as 'bailees' who undertook to produce the animals when they were needed by the unit.[9] But this was not the usual practice and it is unlikely that many brigades adopted it so that most units were dependent on contractors to supply their needs. This state of affairs continued after the end of the First World War and only came to an end when units were mechanised.

> This was the occasion when I saw some of the difficulties under which the TA of those days operated. One of the first things the unit had to do was collect their horses, supplied under contract, from the station. A party went down to do this and not long after there was a terrific stampede as most of the animals arrived loose and riderless. Something not quite right about the detraining exercise obviously. Eventually they were all caught and secured in the horse lines and a motley collection they were. They ranged virtually from shire horse to pit pony with all stages in between. Some had never been in harness, some hardly ever out of it. To make up anything like a matching six-horse gun-team was impossible. But teams of sorts they made and out they went on training. To see a lead driver perched on top of a 17 hand shire with a little hack or cob as his off horse was amusing but quite unfair. It was the usual contractual racket.

𝕶𝖆𝖒𝖕 THIRD 𝕶𝖓𝖊𝖜𝖘

THE OFFICIOUS NEWS-ANCE   3ᴿᴰ WEST LANCS. BRIGADE
        OF THE   R.F.A.
                          WEST LANCASHIRE BRIGADE
                          ROYAL FIELD ARTILLERY.
  "If you want to win your battles,   (INCLUDING THE AMMUNITION COLUMN.)
  Take and work your blooming guns."
                          QUO FAS ET GLORIA DUCUNT

No. 19.   LARK HILL CAMP, 28th JULY, 1914.   ALL RIGHTS DESERVED.

The manly part is to do, with might and main, what you can do.—*Emerson*.

* * * *

siege though fair was bare, and recalled the lines in the Ingoldsby legend :—

O, Salisbury Plain is bleak and bare,—
At least, so I've heard many people declare,
For I fairly confess I never was there :—

PLATE 35: The camp newspaper of the 3rd West Lancashire Brigade Territorial Force, published at Larkhill a week before the beginning of the First War. (*Mrs M.H. Fallon*)

If it had four legs and could stand, send it and totally ignore its suitability or otherwise.[10]

In spite of the various obstacles which confronted the Territorial Forces their morale was high and their enthusiasm unbounded. The 3rd West Lancashire Brigade published its own newspaper – *Kamp Knews* – when it was at Larkhill in July 1914 and the heading of this entertaining publication is reproduced as Plate 35 (above). After war was declared, many Territorial brigades were sent to Larkhill for two or three days' firing before leaving for France, in the same way that their successors were in 1939. On 9 January 1915, the 3rd South Midland Brigade travelled from their concentration area near Chelmsford, Essex, to Rollestone Camp for firing practice and this occasion has been described by one of the officers, Major H.P. Haynes, MC who, at the time, was a captain in the 1st Warwickshire Battery.

January 9th. Left Galleywood 10.00 p.m., marched to Chelmsford; left by 12.30 train.

January 10th. Arrived Amesbury 6.30 a.m. dark but fine. Marched to Rollestone via Stonehenge and Fargo. Found nothing to eat on arrival in camp but eventually Harrods arrived with breakfast at 11.00 a.m.

January 11th. Marched to Silver Barrow for gun practice. Fired 50 rounds in five series. Poor shooting.

January 12th. Marched with Battery to West Down Plantation for firing by 2nd and 3rd Batteries. Back at 1.30. Left Rollestone Camp 3.30 and caught the 5.49 from Amesbury for London. Out to Chelmsford by 11.30 p.m. train. Marched to Galleywood, reached there at 1.45 a.m. on 13th. Marched about 20 miles today.[11]

Between the two World Wars, it was usual for Territorial artillery brigades to attend a practice camp every other year but after 1947 regiments normally practised every year. Since 1908 the Territorial Army has seen many changes and not the least of these have been in respect of its title. After the First World War the Territorial Force was disbanded, but was reformed in 1920 as the Territorial Army which in turn was disbanded in 1946 and reformed in 1947. In 1967 the Territorial and Army Volunteer Reserve (TAVR) was established and replaced the Territorial Army but twelve years later the position was reversed when, in 1979, the TAVR was terminated and once again the Territorial Army came into existence.

No account of Territorial Gunners and practice camps would be complete without reference to the competitions that have been held by the National Artillery Association since 1865. The Association was formed in 1863 with the object of holding competitions between Volunteer Artillery units in order to encourage and improve their efficiency in the firing and handling of equipment. The first competition was held at Shoeburyness in August 1865 when twenty-five gun detachments took part and prizes were presented by HM The Queen, HRH The Prince of Wales, the Commander-in-Chief and the Association. The competition was conducted between individual gun detachments and not between batteries, as was the case in later years, and the premier award known as HM The Queen's Prize was won by No. 2 Detachment of the 1st Sussex Artillery Volunteers.[12]

After the formation of the Territorial Force in 1908, provision was made for horse and field batteries to take part and the emphasis began to pass from coast-defence artillery to field. Three prizes were awarded: HM The King's Prize for Field Artillery, The King's

Prize for Heavy Artillery and HRH The Prince of Wales's Prize for Medium Artillery. In 1910 the competitions were held at Oke-hampton but already some doubts were being expressed as to their value and Colonel S.C. Smith, Chief Instructor, Horse and Field School of Gunnery, included the following remarks in his report:

> The National Artillery Association held their competitions at Okehampton this year for the first time. This enabled more up-to-date conditions to be enforced, tactics and manoeuvre being added as qualifications. It is, however, a matter for consideration whether these competitions now serve any specially useful purpose.[13]

The next year the event took place on the West Down ranges and in the meantime Colonel Smith's views had become rather more definite. 'The National Artillery Association held their competitions this year at West Down Camp; I hope that we have now seen the last of this meeting.'[14]

For 1912 the competition for horse and field batteries was restricted to units that had already attended official practice camps, the competitors being judged on their performance at these camps.[15]

This new arrangement did not, however, avoid criticism by Lieutenant-Colonel F.R. Bingham, the new Chief Instructor.

PLATE 36: Territorials firing 15 pr BLC at practice camp *c* 1912. Note the 'rear OP'. (*Mrs M.H. Fallon*)

This year a so-called competition was held between batteries armed with 4.7 in. QF., 15 pr BLC and 5 in. howitzers, for the 'King's Prize'.

I hope this is the last year of this competition. It is manifestly absurd to allow the above natures of guns to compete against each other at such widely different camps as Larkhill, West Down, Trawsfynydd, Okehampton and Ad Fines (Redesdale), under five different umpires. It takes 32 rounds, and in my opinion is a pure waste of ammunition and I cannot see that a competition of this sort conveys conviction to anyone, and it is no test of the comparative merits of the batteries.[16]

His comments appear to have had some effect although the system was still being questioned in the following year:

The prizes were given this year on a different method to previous years; and they were allotted to each camp and the judging entrusted to the Gunnery Instructor. The anomaly, however, still remains, that for the King's Prize batteries compete against each other at different camps. This year a battery at Buddon was allotted 86 per cent of total marks, a battery at Larkhill was allotted 84 per cent. Who knows which is the best battery? I confess I do not.[17]

On account of the war, no competitions were held from 1914 to 1920 but they were re-introduced in 1921 when three prizes, each known as HM The King's Prize, were offered for field, medium and heavy artillery respectively. However in 1930 three separate competitions were established, one for heavy artillery (9.2 in.), one for heavy artillery (6 in.) and one which included horse, field, light and medium artillery,[18] the first winners in the last class being 271 Battery, 68th South Midland Field Brigade with 236 Battery, 59th (4th West Lancashire), Medium Brigade being placed second. In each competition the first prize was known as HM The King's Cup. This arrangement continued until 1938 but mainly as a result of the Second World War the competitions did not take place between 1939 and 1961. Eventually, in 1962 a competition was held once again for horse, field and medium artillery, the first prize now being known as HM The Queen's Cup.

In 1968 the National Artillery Association took over the administration of competitions for air-defence artillery while in recent years the competitions have been extended and the number of awards increased. Despite the difficulties which have, from time to time, confronted the Association and the many changes that have taken place, 'the Association still exists for the purpose for which it was originally formed: to encourage efficiency and esprit de corps in the Volunteer units of the Royal Artillery'.[19]

12. Larkhill Garrison

Larkhill Garrison is situated on the southern slopes of Knighton Down which extend from the Long Barrow to Fargo Road. The area is divided by a shallow depression which runs southwards from the RA Mess to Down Barn and continues across Fargo Road to beyond the junction of the A303 and A344 roads near Stonehenge. It is this feature which accounts for the 'dip' in the Packway between Roberts Barracks and the Garrison Church. The camp which covers 803 acres (325 hectares) has evolved around three principal roads running from west to east. Of these, the Packway is the most important and forms what may be termed the 'base line' on which Larkhill has developed. To the south, Fargo Road runs roughly parallel to the Packway while Brackenbury Road, which leads into Glover Road, forms a stirrup-shaped loop to the north. At the same time, several roads run north and south, the most important links being Willougby Road and its continuation – Watson Road – on the west, and Wood Road on the east. A list of roads and buildings which have been named in commemoration of some of the officers who have been associated with the School, and those who have served with eminence in the Royal Regiment, will be found in Appendix XII.

Much of Larkhill, as it exists today, has been built since 1960 and to the north of the Packway it has been divided into four parts which have been named Alanbrooke Barracks, Stirling Barracks, Robert Barracks and Horne Barracks. Alanbrooke covers the area which lies to the north of Brackenbury Road and Glover Road, from the shelter belt adjoining Watson Road to a line running from grid reference 136446 to 136450, but excluding Knighton Down Sports Ground. It includes the Warrant Officers' and Sergeants' Mess, the Soldiers' Dining Hall, the Gun Club (NAAFI) and the WRAC quarters. Stirling Barracks incorporates the whole of the land north of the Packway as far as Alanbrooke Barracks but excludes Roberts Barracks, the Packway shops and the married quarters in Biddulph Road. Within its boundaries lies the School headquarters, the instructional blocks, the administrative buildings, the gun park, the RA Mess, the Garrison Church and the offices of the Department of the Environment.

The principal area covered by Roberts Barracks is bounded by the Packway, Watson Road, Power Road and Phillips Road together with the Packway Mess. Until the middle of 1983, these barracks were used by the Support Regiment, Royal School of Artillery. Horne Barracks lie to the west of Roberts Barracks and cover a triangular-shaped site which is bounded by the Packway, Brackenbury Road and Watson Road. Only about one quarter of this area is occupied by buildings which house 22 (Gibraltar 1779–83) Locating Battery RA, the RA Mounted Band, the Ministry of Defence Police and No. 1 Troop Wiltshire Army Cadet Force. To the south of the Packway between Willoughby and Watson roads are a group of buildings which include the Stanoc Centre, the Garrison Medical and Dental Centre, the Roman Catholic Church, the County Police Station, the NAAFI shop, the Packhorse Inn and the swimming pool. On the other side of Wilson Road is the Larkhill Primary School while, beyond this, lies the main block of the soldiers married quarters. To the southeast, beyond Down Barn, are the officers' married quarters at Strangways and around Colquhoun Road and Wells Road.

The expansive and well-planned layout of the roads and buildings in the Garrison area has offered considerable scope for planting trees and shrubs and no opportunity has been lost in establishing avenues, ornamental groups, screens and shelter belts. The first evidence of tree planting at Larkhill was a small wood named Larkhill Copse which occupied the site of the present RA Mess and this is shown on the Ordnance Survey map published in 1903.[1] Except for a group of trees surrounding Down Barn, this plantation comprised the only trees at Larkhill at the beginning of this century. The first major planting scheme to be carried out after the School was established, in 1920, was on either side of the Packway and along the original line of Bell Road before it was diverted. This was done in 1929 by Lieutenant-Colonel H.L. Piggot who was the War Department Land Agent and since then large numbers of trees have been planted at Larkhill by the Defence Land Agent's staff.

During the course of its history, at least seven officers' messes have existed at Larkhill and of these the oldest and best known was 'A' Mess (see Plate 26, page 109) which served Gunner officers for no less than fifty-three years. Situated at the eastern end of Brackenbury Road (grid reference 134449), it was built in 1915 and did not finally close until 1968. It was demolished shortly afterwards. 'B' Mess which was built sometime after 1919 (it was in use by 1926), was located in Pownall Road at grid reference 145437. During the winter months it was used as an overflow for 'A' Mess but in the summer the staff manned a tented mess at West Down Camp during the practice season.[2] The history of 'C' Mess is somewhat obscure. It was erected between the two World Wars and the building, which was situated at the junction of Wood Road and Tombs Road with Fargo Road, was still standing in 1983. Like 'B' Mess, it provided additional accommodation when there was a shortage of room in 'A' Mess but in 1924 it was also used by Gunnery Staff Courses and after 1926, by young officers.[3] However in 1953 it ceased to be employed as a mess and was taken over by the Commander Royal Engineers (CRE). Subsequently it was transferred to the Marricd Quarters Administrative Staff who occupied it until 1968 since when it has been used for various purposes.[4]

Between the two wars other messes were formed; one of the first was that of the Survey Company RA and the 1st Survey Company RA which served from 1921 to 1938,[5] Another mess of the same period was the 'RA Mess - The Packway' that was located in 16 Camp which now forms a part of Roberts Barracks. It was used by the Depot Brigades and Regiments (see Appendix VII) and also by 6th Medium Brigade which was stationed at Larkhill under a normal regimental posting.[6] Although the present Packway Mess was built in 1938, the mess in 16 Camp continued in use and it was not until 1949 that 5th Regiment RHA, who were then Depot Regiment, moved into the new mess. This building which stands in an attractive garden contains a dining room, two ante-rooms and forty bedrooms. It has been used by numerous units since 1938, including the Depot Regiments, 192 Survey Battery RA, 22 (Gibraltar 1779-83) Locating Battery RA and the Support Regiment, Royal School of Artillery, as well as providing extra accommodation when the pressure on the RA Mess has proved to be too great.[7]

Although work on the present RA Mess began in 1936, it was not ready for occupation until 1940. The formal opening did not take place until 1941. The delay in completion was due to a number of causes but even before the order was given for the work to start, problems arose:

The siting of the RA Mess is a story within a story. One would think that the present location would have been a natural choice but this is not the case. Briefly, the 'experts' wanted to build a mess near the top of Knighton Down – probably the most exposed spot on Salisbury Plain. The Commandant at the time, Brigadier A.F. Brooke (later Field Marshal the Viscount Alanbrooke) protested vehemently but apparently in vain. It seemed that the officers of the School of Artillery were to be banished to 'Siberia' for ever. But an ally from an unexpected quarter, in the shape of the Inspector of Ancient Monuments, came to our aid and persuaded the War Office to think again, because being on the skyline it would be a blot on the landscape, anyway when viewed from Stonehenge. So all was well, but only just.[8]

There were also two outlying messes; the Range Detachment's Mess at Greenlands Farm and a mess at West Down Camp which was used by units attending practice camps.

Although there have been Warrant Officers' and Sergeants' messes at Larkhill for as long as the camp has been in existence, unfortunately very little information has been recorded about them. A new School Mess was built in 1931[9] but this may have been of a temporary nature since it was not until 1938 that the first buildings that form the present Mess were erected. Three

PLATE 37: Silver centre piece presented to HRH The Duke of Connaught
by the Officers of the Regiment on the occasion of his marriage.
(*RSA Reprographics*)

further extensions were completed in 1964 and 1965 and new kitchens built in the early 1970s.

The RA Mess has been the scene of many outstanding functions and events some of which have been referred to in earlier chapters. Of these the visits of HM The Queen, HRH The Prince of Wales and other members of the Royal Family and the dinners given to members of the Allied Armies between 1942 and 1945 must be accounted amongst the most important. The Mess Building comprises five main rooms on the ground floor: the Baker Room which until May 1976 was known as the Commandant's Parlour, the Mansergh Room, the Alanbrooke Room, the Permanent Staff Ante-room, previously the Billiard Room, and the Dining Room. There are 184 bedrooms.

Owing to lack of space it is not possible to describe the many items which comprise the Mess silver but the following pieces are of particular interest. On the centre table in the entrance hall stands an exceptionally fine group consisting of a 9 pr ML field gun with a detachment of five men. A plaque bearing the following inscription is fixed to the plinth.

Presented to HRH Arthur W.P.A. Duke of Connaught, KG, KT, KP, GCMG, GCSI on the occasion of his marriage with HRH The Princess Louise Margaret of Prussia by the Officers of the Royal Artillery who remember with pride that His Royal Highness in his early military career was associated with their Corps. 1879.

After his death, the following letter from Colonel C.S. Price Davies, Comptroller to the Duke, dated 20 February 1942, was received by the Master Gunner, Field Marshal Lord Milne.

Dear Field Marshal,

Although no special bequest was made in His late Royal Highness' Will, The Duke of Connaught left a list of wishes, which included your Regiment.

Lady Patricia Ramsey now has great pleasure in giving your Regimental Wedding Present to the Duke of Connaught back to the officers of the Royal Artillery in memory of her beloved father, who for so many years was associated with your Regiment . . .

Yours sincerely
Charles S. Price Davies
Colonel
Comptroller and Executor

There are also a large number of silver models of guns and other equipment which include the following: 18 pr, 25 pr, 5.5 in. gun, 9.2 in. howitzer, 3.7 in. heavy AA gun, 'Abbot', 'Rapier', 'Blow-pipe' and 'Thunderbird'. One of the more unusual is that of a pack mule carrying the piece of a 2.5 in. RML mountain gun which has found a unique place in the annals of the Regiment by virtue of Rudyard Kipling's poem 'Screw-Guns'. To mark the amalgamation of Larkhill and Manorbier, 150 silver wine goblets

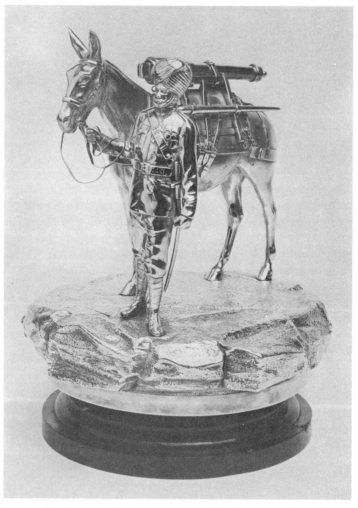

PLATE 38: Silver statuette commemorating the Mountain Artillery.
(*RSA Reprographics*)

were presented to the Mess by past commandants, regiments, unit headquarters and those who had served at the two Schools. One of these was also presented by HM The Queen when she visited Larkhill in April 1973.

The Mess silver also includes a unique collection of five Kadir Cups which have always been regarded as the 'blue riband' of pigsticking, a sport which required great horsemanship in addition to considerable skill and courage. In 1868 a cup was presented by Mr W.A. Forbes, the first President of the Meerut Tent Club 'for horses fairly hunted to pig' and in 1874 this became known as the Kadir Cup, the word *Kadir* being defined as 'a large area of flat plain with tall grass'. One of the leading exponents of pigsticking was Captain P.H.J. Tuck RA (afterwards Brigadier P.H.J. Tuck) who was widely known as 'Friar' Tuck. On his death he left his collection of pig-sticking trophies to the Regiment and these included the two Kadir Cups which he won in 1936 and 1939. The other three cups were won by Captain J. Hamwell, RA, ADC in 1890, Captain C.F. Blane, RHA in 1893 and Lieutenant W.D. Paynter, RHA in 1910. The last competition was held in 1939 and by that year the cup had been won nine times by a Field Gunner and five times by a Horse Gunner.[10]

Two other items which are especially interesting are the cup that was won by Lieutenant H.P. Burnyeats, RA riding his Downpatrick II in the Royal Artillery Gold Cup on 20 April 1906 and the statuette of Lieutenant-Colonel F.W.C. Weldon, MVO, MBE, MC, RA on 'Kilbarry' who together achieved many successes in British and European Horse Trials.

The Mess also has a notable collection of pictures by a number of distinguished artists. In the dining room is a portrait of HM The Queen which is a copy by James Gunn (1893–1964) of his original painting that hangs in the Headquarters Mess at Woolwich and a portrait of HM King George VI by Denis Fildes (1889–1975). At the opposite end of the room are portraits of Field Marshal Lord Milne and Field Marshal Viscount Alanbrooke, both by Sir Oswald Birley (1880–1952). In the reception rooms are a number of pictures by well-known artists and these include two original watercolours by Orlando Norrie (1832–1901) one of which was presented by The Princess Royal when she visited the mess on 9 January 1958. This bears the inscription 'Field Artillery – Orlando Norrie). Presented by HRH The Princess Royal' while the other is simply entitled 'RHA Section'.

There are also two examples of the work of Lucy Kemp-Welch (1869–1958), the first being a signed print with the title of '9.2

PLATE 39: 'The Scent' — a crayon drawing on plywood by Gilbert Holiday.

Gun Team, Bulford Camp 1918' while the other is an original inscribed 'Leaders of the Heavy Gun Team'. In fact, this shows the second pair of horses in the 9.2 gun team and not the leaders. This picture was presented to the mess by Mr L. Hewitt, a Territorial Gunner who remembered Larkhill with affection, in the days when Brigadier A.F. Brooke was Commandant.

Other pictures which are of considerable interest are eight by Gilbert Holiday (1879-1937) of which three are originals and five are signed prints. Holiday, or 'G.H.' as he was frequently known, was commissioned into the Royal Field Artillery in 1915 and continued to serve until 1919 when he returned to civilian life. Of the three originals, the most interesting is a crayon sketch of a hunting scene entitled 'The Scent' which was drawn on the wall of a classroom at Larkhill when G.H. was stationed there, the section of the wall having been subsequently removed. The other two are a pair which were presented to the Mess by four brothers; John, Peter, Mark and Martin Greyson, all of whom were Gunners. One picture is entitled 'Coming into action' while the other shows a battery firing on the ranges over open sights and bears the legend 'Gunnery, Salisbury Plain 1914': both were painted at Larkhill.

Another great Gunner artist was C.J. Payne (1884-1967) who is better known as 'Snaffles'. He enlisted into the Royal Garrison Artillery on 8 May 1902 and after completing three years' service with the colours, transferred to the Reserve in 1905. After six years – three years before his time expired – he was discharged at his own request, on payment of £25, in order to devote the whole of his time to painting. He rejoined the Army when war broke out in 1914, and later went to India. The Mess has an outstanding collection of his paintings comprising seven originals and thirty-one prints of which twenty-five are signed. The originals consist of one of an elephant battery, a 'cartoon' on pigsticking and five of Gunner officers, in varying uniforms. Four of these were painted under the artist's initials 'CJP' before he had adopted the pseudonym of 'Snaffles'. Lionel Edwards (1878-1966), who has been recognised as one of the finest English sporting artists, is represented by six pictures of which four are originals. All but one of these depict scenes at Larkhill, including one of the RA Hunt which was painted in 1952. There are also three delightful pen and ink drawings by Maurice Tullock of 'Friar' Tuck's ponies, Manifest, Miss Fire and Squeaker.

When the events of the 50th Anniversary of the School were being planned, it was felt that it would be appropriate if the occasion could be commemorated by a painting and, through the

PLATE 40: 'Gunnery, Salisbury Plain, 1914' by Gilbert Holiday.

generosity of Colonel Sir Desmond Brayley, MC, the School was able to commission Miss Wanklyn. However, it was later decided to increase the number of paintings to three.[11] The largest of these shows the 'Abbots' of 2nd Field Regiment RA driving across the arena at Knighton Down on Artillery Day 1970, while the other two are composed of individual scenes at Larkhill, one covering the period from 1920 to 1945, and the other from 1945 to 1970. There are two other pictures by Miss Wanklyn, the first of which shows HM The Queen on the point-to-point course during her visit to the School in April 1973. The second portrays the Master Gunner greeting Her Majesty inside the West Door of St Paul's Cathedral on 8 July 1966, at the Thanksgiving Service to commemorate the 250th Anniversary of the formation of the Regiment. In the entrance hall are two large oil paintings by H. Septimus Power (1879–1951), one depicting heavy artillery going into action before Passchendaele on 9 October 1917 and the other field artillery advancing before Harbonnieres on 8 August 1918.

In order to ensure that a mess runs smoothly and efficiently, it is essential to have a competent mess secretary who is supported by an experienced and proficient staff and in these respects the School has been especially fortunate. The following is a list of those who have held the position of mess secretary from 1924 to the present time, except for the period from 1932 to 1936:

1924–8	Captain F.A.L. Cooper, RA
1928–32	Captain J.H.W.G. Richards, RA
1932–6	No record
1936–49	Major H.S. Crane, MBE
1949–52	Colonel R.G.R. Thompson, OBE
1952–62	Lieutenant-Colonel R.B. Greig, DSO
1962–79	Major F.M. Robertson, MC
1979–	Major E.G. Stadward, TD

Over the years there have been many instances of long and outstanding service by members of the mess staff and amongst these the following may be mentioned: Mr R.W. Edwards, BEM who was chief steward, and had worked in 'A' Mess and the RA Mess for thirty-three years from 1925 to 1958; also Mr M. McCoy, BEM who after serving in the Regiment for some eight years, later became Chief Steward, a position that he held for over twenty-five years. Another well-known member of the staff was Private P.M. Smith of No. 9 Independent Company, WRAC who, in 1960, completed eighteen years' service in 'A' Mess, where she was

PLATE 41: 'The RA Hunt' by Lionel Edwards, 1952. The covert on the right is Shrewton Folly and on the left, Old Farm Clump. The central figure is the Master, Lt.-Col. H.C.R. Gillman.

affectionately known as 'Phyllis'. On 26 January 1960 she received the Long Service and Good Conduct Medal from the DRA, Major-General E.D. Howard-Vyse, CB, CBE, MC.[12] Mr Reggie Smith, who joined the staff in 1947, was still an active member of it twenty years later. Another stalwart was Mr I.E. Curtis, who joined the Royal Corps of Signals in 1940, served in North Africa and Italy and was subsequently invalided out of the Army. He became a member of the mess staff in 1952 and continued until his death in 1976. Mention must also be made of Mr W.S.H. Clarke, universally known as 'Nobby' who, after serving in the Regiment from May 1940 until 1946 was appointed mess barber in that year. He was still at work in 1983 – some thirty-seven years later – which must be a unique record of service to the Royal Regiment.[13] To complete the picture, it is only necessary to add that Mr J.C.M. Campbell the present Chief Steward has already served for over twenty years in the Mess.

The Warrant Officers' and Sergeants' Mess has sixty rooms which are available for those attending courses and over the years accommodation has been provided for senior NCOs from every regiment in the British Army and many from overseas. Members of the Royal Navy, the Royal Air Force as well as civilians have also stayed in the Mess from time to time. Among the items belonging to the Mess are two of particular interest. The first is a barometer

PLATE 42: The Warrant Officers' and Sergeants' Mess, 1983.
(*RSA Reprographics*)

presented by Brigadier and Mrs A.F. Brooke (afterwards Field
Marshal Viscount Alanbrooke and Viscountess Alanbrooke) when
he was Commandant of the School from 1929 to 1932. The other
is an exceptionally fine model of a 6 in. howitzer and limber, the
working parts of which all operate correctly and which bears the
following inscription:

Made at
Military College of Science
Workshop
Woolwich
1938

PLATE 43: Model of 6 in. howitzer and limber. Warrant Officers' and Sergeants' Mess.

The original Garrison Church which was built in 1914 was a
wooden hut that stood on the north-east side of Lawrence Road
adjoining the site of the present church. By 1936, the War Department had decided to provide a new church as part of the recon-
struction of Larkhill and building operations began on 15 October
1936. The Foundation Stone was laid by General Sir John Burnett-
Stuart on 22 January 1937 in weather that was described as
'Salisbury Plain at its very worst – a howling gale and torrential
rain'.[14] The stone which was blessed by the Chaplain-General,
bears the following inscription:

TO THE GLORY OF GOD
THIS STONE WAS LAID BY
GENERAL
SIR JOHN T. BURNETT-STUART, KCB,
KBE, CMG, DSO
GENERAL OFFICER COMMANDING-IN-CHIEF
SOUTHERN COMMAND
22 JANUARY 1937

On 20 December the bell was dedicated, followed by the dedication of the cross over the East End on 1 February 1938.

Exactly sixteen months after the laying of the Foundation Stone, the building of the Church was completed and it was dedicated to St Alban the Martyr on 21 May 1938 by the Chaplain-General, the Reverend E.H. Thorold, CB, CBE and on this occasion the weather was perfect. St Alban was the first British martyr who was put to death, probably in AD 212. In the past some authorities have considered that he was a Roman soldier but more recently this view has been questioned, since it has not been proved beyond doubt.[16] It is probably the supposition that he was a soldier, as well as being the first Christian martyr, that led to the decision to dedicate the Garrison Church to this Saint. The building was designed by Mr W. Ross, FRIBA, and over half a million bricks were used in its construction while the roof was covered with some three tons of copper. The organ was built by Messrs. A.H. Stanton of Walsall.[11]

In 1954 the original brick pulpit was replaced by one of oak which was given by the Reverend Colonel R. Atkinson, OBE, MC, TD. He had joined the Regiment as a boy in 1900, had risen to the rank of colonel and, at the age of sixty-five, had been ordained.[18] During 1960 it was felt that some action should be taken to introduce more colour and character into the church and it was decided to instal a new window. The subject chosen was St Barbara, the Patron Saint of Artillerymen, and the work was completed in November 1961. The window was dedicated on 3 December, the Sunday nearest to St Barbara's Day (4 December), by the Chaplain-General, The Venerable Archdeacon I.D. Neill, CB, OBE.[19] To enhance the East End a crusader cross, made by the Garrison Engineer, was fixed to the wall of the apse and two tall candlesticks, the gift of the Deputy Commandant, Colonel B. Cocks, GM, TD, were placed on either side of the altar.

The accoustics in the church had always been poor and in 1961 it was decided to consult an expert on the matter. Subsequently it

PLATE 44: Interior of the Garrison Church of St Alban, 1982.
(RSA Reprographics)

was suggested that if something could be done to break the sound
waves, the situation would be improved. As the question of providing a memorial of some kind to Gunners of countries that had
fought with Britain in the Second World War was under consideration, the idea of hanging flags of different artillery formations
came to mind. This would also bring more colour and life into the
church, and the idea was adopted with excellent results.[20] The
flags were dedicated on 10 May 1964. In the following year the
'Stars and Stripes' that had been flown at half-mast at the United
States Field Artillery School at Fort Sill, on the death of Sir
Winston Churchill, was presented to the School and hung in the
church. Other flags have been added from time to time, and a
description of each one with a plan showing its position has been
placed in the aisle.

During 1962 the first of the memorial plaques in commemoration of past commandants was erected and four stained-glass
windows have since been installed. These have been given by the
Mother's Union (May 1970), the Guild of St Helena (November
1970), the Corps of Royal Electrical and Mechanical Engineers
– a window dedicated to St Eligius (December 1970), and the

Larkhill Garrison – a window dedicated to St George (October 1971). The following Collect of the Royal School of Artillery was written in 1970 and is now used in the Garrison Church on St Barbara's Day:

> Almighty God, who has defended and guided us to this hour and supplied all our needs; may we look wide; fill us with high ideals; and fire us with the message of compassion and good will to all. Help us to think and plan; to work and play, to teach and learn, and to pray together, that the Royal School of Artillery may be perfectly fitted to serve you, our fellow men, and the Royal Regiment of Artillery in the work to which you have called us; through Jesus Christ our Lord. Amen.

A list of Church of England chaplains who have served at the School from 1918 to 1982 and Roman Catholic chaplains who have served from 1969 to 1982, will be found in Appendix VI.

Little information is available regarding the first Roman Catholic church at Larkhill but the Ordnance Survey '25 inch sheet' of the 1939 revision,[21] marks 'St. Anthony's Catholic Church' about 90 metres north of the Packway, opposite Lightfoot Road (grid reference 131443). The Ordnance Survey '6 inch sheet' dated 1926[22] shows the same building and although unnamed, it would seem very probable that it was the Catholic Church at that time. Later the church moved to a hut on the north-west corner of the junction of Gore Road and Alanbrooke Road. In 1965 it was decided that a new church should be built and the foundation stone was laid in January 1967, bearing the following inscription,

TO THE GREATER GLORY OF GOD
THIS STONE WAS LAID BY
THE RIGHT REVEREND GERARD W. TICKLE
ROMAN CATHOLIC BISHOP-IN-ORDINARY
TO HER MAJESTY'S FORCES
ON 12TH JANUARY 1967

The church was dedicated by the Bishop to St Barbara and St Anthony on 22 September 1968.[23] It thus incorporated the name of the previous church with that of St Barbara, the Patron Saint of Gunners. Its somewhat unconventional design allows natural light to enter from above and this has resulted in an unusually bright and cheerful building which can seat 175 people.

A number of services and amenities are available for personnel

PLATE 45: Interior of the Roman Catholic Church of St Barbara and St Anthony, 1982. (*RSA Reprographics*)

living in the Garrison area. Medical treatment and dental care is provided by the Royal Army Medical Corps and the Royal Army Dental Corps at the Garrison Medical and Dental Centre. Social services, welfare and housing are covered by the Families, Housing and Welfare Service which operates under the Garrison Housing and Welfare Commandant while the Wiltshire Education Authority provides for the education of the young at the Larkhill Primary School. As regards amenity, the Sharp Hall provides excellent facilities for social occasions such as dances, wedding receptions, the Garrison Flower Show and so on. The hall was originally built by the Young Men's Christian Association – the YMCA – which had been at Larkhill since the First World War, but when the demand for the Association's services declined, the hall was let to the School and renamed the Packway Hall. By the end of 1976 it had fallen into a very poor state of repair and, in view of the heavy cost involved, the Association decided to demolish it. However, when representations were made to the YMCA, it kindly agreed to give the hall, in its state of disrepair, to the School and this gift came into effect in 1977. It was subsequently repaired and refurnished with the help of financial assistance provided by the defence industry. A plaque bearing the following inscription has been placed in the entrance hall:

SHARP HALL
This hall, originally the YMCA, and then the Packway Hall,
was reopened and renamed Sharp Hall on 19 November 1978.
Refurbishing was made possible by the generosity of the
United Kingdom defence industry and in particular of
Marconi Space and Defence Systems Ltd.
whose Managing Director Mr. A.S. Walsh
performed the opening ceremony in the presence
of Lady Sharp.
The hall is named after
General Sir John Sharp KCB, MC, ADC (Gen) MA
Commandant School of Artillery 1964–1966.

A short distance from the Sharp Hall is the Pack Horse Inn which was built at the suggestion of the School in 1962.

Amongst the various social amenities, one of the oldest is the Larkhill Amateur Dramatic Society which was formed in the 1930s and, except for the war years, has given regular performances of well-known plays. The first post-war play was *Laburnum Grove* by J.B. Priestley which was produced in December 1946,[24] and subsequently the Society won the Army Drama Festival in 1968 and 1967. In March 1983, the Society was placed first in the Salisbury Playhouse Amateur One-Act Play Festival for their performance of Tom Stoppard's *After Magritte* and Lieutenant-Colonel G.G. Freeman, RA (Guided Weapons Wing) received the award for the best actor.

The Guild of St Helena, which has a branch at Larkhill, was formed in order to bring together the wives, mothers and daughters of service men of any Christian denomination, irrespective of age or rank. Money which is raised by the Guild is used in a number of ways such as helping widows of service men and handicapped children in service families and in contributing to service charities. Three organizations are concerned with young people: the Army Cadet Force, the Larkhill Guides and Scouts and the Girls Venture Corps. No. 1 Troop, Wiltshire Army Cadet Force was formed in 1962 and now occupies headquarters in Ross Road. Their Corps of Drums which was formed in 1967 played at the Royal Tournament in the following year.

The 1st Larkhill (Stonehenge) Scout Group is composed of a Scout Troop, Cub Scout Park, Guides and Brownies, the leaders of each being members of the School or Garrison or their wives. In 1980 the Scout Troop won the National Scout Car Race. The Girls Venture Corps, which has a Unit in Larkhill, was formed in 1964 after the amalgamation of the Women's Junior Air Corps and the Girls Training Corps and provides for girls between the ages of thirteen and eighteen years. Their activities range from gliding, canoeing, skiing and rifle-shooting to dance, drama and community work.

Those who wish to play games have a large number from which to choose, and arrangements exist for the following: association football, Badminton, basket ball, cricket, golf, hockey, Rugby football, squash and tennis. At the end of 1982, there were six separate sports grounds which provided facilities for athletics, association and Rugby football, cricket and hockey in addition to tennis and squash courts.

As regards field sports, hunting can claim pride of place, for not only are the Kennels of the Royal Artillery Hunt less than four miles distant but it is the only pack of hounds in this country which is maintained by a regiment of the British Army. Its origins lie in the fact that in 1907, Captain A.E. Hussey, MFH generously made over part of the country that was hunted by the Tedworth Hounds to the Regiment. As a result, a pack of harriers was formed under the Mastership of Major J.G. Geddes which hunted hares until 1917, when sadly the hounds were put down. However the pack was reformed in 1919 and continued until 1939 but from the beginning of the second war until 1941, there was no hunting.

In 1942 it was decided to replace the harriers by fox hounds, a decision that was influenced by the fact that since they would hunt foxes, rations could be obtained for hounds that destroyed vermin and this enabled the Hunt to survive. The kennels which were built in 1934 are situated at Bulford Camp and in October 1982 the pack comprised 22½ couple. The Hunt uniform is green with a red collar – a legacy from the days when the hounds were harriers. A list of masters from 1907 to 1983 will be found in Appendix XVI.

Closely connected with the Hunt is the RA Saddle Club which was formed on 27 February 1946, largely due to the enthusiasm and encouragement of the Commandant, Brigadier G.W.E. Heath. The Club was originally known as the RA Hunt Club but adopted its present title in September 1946 and members are now able to hire horses through the Club, for hunting or riding. The Club at first managed the point-to-point course which was built on Knighton Down during the winter of 1946 and is the only regimental race

PLATE 46: The Larkhill Point-to-Point Course. 1974. (*RSA Reprographics*)

course in the country. The first meeting which was held on 23 April 1947 was ruined by appalling weather when every tent was blown down except the weighing-in tent. Despite this unfortunate start, the course has proved to be a tremendous success and in 1983 six meetings were scheduled to be held – the RA Hunt, four local hunts and the United Services Point-to Point.

After the course was finished in 1931, the Royal Artillery Hunter Trials were held at Larkhill until 1965 except for the ten years from 1939 to 1949. In 1965 these were combined with the Army Hunter Trials and have since been known as the Army and Royal Artillery Hunter Trials. In 1974, HRH The Princess Anne, Mrs Mark Phillips, GCVO, graciously agreed to become Patron. At the 1976 trials, Her Royal Highness and Captain Mark Phillips entered three horses. Another close connection with RA Hunt is the Royal Artillery Hunt Pony Club.

Brigadier Heath was not only the moving spirit behind the formation of the Saddle Club and the building of the point-to-point course but he also encouraged the establishment of a pack of beagles at Larkhill in 1947. The work of forming the pack was carried out by Lieutenant-Colonel W.E. Hulse who was commanding 124th Field Regiment RA and became the first Master. In

1948 he was appointed to command 5th Regiment RHA and his second-in-command, Major R.J. Uniacke, DSO, RHA succeeded him as Master. He was later followed by an infantry officer. The hounds were kennelled at Larkhill with Lieutenant D.F. Ryan, RHA (afterwards Brigadier D.F. Ryan, OBE) as secretary and Major J.E. Little, MC (afterwards Lieutenant-Colonel J.E. Little) as whipper-in but the pack was disbanded in 1952.[25]

The first record of a shoot at Larkhill is to be found in 1928 and although partridges were originally the predominant game bird, rabbits also provided both sport and income. The largest number that were shot in any one season was in 1935–6 when 1,323 were accounted for. As the number of partridges declined both nationally and locally, steps were taken to increase the stock of pheasants and the successful outcome of this has been due, very largely, to the hard work undertaken by members of the shoot.[26] In 1983 there were two shoots each covering about 14,000 acres, the first – known as the School Shoot – being mainly for those serving at the School while the second, the Garrison Shoot, providing for those in other units at Larkhill and, subject to there being vacancies, for those in HQ UKLF and other small units. All ranks are eligible for membership of either shoot while a limited number of retired officers living in the district may also join. The dividing line between the shoots is the road from The Bustard to Redhorn Hill, the School Shoot lying to the east and the Garrison Shoot to the west.[27]

A mile and a half or so to the east of Larkhill flows the River Avon, more correctly known at this point as the Upper Avon, which provides first-class trout and grayling fishing. Since the early years of this century, several miles of the river between Combe Mill and Bulford have been leased to the Services Dry Fly Fishing Association which in its early days was known as the Officers' Fishing Association. Although the membership of the Association is made up of those serving in all three services, Gunners have always taken a major part in its affairs.[28] Those whose fishing interest lies in the sea rather than the river are catered for by the Garrison Sea Angling Club which has been described as 'an Army club run on civilian lines'.

As well as games and field sports many other activities are available at Larkhill. These include athletics, boxing, judo, cross-country running, orienteering, canoeing, caving, mountaineering and skiing. Provision has also been made for those who wish to take part in flying, motor sports, sailing, sub-aqua diving and rifle shooting. It would be difficult to find a larger selection.

13. The Royal School of Artillery

The duties and responsibilities of the School are laid down in a succession of Charters that are issued by the Director Royal Artillery, as and when such action is thought to be necessary. During the past decade Charters have appeared in 1973, 1976, 1978 and 1980 and a new one is expected in 1983. This procedure has been followed for many years and an early example which was issued in respect of Shoeburyness on 10 March 1862 carries the unusual and prophetic title of 'Charter for the Royal School of Artillery – 1862. School of Gunnery'.

In 1983 the work of the School was summarised as follows:

> It is responsible for instruction, research and technical advice on all aspects of field, air defence and anti-tank artillery and for user trials of equipment. It is also responsible for the writing of all artillery drills and training manuals.[1]

Although the School is under the command of the GOC South West District, it is controlled by the Director Royal Artillery in all matters concerning arms and equipment. At the present time it is composed of five wings and the Young Officers' Branch but as these have already been described at some length in Chapter 9 it is not intended to add anything more. However, details regarding the Support Regiment which absorbed the Administrative Wing in January 1983 will be found in this chapter with an account of 22 (Gibraltar 1779–83) Locating Battery, RA which is under the command of the School.

The present organisation is shown in Figure 9.1, and two subdivisions of Headquarters which are concerned with specialised aspects of the School are the Badley Library and Reprographics. The library was opened on 28 April 1978 by the Commandant, Brigadier J.S. Badley, and it was largely due to his interest and support that it had been formed. Although the library is mainly intended for the use of the School, its services are available to the whole of the Regiment and to all other Ministry of Defence

211

establishments. It now contains a large number of books, publications and periodicals on gunnery and other allied subjects and has proved to be a valuable asset to the School.

Reprographics produce photographs, slides, training pamphlets and *aides-memoires* for all sections of the School and Garrison as well as for United Kingdom Land Forces, HQ Director Royal Artillery, HQ South West District and when possible for Territorial Gunner regiments. It also provides display boards and posters for the Royal Tournament and the Royal Military Academy Sandhurst, for recruiting and for the School itself. During the course of 1982 the output from the printroom was nine million impressions and five million photocopies, while four thousand pamphlets were produced in March 1983 alone. This impressive output of high quality material is due to a select team of printers, photographers, draughtsmen and a model maker, under a succession of notable officers who have been in charge of the Section. It will be seen from the List of Illustrations that a number of excellent photographs in this book have been taken by the staff of Reprographics while some of the old ones have been rephotographed by them.

The School's year is divided into three terms – Spring, Summer and Autumn – and these usually run from about 4 January to 8 April, 22 April to 6 August, and 2 September to 22 December respectively. During 1982 a total of 177 courses were held which were divided between the Wings as follows: Gunnery, 69; Guided Weapons, 76; Tactics 13; Signals, 15 and Young Officers Branch, 4. The School is under the command of the Commandant (brigadier) who is also the Commandant of the Larkhill Garrison and although there had been a Deputy Commandant since 1950, this appointment was terminated in 1983. The Co-ordination, Development and Automatic Data Processing sections of Headquarters are each the responsibility of a Staff Officer Grade 1 (SO1), a lieutenant-colonel, while Personnel and Logistics are under a Staff Officer Grade 2 (SO2) – a major.

Gunnery Wing is commanded by a Chief Instructor – CIG – who is a colonel with two Senior Instructors (lieutenant-colonels), one for Field – SI (Fd) – and one for Development – SI Dev (Fd). Guided Weapons Wing is also under the command of a Chief Instructor – CIGW – (colonel) with two Senior Instructors, one of whom is concerned with Guided Weapons – SIGW – and the other with Developments – SI Dev (GW), both of whom are lieutenant-colonels. A Chief Instructor Tactics – CIT – who is a colonel, commands Tactics Wing with three Staff Officers Grade 1 (lieutenant-colonels) for Tactics, Combat Development and All Arms Courses, respectively. Signals Wing is under the command of a Senior Instructor – SI Sigs – who is a lieutenant-colonel of the Royal Signals while REME Wing is under a Commanding Officer (colonel) with a Second-in-Command and a Production Manager both of whom are lieutenant-colonels. The Young Officers Branch is commanded by a Senior Instructor (major) with an IG (major).

The Headquarters Staff also includes an officer in charge of the School Booking Centre, a Range Liaison Officer, Librarian, Reprographics Officer, Chaplains of three denominations and French and German Liaison Officers. Gunnery Wing also has on its strength 14 IGs, 10 TIGs, 3 Staff Officers Grade 3 (SO3), the officer commanding the RA Sales Demonstration Team, an adjutant and a Wing Master Gunner. On the staff of Guided Weapons Wing are also 10 IGs, 4 TIGs, 1 Staff Officer (SO3), 2 instructors from the RAF and one from the Royal Tank Regiment, 3 civilian lecturers and a Wing Master Gunner. Tactics Wing has in addition an IG, 7 staff officers (SO2) and an adjutant while Signals Wing includes a Deputy Senior Instructor (RA), 2 Troop Commanders, an adjutant and two WOIs. REME Wing also has 7 officers of the rank of major, 2 captains, an adjutant and one civilian.

Quite apart from the main constitution of the School, a brief

PLATE 47: The original School Headquarters which were demolished in the late 1960s. (*T.L. Fuller*)

outline of which has been given in the preceeding paragraphs, there is a separate establishment which is known as the Gunnery Staff, This has been described as 'an institution peculiar to the Royal Artillery whose duty it was and still is, to go wherever the units of the Royal Artillery happen to be stationed and propagate the gospel according to Larkhill'.[2]

Its personnel can be divided into four categories, firstly, Instructors in Gunnery; secondly, Technical Instructors in Gunnery, who are commissioned from Warrant Officers Class 1 (Master Gunners); thirdly, Warrant Officers Class 1 (MG), who are promoted from Warrant Officers Class 2 (Sergeant Major Instructors in Gunnery); and fourthly, Warrant Officers Class 2 (SMIG). All must have qualified on a Gunnery Staff Course at the School. The functions of the Gunnery Staff may be summarised as follows:

To instruct at the Royal School of Artillery and the Royal Artillery Gunnery Training Establishment (RAGTE) in order to maintain a standard of technical excellence within the Royal Regiment.

To provide assistance and technical advice in gunnery at practice camps and on exercises.

To fill appointments in the Proof and Experimental Establishments.

To carry out the development and trials of new or existing weapon systems.

To fill Gunnery Staff appointments in the organisation for selling British equipment.

To provide foreign armies with technical assistance in gunnery.[3]

Shortly after the end of the Second World War an arrangement was made with the Royal Canadian Artillery for an exchange of British and Canadian IGs. This began in 1949 when Captain W. Simcock (afterwards Lieutenant-Colonel W. Simcock) arrived at Larkhill and since then fifteen Canadian Officers have been attached to the School, and their opposite numbers have proceeded to the Canadian School of Artillery. The usual duration of each attachment has been approximately two years although in certain cases this has been increased to three, Major G.D.C. Scott, CD, holding this appointment in 1983.

In September 1964, after a similar arrangement had been made with the United States Army, Major R.M. Clewell was posted to Larkhill and since that date eight American IGs have each spent two years at the School, the present officer being Major D.L.

Radnotti. Two years later the scheme was extended to the Australian Forces and in December 1966, Captain I.G. Darlington (afterwards Lieutenant-Colonel I.G. Darlington) arrived at the School and, by 1983, a further six Australian IGs had followed him, Major P.J. Lawrence occupying this position in 1983.

In 1957, Lieutenant-Colonel M. de Vallet was appointed as the first Liaison Officer from the French Army. He has been followed by eight others, each of whom have been attached to the School for a three-year period, the present Liaison Officer being Lieutenant-Colonel J. Pasquier. On 1 May 1970 Oberstleutnant George Grimm became the first German Liaison Officer and since then, three other officers have succeeded him, each serving for a period of three years, Oberstleutnant J.W.K. Böthling holding this appointment in 1983.

Shortly after the School of Artillery was established in 1920, it was decided to appoint a brigade that could carry out certain duties connected with the School. These included the provision of personnel and equipment for course shooting and demonstrations, testing fuses and ammunition and work on the ranges such as towing moving targets. From time to time the Depot Brigade was assisted by one of the regular brigades that were usually stationed at Larkhill between the wars.

The first unit to hold the position of Depot Brigade was the 15th Brigade, Royal Field Artillery and from then until April 1982 when the support Regiment, Royal School of Artillery was formed, sixteen brigades or regiments held this appointment. From 1920 until 1965 these were known as Depot Brigades or Regiments but after that year the title was changed to Support Regiment. During the course of the past sixty-two years, the longest tour of duty carried out by one unit was that of the 18th Medium Regiment RA which completed eleven years from 1951 to 1962. Two brigades or regiments have performed three tours of duty, namely, the 2nd Field Brigade RA (afterwards 2nd Field Regiment RA) in 1928, 1932 and 1979 and the 26th Field Brigade RA (afterwards 26th Field Regiment RA) in 1930, 1934 and 1971. Two tours were undertaken by the 6th Field Brigade RA (afterwards 6th Field Regiment RA) in 1925 and 1962 and by the 25th Field Brigade RA (afterwards 25th Field Regiment RA) in 1924 and 1966.

In April 1982 a complete change in policy took place when a new regiment was formed with an establishment specifically designed for carrying out the duties required by the School. This was the Support Regiment, Royal School of Artillery, which was composed of 132 Field Battery (The Bengal Rocket Troop) RA and 176 (Abu Klea) Field Battery RA, both batteries having previously formed part of the 39th Field Regiment RA, together with a new Headquarters Battery. At the time of its formation, the Regiment's chief responsibility was to provide personnel and guns for course shooting and fire-power demonstrations at Larkhill and for the School of Infantry at Warminster, the Junior Division of the Staff College and the Army Air Corps Centre. Each battery is equipped with six 105 mm L.119 Light Guns while 132 Field Battery also holds four 5.5 in. guns and is required to man the following equipments which are held by the School Gun Park: three 155 mm howitzers, FH 70; two 175 mm SP guns, M107; two 8 in. SP howitzers, M110 and three 155 mm SP howitzers, M109. In addition to their six light guns, 176 Field Battery also holds six 105 mm SP field guns (Abbots) and six 105 mm L5 pack howitzers.

On 10 January 1983, the Regiment took over the duties of Administrative Wing which was then terminated, and so became responsible for the executive side of the administration of the School. It also deals with officers' documentation, the administration of all other ranks who are on the strength of the School, that is to say, their postings, appointments, promotion, leave, discipline and employment. In addition, it is concerned with the basic military training of all other ranks, the organisation of the messes, the provision of transport and equipment for the School as well as firing on the ranges. Consequently the Regiment covers a much larger field than was previously the case and some idea of the scope of its operations can be gained from Figure 13.1.

The Regiment now consists of Headquarters and four batteries, the Headquarter Battery comprising five sections – Quartermaster, Quartermaster (Technical), Pay, Messes and Students. The Technical Quartermaster is responsible for the work that was previously carried out by the Equipment Officer and also for the Fargo Ammunition Depot while many of the duties in the Battery are discharged by members of the WRAC. The Support Battery – 1st Battery (The Blazers) – is composed of the Mechanical Transport (MT) Troop, the Guided Weapons Troop, Range Detachment, Gunnery Trials Detachment with the RA Sales Team attached. The two firing batteries, to which reference has already been made, are 132 Field Battery which includes Battery Headquarters, two gun troops and a maintenance troop and 176 Field Battery made up of Battery Headquarters and two troops.[4]

The RA Sales Team was formed in 1972 following the decision

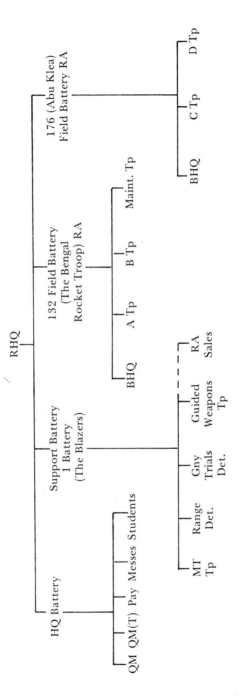

Figure 13.2   The Support Regiment RSA, 1983

of the Ministry of Defence to assist the defence industries by demonstrating military equipment, after foreign delegations had seen sale displays. These demonstrations are given either in the United Kingdom or in the interested country. The Team's first expedition was to the Far East in the summer of 1972 and this was followed by a visit to North and West Africa during the winter of that year. From then until 1980, except for 1979, the team paid visits to two countries or groups of countries each year but in 1981 the emphasis changed to after-sales service. The School has provided administrative support and has given valuable assistance to the Team since it was formed and this has been reciprocated in a number of ways.[5]

The link between 22 (Gibraltar 1779-83) Locating Battery RA and Larkhill began in 1950 although the Regiment to which it belonged can be traced to August 1939 when 2nd Survey Regiment RA was formed following the division of 1st Survey Regiment, then at Larkhill, into two parts. After service in France in 1940, the 2nd Regiment subsequently embarked for the Far East in March 1943 and, by the end of the war with Japan, was stationed in India. In January 1947 the Regiment proceeded to Palestine and on 1 April of that year it became the 52nd Observation Regiment RA and was joined by 22 Battery. During 1949 the Regiment was divided into two parts, the larger proceeding to Hong Kong as an independent battery while the remainder returned to England in 1950.

In June 1961 the Regiment was renamed 52nd Locating Regiment and moved to Roberts Barracks, Larkhill, in March of the following year. On 18 August 1958, 22 Battery was reformed as an independent locating battery with the title of 22 (Gibraltar) Composite Divisional Locating Battery RA and after the disbandment of 52nd Locating Regiment the Battery took over the Regiment's property. Finally on 1 October 1963 the Battery was amalgamated with 160 (Middleton's Company) Battery and was renamed 22 (Gibraltar 1779-83) Locating Battery.[6]

The Battery is a field force unit but it also assists Gunnery Wing in battlefield surveillance, electronic procedure and trials of new equipment. It comprises three troops, A Troop which is concerned with the Artillery Meteorological System (AMETS) and Light Weight Meteorological and Survey for the Allied Command Europe (ACE) Mobile Force, B Troop which operates drones (miniature aircraft) and C Troop which deals with survey and sound ranging.[7]

Although members of the Auxiliary Territorial Service – the ATS – which on 1 February 1949 became the Women's Royal

Army Corps (WRAC), have served at Larkhill for over forty years, the School Establishment for September 1940 made no mention of them. The subsequent Establishment for 1941 however, contains the first two references to the Service; one under Headquarters Wing states that of nine drivers, '4 may be ATS', while the other, under Anti-Tank Wing reads, 'Clerks (may be ATS) .... 2'.[8] The following Establishment for 1942 presents a very different picture and instead of there only being the possibility of six ATS at the School there were now 639 and a year later the figure had risen to 695.[9]

After the end of the war the numbers on the Establishment fell to 295 in 1946 and a hundred in 1948 while in 1982 the total strength was seventy-nine including two officers and five senior NCOs. After February 1949 the title of the Larkhill unit was 9 Company, WRAC but in October 1968 it was renamed WRAC Battery. In 1981 it became HQ Battery, Administrative Wing, but when the Support Regiment replaced the Wing in January 1983, those serving in the WRAC became integral members of the Regiment.

Two units which have enhanced many ceremonial occasions at the School as well as giving much pleasure to those serving at Larkhill are the RA Mounted Band and the RA Alanbrooke Band whose headquarters have been in Horne Barracks. During the past sixteen years a number of changes have taken place in the bands of the Regiment as well as in their titles. In 1967 the RA (Portsmouth) Band which was formed in 1903 was transferred to Larkhill and renamed the RA (Larkhill) Band but four years later its title was changed to the RA Alanbrooke Band. In 1972 the Band changed stations with the RA Mounted Band which was in the British Army of the Rhine, and moved to Germany where it remained until 1977. During that year the Alanbrooke Band returned to Larkhill and the Mounted Band reverted to Germany and this process was repeated again in 1982. Since 1967 the following Directors of Music have been appointed:

1967	Captain W. Allen, RA	RA Larkhill Band
1970	Captain A.R. Pinkney, RA	RA Larkhill Band
1972	Captain G.E. Evans, RA	RA Mounted Band
1972	Captain T.A. Kenny, RA	RA Mounted Band
1977	Major A.R. Pinkney, RA	Alanbrooke Band
1979	Captain D.H. Mackay, RA	Alanbrooke Band
1982	Captain B.E. Hicks, RA	RA Mounted Band
1983	Captain F.A. Renton, RA	RA Mounted Band

There are several military establishments at Larkhill which, although their activities are not solely concerned with the School, may have a bearing on its work. On 1 January 1982 the Headquarters 21 Artillery Group which was located at Woolwich, moved to Larkhill with the new designation of Headquarters Royal Artillery (South).[10] On the same date the Commander of 21 Artillery Group became Commander Royal Artillery South – CRA South – with special responsibility for all RA Units in the United Kingdom Field Force and adviser on artillery matters to HQ United Kingdom Land Forces.

In May 1979 a team was formed at Larkhill which was concerned with Automatic Data Processing (ADP) otherwise known as the Battlefield Artillery Target Engagement System (BATES). The team's primary purpose is to disseminate a knowledge of the subject throughout the School and at the same time to provide a close liaison between it and the BATES Project Management.

On 1 September 1981, in view of the research and developments which had been carried out by the United States Military Authorities on surveillance, target acquisition, night observation and counter-surveillance, a centre for dealing with the matters was established at Larkhill. Under the title of its acronym – Stanoc – each section is respectively the responsibility of an officer of the Intelligence Corps, the Royal Artillery, the Royal Signals and the Royal Engineers.[11] The STANOC Centre works under the direction of the Assistant Chief of the General Staff (operational requirements) at the Ministry of Defence, but relies on the Garrison for administrative support.

Early in 1969 a Training Evaluation Section was formed at the School which was mainly concerned with matters relating to pay reviews and 'job descriptions'. In 1973 the Section was renamed the Training Development Team, Royal Artillery (TDT RA) and was transferred to the Director Royal Artillery although its personnel remained at Larkhill. The Team, which is under the direction of a Controller (lieutenant-colonel), consists of three officers, three warrant officers Class 2 and two civilian clerical officers. Its principal task is to apply what is known as the 'Systems Approach to Training', to the employment structure of the whole of the Royal Regiment and this is achieved in four stages. After analysing each type of employment, a 'job specification' is written which describes the tasks involved and from this, 'training objectives' are drawn up setting out the standards which should be achieved. Lastly, in order to ensure that these standards are reached, 'employment tests' are held by specially appointed examination

PLATE 48: The Newcome Hall which was completed in 1966 with the School flag flying from the flagstaff. (*RSA Reprographics*)

boards. If these are to be written tests, they are set by TDT RA in order that a universal standard is maintained.[12] The School's Learning Resources Section is also under the control of the Team.

Facilities for various aspects of education are provided by No. 12 Army Education Centre at its headquarters and library in Whinyates Road. These include preparation for the Education Promotion Certificate at both minor and advanced levels, advice and assistance in respect of the resettlement of soldiers who are leaving the Army and the arrangement of vocational and resettlement courses. In addition correspondence courses can be organized for any serving soldier, irrespective of rank, in any academic subject, for business studies, for the City and Guilds examinations, and so on. The library is available for the use of all ranks and their families and any books not in stock can be obtained at short notice.

There are also several organizations at or near Larkhill whose work affects the School to a greater or lesser degree. Adjacent to the Amesbury-Devizes road (A360), and about a mile to the south of West Lavington, is the Lavington range of the Proof and Experimental Establishment. Opened in December 1960, the range is used for the testing and recovery of fuses after they have been fired. Earlier experiments had shown that shells fired almost vertically remained in a vertical position throughout their flight and returned to earth base first, thus avoiding damage to the fuses. Specially modified equipment has been installed so as to enable vertical firing to take place while the chalk subsoil provides a suitable landing bed for the descending shells. Trials are carried out for several departments including the Royal Armament Research and Development Establishment (RARDE) and the Ordnance Board.

The Royal Aircraft Establishment, which is one of the Research Establishments of the Ministry of Defence, began its connection with Larkhill in 1947 when it became necessary to find a suitable area from which missiles could be recovered. At first the use of the ranges was rather limited and arrangements were of a somewhat temporary nature but in 1951 the construction of permanent OPs began so that in 1958 the Establishment was able to use the ranges on a fulltime basis. During recent years, work at Larkhill has included the testing and development of 'Blowpipe', 'Swing fire', aircraft ejector seats and trials of parachute equipment.[13]

As might be expected, work of this kind has sometimes produced moments of excitement and even drama. In 1958 two members of the Establishment were working on a research project in a cage which was attached to a captive airborne balloon; suddenly the balloon anchorage cable parted from the winch drum and as the balloon rose the telephone line snapped so that communication with the ground ceased. The occupants of the cage were so intent on their work that they were unaware of what happened, while those on the ground were unable to let them know. Shortly before the balloon reached the height at which it was liable to explode, the men realised what had happened and parachuted to the ground. On another occasion, the cable to which an unmanned balloon was tethered was severed by a round from a gun which was firing on the ranges in the course of normal practice, although the chances of this happening must have been extremely remote. When freed, the balloon drifted eastwards from Larkhill dragging some 500 feet of cable below it and eventually took a course along the middle of the Basingstoke-Camberley road (A30) at Hartney Wintney.[14] Here it understandably caused some confusion amongst motorists of whom, by a remarkable coincidence, the author was one.

I was driving along the A30 towards Basingstoke at a point where the road was lined with trees. To my surprise I saw a rope stretching up through the trees, moving along the road towards me, as if some invisible magician was performing the Indian rope trick. Motorists promptly took avoiding action by driving on to the verges and looking up one could see a balloon drifting over the tree tops.[15]

It finally became entangled around an aerial and was later recovered.

The Royal Artillery Target Operation Group, which has its headquarters at Rollestone Camp, is a part of Short Brothers Air Services Ltd, a subsidiary of Short Brothers Ltd of Belfast. The Group operates the 'Skeet' miniature aircraft which has been developed from the Model Aircraft Target System (MATS 'B'), and is a close-range aerial target system used exclusively for target training. The aircraft are purchased by the Ministry of Defence and at the present time are operated by Short Brothers Air Services under contract.[16]

An event which was to have a far-reaching effect not only on gunnery but also in many other spheres, was the setting up of a meteorological office near Larkhill during the First World War, probably in 1916. It was located at Butler's Cross (reference 023502) which lies about one and a half miles to the north of Tilshead but after a short time it moved to West Lavington and later to the vicinity of Stonehenge, finally establishing itself at

Larkhill. In the period between the two wars an office was maintained at the School and this was located in two huts beside the
Gun Park. In 1965 these were destroyed by a gas explosion and
fire which burnt many valuable weather records and instruments
although a lead water-pipe, which melted in the heat, protected
the money in the tea kitty!

Larkhill played an important part in the development of equipment to measure the upper winds and temperatures that are
significant in accurate gunnery, and prior to 1940 upper winds
were measured by optically tracking a small hydrogen-filled balloon using theodolites. The pillars on which these were mounted
can still be seen on the ranges. For windfinding at night, a candle-
lit lantern was attached to the balloon. Shortly before the Second
World War, balloons were tracked by fastening a radio-transmitter
to them and locating their position by direction-finding stations
which were sited at Larkhill, Broadchalke and Chitterne.

In 1943 this method was replaced by the first radar windfinding system which remained in use until 1973 when the present
procedure came into use. In 1959 it was decided that Army
personnel should be trained in meteorological work and the office
has always worked in close co-operation with Locating Wing and,
subsequently, Gunnery Wing, in this matter. The Army and the
meteorological office at Larkhill also helped to develop the
Army's radio-sonde system, AMETS, which came into service in
1974.[17]

The responsibility for the management of much of the land
which forms Salisbury Plain lies with the Defence Land Agent
whose headquarters are at the Estate Office in Durrington, a little
over a mile to the east of Larkhill. The first purchases of land were
made by the War Department in 1897 and by 1902 the area that
had been acquired amounted to some 42,000 acres. It was at this
point that it was thought prudent to appoint a full-time land agent
to look after this large area which extended for almost 'an equal
distance east and west of the River Avon, from Upavon on the
north to Bulford on the south'. Today the estate covers some
91,000 acres, more than twice the size it was in 1902 and the
work of the Agent has increased accordingly. In addition to
managing land which is used for military purposes, and this includes Larkhill and the ranges, he is responsible for a considerable
number of farms which are let to tenants, many houses and cottages and a large area of woodland.[18]

Two other organisations whose work is of importance to the
School are the Ministry of Defence Police and the Department of

FLAGS FLOWN AT LARKHILL 1983

The Royal Artillery Standard

The Regimental Flag

The Royal School of Artillery Flag

The Support Regiment, The Royal
School of Artillery

1 Battery, Royal Artillery

132 Field Battery (The Bengal
Rocket Troop) R.A.

176 (Abu Klea) Field Battery R.A.

FLAGS FLOWN AT LARKHILL 1983

22nd Locating Battery Royal Artillery

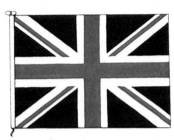

The Union Flag

Corps of Royal Electrical and Mechanical
Engineers

Women's Royal Army Corps

Royal Aircraft Establishment

Proof and Experimental Establishment

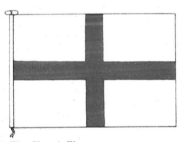

The Church Flag

PLATE 49: Aerial view of the School Headquarters and surroundings, 28th April 1982. (*RSA Reprographics*)

the Environment. The Ministry of Defence Police Force was formed on 1 October 1971 after the Admiralty, Army Department and Air Force Department Constabularies were amalgamated, and is responsible for the policing of Ministry of Defence establishments throughout the United Kingdom. At Larkhill the Force operates from its headquarters in Ross Road. The work of the Department of the Environment, which is located in Watson Road, was originally the responsibility of the Garrison Engineer under the Commander Royal Engineers (CRE) but later the Ministry of Works took over. Subsequently the Ministry was replaced by the Department of the Environment (Property Services Agency).

No account of the Royal School of Artillery would be complete without referring to the close relationship which has existed between the Royal Navy and the Royal Artillery. This first became evident when 'bomb ships' armed with heavy mortars were introduced into the Navy and small detachments of the Royal Regiment were employed to fire the mortars while the naval crew navigated the ships. This practice continued from shortly after the formation of the Regiment on 26 May 1716 until 1804 when the Admiralty raised the Royal Marine Artillery. On the other hand, during the Crimean War and the Indian Mutiny the Royal Navy provided landing parties, which then manned shore-based guns.[19] During the Boer War, the Naval Brigade from HMS *Powerful*, distinguished itself with its 4.7 in. guns at Ladysmith while at the battle of Colenso the naval presence was such that one prominent feature was named Naval Gun Hill.[20]

When in 1940 the Royal Navy was unable to provide all the trained personnel to man the anti-aircraft defences in merchant ships, the Maritime Regiment RA was formed and its members served afloat until hostilities ceased.[21] During the war close liaison was maintained between Larkhill and HMS *Excellent*, the Royal Naval Gunnery School at Whale Island. Every Gunnery Staff Course visited HMS *Excellent* and each Naval Gunnery Course paid a visit to Larkhill.[22] Other Gunner officers attended courses at Whale Island in order to learn how to observe naval gunfire when acting as Forward Observation Officers (FOOs) during a landing and how to carry out the duties of Army Liaison Officers in HM ships. So successful was this co-operation that in spite of the inevitable reductions that became necessary when the war ended, a Royal Artillery Liaison Officer (RALO) continued to be based at Whale Island. Although the war was over, it did not mean that they could carry out their duties with any less circumspection or forethought.

I served on the Staff of Commander G, a small but fiery officer whose gaiters were so highly polished that he was believed to use them as a shaving mirror. At my first interview with him he said 'let me have none of your b———— abbreviations'. A week later I wrote a letter for him to sign; it arrived back on my desk with the letters WRTYL PSM written on it so I walked into his office and told him I did not understand his b———— abbreviations (*with reference to your letter please see me*). After that we got on very well.[23]

In 1945 the School received a challenge from HMS *Excellent* to take part in 'a multitude of divers games and contests, requiring consummate skill, infinite patience, steadfast courage and great endurance'. This document was dropped at Larkhill from a naval helicopter and the School's acceptance duly arrived at Whale Island by way of an 'Auster' light aircraft. The trophy took the form of a 'golden gun' which was a model of a 32 pr and was presented by HMS *Excellent*. The event which was known as the Barbara Games, was still held until 1982. In recent years with the changing face of HMS *Excellent*, the games have been reduced to one with the visiting Advanced Warfare Officers' Course from HMS *Dryad*, who currently hold the trophy known as the Barbara Gun.[24] At the time of writing no visit had been planned for 1983.

A further link was forged with the Royal Navy when the following letter was written by the Captain of HMS *Vanguard* – Captain G.V. Gladstone, RN – to the Master Gunner – Field Marshal Lord Alanbrooke – on St Barbara's Day 1949 suggesting that a Fellowship should be established between HMS *Vanguard* and the Royal Regiment.[25]

My Lord,

   I have the honour to invite Your Lordship's approval for a Fellowship between His Majesty's Ship Vanguard and the Royal Regiment of Artillery.

   I am sure it is Your Lordship's view that the several arms of His Majesty's Forces should be linked in peace and war by ties of mutual interest for the better achievement of our common purpose, the Defence of the Realm.

   This ship, which I have the honour to command, mounts the greatest guns in the Royal Navy, and it seems fitting to her Officers and Company that we should look for friendship to the Royal Artillery.

   If your Lordship will be good enough to signify your approval, and to inform accordingly those detachments who may be

in the neighbourhood of HMS Vanguard, I believe it can be left
to the Commanding Officers concerned to take the appropriate
action.

    I have the honour to be, My Lord,

Your Lordship's most obedient servant,

G.V. GLADSTONE,

Captain, Royal Navy.

On 1 January 1950, the Master Gunner replied as follows:

Sir,

    On behalf of the Royal Regiment of Artillery, I thank you
for your letter dated on St. Barbara's Day 1949.

    Your proposal for a Fellowship between His Majesty's Ship
VANGUARD and the Royal Regiment of Artillery is very
warmly welcomed, and much appreciated by all ranks.

    I am taking steps to ensure that the inauguration of this
Fellowship shall be made known throughout the Royal Regiment, and the Commanding Officers of units at present serving
in the neighbourhood of HMS VANGUARD will be notified.

    In conclusion, I express the hope and indeed the belief, that
this Fellowship will always remain a very real one, and will
provide a bond of friendship which will be to our mutual advantage.

    I have the honour to be, Sir,

Your obedient Servant,

ALANBROOKE,

F.M.

Master Gunner, St. James's Park.

HMS *Vanguard* was laid down in the yard of John Brown & Co.
Ltd, on Clydebank in 1941; she was launched by HRH Princess
Elizabeth in November 1944 and was completed in August 1946.
From 1950-4 she was Flagship of the Home Fleet and from 1946-
60, Flagship of the Reserve Fleet, but in August 1960 she was
towed to Faslane to be broken up. During the period when she
was in the Reserve Fleet, 18th Medium Regiment RA, which was
then Depot Regiment at Larkhill, established an affiliation with
her. Later in 1965, the Regiment were chosen by the Admiralty
Board to receive the Ship's Bell for keeping, in perpetuity. However, when the Regiment was disbanded in February 1969, it was
the Regiment's wish that the bell should be presented to the
School of Artillery in view of the long association between the

PLATE 50: Artillery Day. One of the displays and a small section of the spectators. (*RSA Reprographics*)

School and the Regiment from 1951 to 1962. The Bell now hangs in the entrance vestibule of the School Headquarters.

Demonstrations and displays of weapons and firepower have formed an important part of the work of the School for many years. At first these were designed to illustrate the use of artillery and its potentialities to the other services, other arms and cadets and they were frequently referred to as 'exercises'. One of the first was 'Exercise Scapa' which was held in 1949 and was divided into two parts: a procession of weapons then in use, followed by a 'mock engagement'.[26] In 1952 a demonstration entitled 'Ambassador I' was held and this was followed by Ambassador II, III and IV in 1953, 1954 and 1955 respectively. In 1957 'Exercise Young Ambassador' took place,[27] and in August 1961 an 'open day' was arranged for contingents of the Combined Cadet Force and also for the general public, which was described as 'the first of this particular kind to be staged at Larkhill'. This presumably referred to the fact that the public were admitted. In 1962 the open day was named 'Larkhill Day' and it proved to be an outstanding success.

Spring cottage,
Shottery,
Stratford-on-Avon,
Warks.
10th. July, 1977.

The Commandant.
Royal School of Artillery.
Lark hill.
Wiltshire.

Dear Sir,

Thank you very much for putting on a very nice display, on July ninea at lark hill. The Soldiers in the tents were very helpful in exSplaning things. I came with my family, Daddy Says he will bring me again next year.

from Matthew John Price.

Striker-Anti-tank-missile carrier.

PLATE 51: A letter of appreciation.

people flocked in their thousands to see current artillery equipments and view the massed fire power of over 70 guns, culminating with the firing of an Honest John Rocket from the racecourse area across to Imber Ranges. What a marvellous day it was for everyone involved, spectators and staff alike.[28]

Larkhill Day was held again in the following year but in 1964 it only took the form of a demonstration for regular troops and contingents of the Combined Cadet Force.[29] However, in 1965 the occasion was restored to its former standing and was again known as Larkhill Day, the public once again being admitted. To mark the 50th Anniversary of the School in 1970, the occasion was renamed Artillery Day and a record of these will be found in Appendix X with the names of the officers who took the salute. There can be little doubt that Artillery Days are greatly enjoyed by members of the public as the letter from Master Matthew John Price which is reproduced as Plate 51 (page 230) testifies.

In addition to demonstrations and displays, exercises in the more usually accepted military meaning of the word, are held from time to time, one of the more recent being 'Exercise Avon Express' which occurred in 1977. A limited number of conferences also take place at the School.

Although not necessarily an annual event, the Wilkinson Cane may be awarded to

the member of the permanent staff of the School (excluding officers) who, in the opinion of the Commandant, has by his general efficiency, personal efforts, merit and devotion to duty, done most to bring credit to the School during the calendar year.[30]

Those eligible for the award must be soldiers of the rank of Warrant Officer Class 2 and below (at the time of the award) who have completed a minimum of twelve months on the strength of the School or REME Wing. The following have won the award since 1960:

1960	WO2 (AIG) H.E. Baker
1961	WO2 (AIG) E.R. Clarke
1967	WO2 (CSM) W.G. Pratt
1969	WO2 (BSM) H.W. Pratt
1970	S/Sgt S. Dowell (REME Manorbier)
1971	WO2 (AIG) F.A.G. Seymour (Gunnery Wing)
1972	S/Sgt (AC) H. Lomax (Gunnery Wing)
1973	WO M. Nicholson, RAF (Air Defence)
1975	Sgt G. Murray (Air Defence)
1976	Bdr B.M. Siddell (Gym)
1977	A/Sgt A.J. McKeever (Administrative Wing)
1978	A/Sgt E.C. Robertson (Administrative Wing)
1979	Bdr D.R. Bennett (Medical Centre)

1980   Bdr P. Allen (Mechanical Transport)
1981   WO2 C.S. Jones (REME Wing)
1982   Sgt F.C. Martin (Tactics Wing)

Flags are much in evidence at Larkhill and in addition to those hanging in the Garrison Church to which reference has been made in Chapter 12, there are fourteen flags which may be seen flying in or near the Garrison area (see illustrations facing pages 224 and 225). The Union Flag is flown every day from the flagstaff at the southern junction of Glover Road and Bell Road while the School's flag normally flies from the flagstaff which stands between the School Headquarters and the Newcome Hall. However the Royal Artillery Standard is flown in its place on the following occasions: visits by Royalty, visits and inspections by Major-Generals and above, and visits of senior civilians or allied officials of comparable rank.[31] The Regimental Flag is flown every day outside the Guard Room. Other flags which are to be seen at Larkhill are those of the Support Regiment, 1 Battery RA (The Blazers), 132 Field Battery (The Bengal Rocket Troop) RA, 176 (Abu Klea) Field Battery RA, 22 (Gibraltar 1779–83) Locating Battery RA, the Corps of Royal Electrical and Mechanical Engineers, the Women's Royal Army Corps, the Royal Aircraft Establishment and the Church Flag (St George's Flag). The flag of the Proof and Experimental Establishment is flown at the headquarters at Gore Cross, near West Lavington.

In recent years there have been three occasions when flags have had a special historical significance. In 1965, the United States Flag, which had been flown at Fort Still during the week of mourning ordered by President Johnson after the death of Sir Winston Churchill, was presented to the School and now hangs in the Garrison Church. On 30 April 1969, the Regimental Flag which had been flown at half-mast at the School to mark the funeral of General of the Army Dwight D. Eisenhower, was handed to Colonel Ralph A. Starner, United States Army, by the Commandant, Brigadier G. de E. Collin.[32] A similar ceremony took place on 20 November 1970 when Brigadier Collin handed the flag which had been flown to mark the funeral of General de Gaulle, to Chef d'Escadron B. Fournier. On 21 December it was received by the Commandant of l'Ecole D'Application de l'Artillerie, General Coulloumme-Labarth at Chalons-sur-Marne.[33]

There can be few better ways of bringing the story of Gunners at Larkhill to an end, than by recording the service of members of the Royal School of Artillery in the Falkland Islands during 1982.

Major A.J. Craigie, RA of Guided Weapons Wing held the position of SO2 RA Force Headquarters; WO2 S.J. Absolon of Signals Wing was RA Signals representative, and Staff Sergeant P. McMahon, Sergeant D.P. Leary, Sergeant J.C. Blears, Corporal S.D. Bushell and Craftsman C.J. Botto – all members of REME Wing – were attached to 12 Air Defence Regiment RA Workshops. Sixteen members of 132 Field Battery (The Bengal Rocket Troop) RA of the Support Regiment RSA provided artillery support for 1/7th Duke of Edinburgh's Own Gurkha Rifles during the attacks on the north-east Knoll of Mount Tumbledown and Mount William. The fire support included naval gunfire and air strikes by Harrier aircraft and, during the course of these operations, one officer and two soldiers received wounds from which they fortunately recovered.

The following members of the Battery took part in this campaign:

Major M.H. Fallon, RA – Battery Commander
Captain G.M. Pugh, RA
Captain K. Swinton, RA
Bombardier J. Batchelor
Bombardier R. Bowley
Lance-Bombardier A. Gibson
Lance-Bombardier K. Henderson
Lance-Bombardier J. Jackson
Lance-Bombardier A. Neil
Gunner K. Blake
Gunner M. Bradbury
Gunner D. Cecil
Gunner S. Crisp
Gunner M. Ryan
Gunner A. Warren
Gunner J. Williams

QUO FAS ET GLORIA DUCUNT

References

1 The Evolution of the Practice Camp
1. War Office Salisbury Plain Committee, 1897–1902.
2. Lieut. Col. A.H. Burne, *The Woolwich Mess*, revised by Hogg, Brig. O.F.G., 1971.
3. Maj.-Gen. Sir Charles Callwell and Maj.-Gen. Sir John Headlam, *The History of the Royal Artillery*, vol. I, 1931.
4. Ibid.
5. *Memorandum relative to the employment of Horse and Field Artillery*, 1871.
6. Callwell and Headlam, *History of the R.A.* vol. I.
7. *Report of the Special Committee on Rifled Field Guns and High Angle Fire on the Artillery Experiments at Okehampton in August and September*, 1875.
8. Callwell and Headlam, *History of the R.A.* vol. I.
9. Maj. D. Rollo, 'The National Artillery Association', *Journal of The Royal Artillery*, vol. CIX, No. 1, 1982.
10. *Report of the Special Committee on Rifled Field Guns*, 1875.
11. Callwell and Headlam, *History of the R.A.*, vol. I.
12. Ibid.
13. Ibid.
14. Ibid.
15. Army Order 96, June 1899, Royal Regiment of Artillery.

2 The Establishment of Larkhill and West Down
1. John Evelyn, *Kalendarium. My Journal etc.* 1620–49, *The Diaries of John Evelyn*, ed. E.S. De Beer, vol. III, 1955.
2. Ordnance Survey, Map to the scale of two inches to one statute mile, *War Department Land on Salisbury Plain*, surveyed 1872–84, revised 1894–9, published 1903.
3. Directorate of Military Survey, Ministry of Defence, Map to scale of 1:25,000, *Salisbury Plain (East) including Larkhill and West Down*, 1980.
4. A. Cossons, *Victoria County History – Wiltshire*, vol. IV, 1959.
5. *Annual Report of the School of Gunnery for Horse, Field and Heavy Artillery*, 1912, Chief Instructor's letter.
6. *An Act to consolidate and amend certain Enactments relating to the Acquisition of Land for Military Purposes*, 1892, 55 and 56 Vict. c. 43.

7. Chief Surveyor of Defence Lands, Tolworth Tower, by communication.
8. Defence Land Agent, Durrington, by communication.
9. Maj.-Gen. Sir John Headlam, *The History of the Royal Artillery*, vol. II, 1937.
10. *Army Council Instruction 120*, 12 February 1915, 'Establishment of New School of Instruction for R.H. and R.F.A. near Larkhill, Salisbury Plain'.
11. *Annual Report of the School of Gunnery – Horse and Field Artillery at Home*, 1899.
12. Headlam, *History of the R.A.*, vol. II.
13. *Annual Report of the School of Gunnery*, 1901, para. 89.
14. Ibid. para 62.
15. Ibid. para. 87.
16. Headlam, *History of the R.A.*, vol. II.
17. Ibid.
18. *Annual Report of School of Gunnery*, 1901, para. 77.
19. *Annual Report of School of Gunnery*, 1902, para. 171.
20. *Territorial and Reserve Forces Act*, 1907, 7 Edw. 7., c. 11.
21. Headlam, *History of the R.A.*, vol. II.
22. *Annual Report of School of Gunnery*, 1906, para. 64.
23. *Annual Report of School of Gunnery*, 1911, para. 7.
24. *Annual Report of School of Gunnery*, 1909, paras. 11-15.
25. *Annual Report of School of Gunnery*, 1910, paras. 6, 8-11.
26. *Annual Report of School of Gunnery*, 1912, para. 16.
27. *Annual Report of School of Gunnery*, 1913, para. 22.
28. Ibid. para. 9.
29. *Annual Report of School of Gunnery*, 1912, para. 7.

3 Flying at Larkhill

1. Brig. P.W.L. Broke-Smith, *The History of Early British Military Aeronautics*. 1952.
2. A. Conan Doyle, *The Great Boer War*, 1900.
3. *The Monthly Army List*, April 1893.
4. Broke-Smith, *Military Aeronautics*.
5. *The Monthly Army List*, December 1911.
6. *The Monthly Army List*, June 1912.
7. *Annual Report of School of Gunnery*, 1906, para. 66.
8. *Annual Report of School of Gunnery*, 1907, para. 150.
9. *Annual Report of School of Gunnery*, 1902, para. 172.
10. *Annual Report of School of Gunnery*, 1907, para. 150.
11. *Annual Report of School of Gunnery*, 1909, para. 104.
12. Ministry of Defence, Air Historical Branch, 5 (RAF), by communication.
13. Lieut.-Col. J.R. Guy, *A History of Gunnery Wing, Royal School of Artillery*, 1981.
14. Maj. A.F. Stevens, by communication.

15. Anonymous, *History of Larkhill and Netheravon*, Ministry of Defence, Air Historical Branch paper, 1981.
16. The Monthly Army List, October 1909.
17. N.C. Parker, by communication.
18. Ibid.
19. Ibid.
20. Anonymous, *A Short History of No. 3 Squadron*, undated.
21. Ibid.
22. Ibid.
23. *The Monthly Army List*, December 1911.
24. *The Monthly Army List*, June 1912.
25. *The Monthly Army List*, September 1913.
26. *The Monthly Army List*, June 1915.
27. Maj. D.F. Ryan, 'Larkhill, the Early Days', *Journal of the Royal Artillery*, vol. XCVII, No. 1, 1970.
28. Ibid.
29. Anonymous, *A Short History of No. 3 Squadron*.
30. *Annual Report of School of Gunnery*, 1913 para. 37.
31. N.C. Parker, by communication.

4 The First World War

1. Maj.-Gen. Sir George Scott-Moncrieff, 'The Hutting Problem in the War', *The Royal Engineers Journal*, vol. XXXVII, 1924.
2. *Annual Report of the School of Gunnery for Horse and Field Artillery at Home*, 1904, para. 53.
3. Maj. E. Clarke-Smith, *The Larkhill Guide*, Part I, c. 1969.
4. Scott-Moncrieff, *The R.E. Journal*.
5. Ibid.
6. *Who Was Who, 1916–1928*.
7. Maj. D.F. Ryan, 'Larkhill, the Early Days', *Journal of the Royal Artillery*, vol. XCVII, No. 1, 1970.
8. E.J. Chivers, by communication.
9. Lieut.-Col. E. Woodhouse, *Notes on the History of the Transportation Centre, Longmoor, 1904–1930 with details of the work of 8 Railway Coy, 1914–15*, 1938.
10. Lieut.-Col. P. de N. Ramus, by communication.
11. C. Maggs, '75 years since rail line to Bulford opened', *Amesbury Journal*, 4 June 1981.
12. E.J. Chivers, by communication.
13. *The Journal and Transactions of the South Wiltshire Industrial Archaeology Society*, part 5, 1974.
14. Ryan, 'Larkhill, the Early Days'.
15. Ordnance Survey, Map to scale of two inches to one statute mile, *War Department Land on Salisbury Plain*, revised by War Department 1914.
16. Brig. P.W.L. Broke-Smith, *The History of Early British Military Aeronautics*, 1952.

17. R.W. Kidner, *Military Traction Engines and Lorries 1858-1918*, The Oakwood Press, 1975.
18. Cecil Chivers, *Salisbury Plain*, unpublished paper, undated.
19. T.H.J. Heffernan, by communication.
20. Ibid.
21. Cecil, Chivers, *Salisbury Plain*.
22. T.H.J. Heffernan, by communication.
23. Ordnance Survey Map, 1914.
24. Ryan, 'Larkhill, the Early Days'.
25. J.E.B. Gover, A. Mawer and F.M. Stenton, *The Place-Names of Wiltshire*, 1939.
26. Maj. W.A. Wilson, Personal account (unpublished).
27. Ibid.
28. Brig. F. FitzGibbon, Personal account (unpublished).
29. *Army Council Instruction 120*, 12 February 1915, 'Establishment of New School of Instruction for R.H. and R.F.A. near Lark Hill, Salisbury Plain'.
30. Ibid.
31. Brig. F. FitzGibbon, Personal account (unpublished).
32. Maj. T.F. Coupar, by communication.
33. Maj. A.J.W. Harvey, 'Army Schools, III. The School of Artillery', *The Army Quarterly*, July 1954.
34. Ordnance Survey, Map to the scale of 1:20,000 GSGS 2748, Chitterne (North), December 1916.
35. The Monthly Army List, September 1918.
36. *Army Council Instruction 660*, 4 December 1919, 'School of Artillery'.
37. Lieut.-Col. P. de N. Ramus and Maj. A.F. Stevens, by communication.
38. *Annual Reports of the School of Gunnery*, for years 1905, 1907 and 1908.
39. Ryan, 'Larkhill, the Early Days'.
40. Brig. B.G. Mason, Personal account (unpublished), 1968.
41. Lieut.-Col. John McCrae, 'In Flanders Fields', *Punch or The London Charivari*, vol. cxlix, 8 December 1915.

5 **Between the Wars**

1. Brig. C. Childs, 'One April Morning', *Gunner*, No. 138, May 1982.
2. *Army Council Instruction 660*, 4 December 1919, 'School of Artillery'.
3. Maj. D. Rollo, by communication.
4. *The Monthly Army List*, September 1918.
5. Lieut.-Col. J.R. Guy, *A History of Gunnery Wing, Royal School of Artillery*, 1981.
6. Maj. D.F. Ryan, 'Larkhill, the Early Days', *Journal of the Royal Artillery*, vol. xvcll, No. 1, 1970.
7. Guy, *History of Gunnery Wing*.
8. Anonymous, 'Larkhill 1892-1976', *Plain Talk*, No. 5, 1976.
9. Guy, *History of Gunnery Wing*.

10. Maj. A.F. Stevens, 'N.C.Os Gunnery Staff Course in the Mid 1930s', *Gunner*, No. 137, April 1982.
11. Ibid.
12. *Plain Talk*, No. 5, 1976.
13. Anonymous. *Outline History of the School of Artillery, Larkhill, 1914–65*. Undated typescript.
12. Mrs G.G. Ford and Miss A. Thompson, by communication.
15. Ibid.
16. Maj.-Gen. J.E.T. Younger, 'Early Days at the Royal School of Artillery,' *Gunner*, Issue No. 8, July 1971.
17. Lieut.-Col. H.N. Cole, unpublished MSS, 1977.
18. Anonymous, *Outline History of the School, 1914–65*.
19. Brig. J.H.W.G. Richards, by communication.
20. *History of School of Artillery*, Annual Records, 1920–64, unpublished MSS.
21. Maj. F.M. Robertson, by communication.
22. Col. J.F. Williams-Wynne, by communication.
23. *Plain Talk*, No. 5, 1976.
24. Col. F.V. Bennett, 'Red Band', *The Gunner*, vol. 38, June 1956.
25. Guy, *History of Gunnery Wing*.
26. Maj.-Gen. W.D.E. Brown, by communication.
27. Ibid.
28. Lieut.-Col. P. de N. Ramus, by communication.
29. Maj. A.F. Stevens, by communication.
30. Guy, *History of Gunnery Wing*.
31. Ibid.
32. Air Commodore A.J.W. Geddes, by communication.
33. N.D.G. James, personal note.

6 The Second World War

1. *The Royal Artillery Commemoration Book 1939–1945*, 1950
2. Lieut.-Col. J.R. Guy, *A History of Gunnery Wing, Royal School of Artillery*, 1981.
3. *R.A. Commemoration Book*.
4. Guy, *History of Gunnery Wing*.
5. Ibid.
6. *Plain Talk*, No. 5, 1976.
7. Brig. F. FitzGibbon, unpublished MSS, c. 1948.
8. *R.A. Commemoration Book*.
9. Ibid.
10. Army Council Instruction 2278, 28 October 1942, *Allotment for the Purchase of Training Stores*.
11. Army Council Instruction 100, 20 January 1943, *O.C.T.U. Designations*.
12. *History of Units and Establishments in Larkhill*. Circular letter from School of Artillery, reference 8118/1/GS dated 7 May 1953.
13. Col. C. Scott, by communication.

14. Brig. B.E. Watson, by communication.
15. Lt.-Col. S.M. Cleeve, 'History of the School of artillery,' *Gunner*, Issue No. 9, September 1970.
16. FitzGibbon, unpublished MSS.
17. *R.A. Commemoration Book.*
18. Guy, *History of Gunnery Wing.*
19. *R.A. Commemoration Book.*
20. Lieut.-Col. W.A. Owen, *Royal Artillery Regimental News*, November, 1964.
21. Guy, *History of Gunnery Wing.*
22. *R.A. Commemoration Book.*
23. Col. C. Scott, by communication.
24. *R.A. Commemoration Book.*
25. *Plain Talk*, No. 5, 1976.
26. Army Council Instruction 349, 17 April 1940, *R.A. School of Survey.*
27. *R.A. Commemoration Book.*
28. FitzGibbon, unpublished MSS.
29. Guy, *History of Gunnery Wing.*
30. FitzGibbon, unpublished MSS.
31. Ibid.
32. Maj.-Gen. Sir John Headlam, *The History of the Royal Artillery*, vol. II, 1937.
33. Defence Land Agent, Durrington, by communication.
34. Lt.-Col. T. FitzGibbon, by communication.
35. Army Council Instruction 105, 17 January 1942, *Courses – School of Artillery.*
36. Watson, by communication.
37. Anonymous, *History of School of Artillery*, 1941–5, unpublished MSS.
38. Watson, by communication.
39. Maj. D. Rollo, by communication.
40. Army Council Instruction 2193, 15 October 1942, *Training Units and Schools of Instruction*, Appendix A.
41. *History of Units . . . in Larkhill*, 1953.
42. Lieut-Col. P. de N. Ramus, by communication.
43. *School of Artillery, Home War Establishment*, 18 September 1940.
44. Ibid., 20 November 1945.
45. Ibid., 17 September 1940.
46. Ibid., 17 August 1943.
47. Ibid., 20 November 1945.
48. *History of Units . . . in Larkhill*, 1953.
49. *R.A. Commemoration Book.*
50. Ibid.
51. 'Retired Canadian IG Revisits Larkhill', *Gunner*, Issue No. 126, May 1981.
52. Anonymous, *History of 1 Canadian School of Artillery (Overseas) RCA*, undated MSS.
53. 'Larkhill, 11th–12th December 1942'. *The Gunner*, vol. 25, April 1943.

54. Maj. D.L.S. Langley, by communication.
55. *R.A. Commemoration Book.*
56. Ibid.
57. Ibid.
58. Lieut.-Col. W.A. Owen, by communication.
59. *R.A. Commemoration Book.*
60. Ibid.
61. Guy, *History of Gunnery Wing.*
62. *History of School of Artillery*, Annual Records, 1920–64, unpublished MSS.
63. *History of School of Artillery*, 1941–5.
64. Guy, *History of Gunnery Wing.*
65. Watson, by communication.

7 **The Changing Scene**
1. Lieut.-Col. J.R. Guy, *A History of Gunnery Wing Royal School of Artillery*, 1981.
2. *Royal Artillery Notes*, 38, May 1946.
3. *R.A. Notes*, 39, Aug. 1946.
4. Army Council Instruction 433, 4 June 1947, *Courses – School of Artillery – Joining Instructions.*
5. Guy, *History of Gunnery Wing.*
6. *R.A. Notes*, 38, May 1946.
7. *R.A. Notes*, 41, February 1947.
8. Guy, *History of Gunnery Wing.*
9. *Plain Talk*, No. 5, 1976.
10. 'R.A. Mess, Larkhill', *The Gunner*, vol. 30, April 1948.
11. *History of Units and Establishments in Larkhill.* Circular letter from School of Artillery, reference 8118/1/GS dated 7 May 1953.
12. *R.A. Notes*, 78, Autumn 1961.
13. *R.A. Notes*, 42, May 1947.
14. Pellerau, Maj. P.J.M. Paper read at Larkhill, 1970.
15. 'The Garrison-Larkhill', *The Gunner*, vol. 29, November 1947.
16. Guy, *History of Gunnery Wing.*
17. 'United Nations', *The Gunner*, vol. 31, June 1949.
18. Lieut.-Col. L.W. Huelin, by communication.
19. '5th Regiment, R.H.A. – Larkhill', *The Gunner*, vol. 31, November 1949.
20. *R.A. Notes*, 46, May 1948.
21. *R.A. Notes*, 50, May 1949.
22. *History of Units . . . in Larkhill*, 1953.
23. *R.A. Notes*, 68, September 1956.
24. *R.A. Notes*, 76, Autumn 1960.
25. Guy, *History of Gunnery Wing.*
26. *School of Artillery, Larkhill, Historical Record – 1965.*
27. Maj.-Gen. Sir Cyril Colquhoun, by communication.

28. Ibid.
29. 'The Royal Visit to Larkhill', *The Gunner*, vol. 35, April 1953.
30. 'Other Coronation Celebrations', *The Gunner*, vol. 35, July 1953.
31. Guy, *History of Gunnery Wing.*
32. 'School of Artillery - Larkhill', *The Gunner*, vol. 36, July 1954.
33. *School of Artillery - Lower Establishment*, V/76/12 (LE) (ERE), 6 April 1955.
34. *School of Artillery - Lower Establishment*, V/76/13 (LE) (ERE), 21 November 1956.
35. Guy, *History of Gunnery Wing.*
36. *History of the School of Artillery*, Annual Records 1920-64, unpublished MSS.
37. Ibid.
38. Ibid.
39. Maj.-Gen. A.J.C. Block, by communication.
40. *R.A. Notes*, 74, Autumn 1959.
41. *History of the School*, Annual Records, 1920-64.
42. Block, by communication.
43. *History of the School*, Annual Records, 1920-64.
44. Guy, *History of Gunnery Wing.*
45. Maj.-Gen. P.J. Glover, by communication.
46. *History of the School*, Annual Records, 1920-64.
47. 'School of Artillery, Larkhill', *The Gunner*, vol. 42, November 1960.
48. *R.A. Notes*, 77, Spring 1961.
49. Guy, *History of Gunnery Wing.*
50. Maj. A.O. Taylor, by communication.
51. Programme, Joint Services Demonstration, 1962.
52. Col. J. Fairclough, by communication.
53. 'The Saint Barbara Window, St. Alban's Garrison Church, Larkhill'. *Journal of the Royal Artillery*, vol. LXXXIX, No. 1, Spring 1962.
54. Guy, *History of Gunnery Wing.*
55. *History of the School*, Annual Records, 1920-64.
56. *R.A. Notes*, 80, Autumn 1962.
57. Glover, by communication.
58. *R.A. Notes*, 80, Autumn, 1962.
59. Ibid.
60. Special Army Council Instruction, No. 93 of 1964, 18th March 1964. *Administration and Organization - Royal Artillery - Organization, functions and terminology.*
61. *School, Historical Record - 1963.*
62. Ibid.
63. 'School of Artillery, Larkhill', *The Gunner*, vol. 44, 1962.
64. 'School of Artillery, Larkhill, Wagon Lines Club', *The Gunner*, vol. 45, 1963.
65. *School, Historical Record - 1966.*
66. 'School of Artillery, Larkhill, Official Opening by the Master Gunner', *The Gunner*, vol. 48, 1966.

67. Col. M.G. McComas, by communication.
68. Ibid.
69. *School, Historical Record – 1967.*
70. *School, Historical Record – 1968.*
71. *School, Historical Record – 1965.*
72. Ibid.
73. Ibid.
74. Guy, *History of Gunnery Wing.*
75. *School, Historical Record – 1966.*
76. McComas, by communication.
77. 'FACE', *Gunner*, Issue No. 3, February 1971.
78. Guy, *History of Gunnery Wing.*
79. *School, Historical Record – 1968.*
80. *R.A. Notes*, 80, Autumn 1962.
81. *School, Historical Record – 1968.*
82. Ibid.
83. Guy, *History of Gunnery Wing.*
84. Editorial, *The Gunner*, vol. 52, May 1970.
85. *Artillery Day Larkhill 1970 – Souvenir Programme.*
86. 'Royal School of Artillery', *Gunner*, Issue No. 3, February 1971.
87. Ibid.
88. Ibid.
89. Guy, *History of Gunnery Wing.*

8. The Latter Years

1. *Plain Talk*, No. 1, 1971.
2. 'Royal Visitor to Larkhill', *Gunner*, Issue No. 8, July 1971.
3. 'RSA Report', *Gunner*, Issue No. 9, August 1971.
4. Ibid.
5. Ibid.
6. 'Thunderbird comes to Larkhill', *Gunner*, Issue No. 16, March 1972.
7. *Plain Talk*, No. 2, 1972.
8. 'Visit of Director, U.S. Women's Army Corps', *The Lioness*, Vol. XLIV, No. 1, February 1973.
9. 'Her Majesty The Queen's Visit to Larkhill', *Gunner*, Issue No. 31, June 1973.
10. 'Royal Visit to Larkhill', *Gunner*, Issue No. 30, May 1973.
11. Guy, *History of Gunnery Wing.*
12. *Plain Talk*, No. 3, 1973.
13. Ibid.
14. *Plain Talk*, No. 4, 1974.
15. Guy, *History of Gunnery Wing.*
16. Guy, *History of Gunnery Wing.*
17. Ibid.
18. Col. P.R.R. de Burgh, by communication.
19. Guy, *History of Gunnery Wing.*

20. 'HRH The Prince of Wales visits the Royal School of Artillery', *Gunner*, Issue No. 105, August 1979.
21. Guy, *History of Gunnery Wing.*
22. 'The Royal School of Artillery', *Gunner*, Issue No. 82, September 1977.
23. Guy, *History of Gunnery Wing.*

9 The Wings

Note: In this and future chapters, references to the School Establishments are given as '*Establishment*' followed by the code number and date.

1. *Establishment*, V/1931/76/1, 18 September 1940.
2. *Establishment*, V/76/6, 20 November 1945.
3. *Establishment*, V/76/7, 12 November 1946.
4. *Establishment*, V/76/8, 10 May 1948.
5. *Establishment*, V/76/9, 1 April 1949.
6. *Establishment*, V/76/3, 3 July 1941.
7. *Establishment*, V/76/4, 5 October 1942.
8. *The Royal Artillery Commemoration Book* 1939–1945, 1950.
9. Ibid.
10. Brig. A.B. Davies, by communication.
11. Col. G.N.C. Smith, by communication.
12. Lt-Col. W.A. Owen, 'Some Memories of the Equipment Wing, School of Artillery, Larkhill, 1941–45', *Gunner*, Issue No. 57, August 1975.
13. Ibid.
14. *Establishment*, V/76/6, 20 November 1945.
15. Maj. W.A. Hicks, 'The Equipment Wing, School of Artillery, Larkhill, 1941–45', *Gunner*, Issue No. 58, September 1975.
16. *Establishment*, V/76/5, 17 August 1943.
17. *Establishment*, V/76/9, 1 April 1949.
18. *Establishment*, V/76/1, 24 January 1952.
19. *Establishment*, V/76/10, 1 August 1950.
20. *Establishment*, V/76/14 (P) (ERE), 1 April 1961.
21. *Establishment*, 5/76/18 (P), 1 September 1969.
22. *Establishment*, V/76/18 (P), 1 September 1969.
23. *History of School of Artillery*, Annual Records, 1920–64, unpublished MSS.
24. *Establishment*, V/76/7, 12 November 1946.
25. *Establishment*, V/76/8, 10 May 1948.
26. *Establishment*, V/76/10, 1 August 1950.
27. Ibid.
28. *History of Tactics Wing 1945–68*, unpublished MSS.
29. *School of Artillery, Larkhill, Historical Record*, 1965.
30. Lieut-Col. J.R. Guy, *A History of Gunnery Wing, Royal School of Artillery*, 1981.
31. Army Council Instruction 349, 17 April 1940, *RA School of Survey.*
32. Ibid.

33. Army Council Instruction 231, 19 February 1941. *RA School of Survey*.
34. Army Council Instruction 2168, 5 November 1941, *Courses of Instruction – School of Artillery, Joining Instructions*.
35. Army Council Instruction 15, 6 January 1943, *Courses of Instruction – School of Artillery – Joining Instructions and Objects of the Courses*.
36. Lieut-Col. G.P. Chapman, by communication.
37. *The Radar Wing, School of Artillery*, unpublished MSS.
38. *Establishment*, V/76/6, 20 November 1945.
39. *The Radar Wing*, unpublished MSS.
40. Ibid.
41. *Establishment*, V/76/7, 12 November 1946.
42. *Establishment*, V/76/8, 10 May 1948.
43. *Establishment*, V/76/10, 1 August 1950.
44. Lieut-Col. W.M. Morgan, *Artillery Support, Administration and Equipment Management of The Royal School of Artillery, (The Morgan Report)*, 1981.
45. *Establishment*, V/76/1, 24 January 1952.
46. *Establishment*, V/76/13, (LE) (ERE), 21 November 1956.
47. *History of the School*, Annual Records, 1920–64.
48. Ibid.
49. *Establishment*, V/76/14 (P) (ERE), 1 April 1961.
50. Army Council Instruction 164, 23 May 1962, *Designations – Surface to Surface Artillery*.
51. *Annual Report of the School of Gunnery – Horse and Field Artillery at Home*, 1901, para. 68.
52. *Annual Report of School of Gunnery*, 1906, para. 65.
53. Air Cdre, A.J.W. Geddes, by communication.
54. Maj. F.M. Robertson, by communication.
55. *Young Officers' Branch*, unpublished MSS.
56. *Establishment*, V/76/10, 1 August 1950.
57. *Establishment*, V/76/1 (HE), 24 January 1952.
58. *Establishment*, V/76/14 (P) (ERE), 1 April 1961.
59. *Establishment*, V/76/18 (P), 1 September 1969.
60. Col. P.R.R. de Burgh, *Young Officers' Prize Awards* , unpublished MSS.
61. *RA Notes*, 66, August 1955.
62. *History of the School*, Annual Records, 1920–64.
63. Ibid.
64. *RA Notes*, 72, October 1958.
65. Capt. P.M.R. Stacpoole, 'Ubique quo radar et Doppler ducunt', *Journal of the Royal Artillery*, vol. LXXXVI, No. 3, Winter 1959.
66. *History of the School*, Annual Records, 1920–64.
67. Ibid.
68. *RA Notes*, 81, Autumn 1963.
69. *Establishment*, V/76/16 (P) (ERE), 20 September 1963.
70. Maj.-Gen. Sir John Headlam, *The History of the Royal Artillery*, vol. II, 1937.
71. *Annual Report of School of Gunnery*, 1902, para. 167.

72. *Establishment*, V/76/5, 17 August 1943.
73. *Establishment*, V/76/6, 20 November 1945.
74. *Establishment*, V/76/8, 10 May 1948.
75. *RA Notes*, 54, May 1950.
76. *Establishment*, V/76/1, 24 January 1952.
77. Col. G.W.A. Pearce, *REME at the School of Artillery, Larkhill, 1945-68*, unpublished MSS.
78. Ibid.
79. *Establishment*, 5/3783/1 (P) (W), 1 January 1971.
80. 'School of Artillery – Authority for Amalgamation', *The Gunner*, vol. 52, October 1970.
81. *Establishment*, 5/3783/3 (P) (W), 1 September 1973.
82. Maj.-Gen. P.B. Foster, by communication.
83. *Establishment*, 5/3783/4 (P) (W), 25 November 1977.

10 **The Ranges**
1. *RA Notes* 46, May 1948.
2. Lieut-Col. J.H. Price, by communication.
3. C. Baycliffe, by communication.
4. Col. P.R.R. de Burgh, by communication.
5. Ibid.
6. Maj.-Gen. Sir Peter Gillet, by communication.
7. de Burgh, by communication.
8. Lieut-Col. W.A. Owen, by communication.
9. J. Bridle, BSM (AIG) retired, by communication.
10. Maj. H.G. Bennett, *Salisbury Plain Range Detachment RA, Historical Report*, 1953.
11. Brig. F. FitzGibbon, unpublished MSS, c. 1948.
12. Bennett, *Salisbury Plain Range Det.*, 1953.
13. Brig. C. Childs, 'One April Morning', *Gunner*, No. 138, May 1982.
14. Col. P.R.R. de Burgh and P.W. Browne, by communication.
15. Capt. M.M. Double, by communication.
16. Price, by communication.
17. E. Bowden, by communication.
18. Maj.-Gen. R.H.L. Wheeler, by communication.
19. Maj. W.H. Whitcombe, by communication.
20. *Annual Report of the School of Gunnery – Horse and Field Artillery at Home*, 1901, para. 89.
21. Bennett, *Salisbury Plain Range Det.*, 1953.
22. Brig. D.D.C. Tulloch, by communication.
23. Bennett, *Salisbury Plain Range Det.*, 1953.
24. Col. G.E. Drought, by communication.
25. Ibid.
26. Bennett, *Salisbury Plain Range Det.*, 1953.
27. Maj. D. Rollo, by communication.
28. Bennett, *Salisbury Plain Range Det.*, 1953.

29. Lieut.-Col. J.W. Madden, by communication.
30. *History of Units and Establishments in Larkhill.* Circular letter from School of Artillery reference 8118/1/GS dated 7 May 1953.
31. Maj. H.G. Bennett, *Brief for Garrison Commander on his final visit.* 1961.
32. Col. B. Cocks, by communication.
33. Bennett, *Salisbury Plain Range Det.*, 1961.
34. *Establishment*, 5/76/18 (P) 1 September 1969.
35. *Establishment*, 5/3783/4 (P) (W) 25 November 1977.
36. *Establishment*, V/76/5 17 August 1943.
37. *Establishment*, V/76/10 1 August 1950.
38. *Establishment*, V/76/13 (LE) (ERE) 21 November 1956.
39. *Establishment*, 5/3783/6 (P) (W) 3 November 1980.
40. Bowden, by communication.
41. Maj. P.M. Gell, by communication.
42. Sir Richard C. Hoare, *The Ancient History of South Wiltshire*, Part 1, 1812.
43. J. Speed, *Map of Wiltshire*, 1610.
44. J. Andrews and A. Dury, *Map of Whiltshire*, 1773.
45. J. Cary, *New English Atlas*, 1809.
46. Hoare, *History of S. Wiltshire*, 1812.
47. Ordnance Survey, Map to scale of one inch to one statute mile, published 14 August 1817.
48. *A Narrative of the Life, Confession and Dying Speech of Jarvis Matchan who was on 2d of August 1786, executed . . .*
49. Thomas Ingoldsby, 'The Dead Drummer', *The Ingoldsby Legends*, vol. II, 1870.
50. Maj. C.E. Corke, by communication.
51. B.A. Painter, Chief Forester, Property Services Agency, by communication.
52. Ibid.
53. 'Conservation', 'A Little Help from Her Friends', *Journal of The Royal Artillery*, vol. CVIII, No. 2, 1981.
54. 'S. Small', 'The Other Larkhill', *Journal of The Royal Artillery*, vol. XCVII, No. 1, 1970.
55. N.D.G. James, personal note.
56. *Conservation on Salisbury Plain*, memorandum issued by the Larkhill/West Down Conservation Group.
57. 'Samuel Small', 'The Great Bustard', *Journal of The Royal Artillery*, vol. CI, No. 1, 1974.
58. 'Nature Notes', *The Times*, 18 January 1982.

11 Larkhill and the Territorial Army

1. *Annual Report of the School of Gunnery for Horse and Field Artillery at Home*, 1902, paras. 170-1.
2. *Annual Report of School of Gunnery*, 1909, Chief Instructor's Report, para. 5.

3. *Annual Report of School of Gunnery*, 1908, para. 26.
4. *Annual Report of School of Gunnery*, 1910, Chief Instructor's Report, para. 10.
5. *Annual Report of School of Gunnery*, 1912, Chief Instructor's Report, para. 14.
6. *Annual Report of School of Gunnery*, 1913, Chief Instructor's Report, para. 17.
7. N.D.G. James, *Before the Echoes Die Away*, 1980.
8. Maj.-Gen. Sir John Headlam, *The History of the Royal Artillery*, vol. II, 1937.
9. James, *Before the Echoes*.
10. Maj. A.F. Stevens, 'Working Partners', *Gunner*, No. 126, May 1981.
11. James, *Before the Echoes*.
12. Maj. D. Rollo, 'The National Artillery Association', *Journal of the Royal Artillery*, vol. CIX, No. 1, 1982.
13. *Annual Report of School of Gunnery*, 1910, Chief Instructor's Report, para. 30.
14. *Annual Report of School of Gunnery*, 1911, Chief Instructor's Report, para. 49.
15. Rollo, 'The National Artillery Association'.
16. *Annual Report of School of Gunnery*, 1912, Chief Instructor's Report, para. 33.
17. *Annual Report of School of Gunnery*, 1915, Chief Instructor's Report, para. 40.
18. Rollo, 'The National Artillery Association'.
19. Ibid.

12 Larkhill Garrison
1. Ordnance Survey, map to scale of two inches to one statute mile, *War Department Land on Salisbury Plain*, published 1903.
2. Brig. J.H.W.G. Richards, by communication.
3. Lieut.-Col. P. de N. Ramus, by communication.
4. Maj. F.M. Robertson, by communication.
5. Richards, by communication.
6. Robertson, by communication.
7. Brig. D.F. Ryan, by communication.
8. *Plain Talk*, No. 5, 1976.
9. *History of the School of Artillery*, Annual Records 1920–64, unpublished MSS.
10. Maj. R.C.F. Craven, 'The "Friar Tuck" Collection', *Journal of the Royal Artillery*, vol. CVII, No. 1, 1980.
11. Brig. G. de E. Collin, 'New Paintings for School', *Gunner*, Issue No. 9, August 1971.
12. 'School of Artillery, Larkhill', *The Gunner*, vol. XLII, March 1960.
13. 'Short Back and Sides' – 'Nobby Clarke', *Gunner*, Issue No. 122, January 1981.

14. The Rev. H.G. Williamson, 'The New Garrison Church of St. Alban, Larkhill', *Royal Army Chaplain Department Journal*, Vol. VI, no. 46, July 1938.
15. Ibid.
16. J.G.E. Cox, Keeper of Records, St Albans Cathedral, by communication.
17. H.G. Williamson, 'The New Garrison Church . . .'
18. 'School of Artillery - Larkhill', *The Gunner*, vol. XXXVI, November 1954.
19. 'The Saint Barbara Window, St. Albans Garrison Church, Larkhill', *Journal of the Royal Artillery*, vol. LXXXIX, No. 1, 1962.
20. Col. B. Cocks, by communication.
21. Ordnance Survey Map, 25.334 Inches to a Statute Mile, Wiltshire Sheet LIV.11, 1939.
22. Ordnance Survey Map, Six Inches to One Statute Mile, Wiltshire Sheet LIV.SE, 1926.
23. *School of Artillery, Larkhill. Historical Record*, 1968.
24. 'Larkhill Amateur Dramatic Society', *The Gunner*, vol. 28, February 1947.
25. Col. P.R.R. de Burgh, by communication.
26. Lieut-Col. D.W.O. Price, by communication.
27. Ibid.
28. Brig. E.N. Oldrey, by communication.

13 The Royal School of Artillery

1. *The Royal School of Artillery Larkhill, Role & Organisation & General Information*, 1983.
2. Lieut.-Col. J.R. Guy, *A History of Gunnery Wing Royal School of Artillery*, 1981.
3. *RSA, Role & Organisation*, 1983.
4. Ibid.
5. Maj. P.H. Scott, *RA Sales Team*, unpublished MSS.
6. History of 22 (Gibraltar 1779-83) Locating Battery, RA.
7. *RSA, Role & Organisation*, 1983.
8. *Establishment*, V/76/3, 3 July 1941.
9. *Establishment*, V/76/4, 5 October 1942.
10. 'Farewell to "21" ', *Gunner*, Issue No. 133, December 1981.
11. *The STANOC Centre, Larkhill*, unpublished MSS.
12. *Roles and Functions of TDT RA*, June 1980.
13. I.S. Dyer, *An Outline of the History and Development of the Royal Aircraft Establishment, Larkhill*, 1973.
14. Ibid.
15. N.D.G. James, personal note.
16. Lieut.-Col. D.A. Robson, by communication.
17. A.G. Sills, *Meteorological Office, Larkhill*.
18. *Defence Land Agent, Salisbury Plain, Department of the Environment*, 1978.

19. Lieut.-Col. M.E.S. Laws, 'Royal Navy and Royal Artillery', *The Gunner*, vol. 31, February 1950.

20. T. Pakenham, *The Boer War*, 1982.

21. Laws, 'Royal Navy and Royal Artillery'.

22. Lieut.-Col. J.R. Guy, *A History of Gunnery Wing Royal School of Artillery*, 1981.

23. Col. P.R.R. de Burgh, *Gunner Connection*, Contact between *HMS Excellent* and Royal School of Artillery, 1940–73.

24. Ibid.

25. *Royal Artillery Notes*, No. 53, February 1950.

26. 'Exercise Scapa', *The Gunner*, vol. 31, June 1949.

27. Guy, *History of Gunnery Wing*.

28. Ibid.

29. *School of Artillery, Larkhill, Historical Record*, 1964.

30. *The Wilkinson Cane Terms of Reference*, 17 December 1981.

31. *RA Notes*, 62, August 1953.

32. 'School of Artillery, Larkhill', *The Gunner*, vol. L1, July 1969.

33. 'School presents Historic Flag', *Gunner*, Issue No. 6, May, 1971.

Appendices

**COMMANDANTS, THE SCHOOL OF ARTILLERY AND
THE ROYAL SCHOOL OF ARTILLERY, 1920–82**

1920	Brigadier-General H.W. Newcome, CMG, DSO
1922	Colonel Commandant W. Stirling, CMG, DSO
1926	Colonel Commandant C.C. Armitage, CMG, DSO
1929	Brig. A.F. Brooke, DSO
1932	Brig. J.M.R. Harrison, DSO
1934	Brig. Lord D.M. Graham, CB, DSO, MC
1936	Brig. H.R. Pownall, CB, DSO, MC
1938	Brig. S.R. Wason, MC
1939	Brig. F. FitzGibbon, DSO
1942	Brig. R.H. Towell, CBE, MC
1945	Brig. G.W.E. Heath, CBE, DSO, MC
1947	Brig. G.G. Mears, CBE, DSO, MC, ADC
1949	Brig. R.W. Goodbody, DSO
1951	Brig. C.H. Colquhoun, OBE
1953	Brig. E.D. Howard-Vyse, CBE, MC
1956	Brig. A.J.C. Block, DSO, OBE
1959	Brig. J.M. McNeill, CBE, ADC
1960	Brig. P.J. Glover, OBE
1962	Brig. W.D.E. Brown, CBE, DSO, ADC
1964	Brig. J.A.T. Sharp, MC
1966	Brig. R.S. Streatfeild, MC
1969	Brig. G. de E. Collin, MC
1971	Brig. P.B. Foster, MC
1973	Brig. K.F. McQueen
1974	Brig. J.S. Badley, ADC
1976	Brig. R.N. Ohlenschlager, MBE
1977	Brig. J.D.W. Goodman
1979	Brig. D.M. Jones
1982	Brig. J.B. Bettridge, CBE

Notes
1. The rank of Brigadier-General was abolished under Army Order 545 of 1920 with effect from 1 January 1921, although this did not apply to

those who had been granted the honorary rank of Brigadier-General on retirement.

2. The same Army Order also laid down that in peace time, certain appointments would carry the temporary rank of Colonel-Commandant and included in these was the appointment of 'Commandant, School of Artillery'.

APPENDIX II
COLONEL COMMANDANTS, THE SCHOOL OF ARTILLERY AND THE ROYAL SCHOOL OF ARTILLERY, 1968-78

1968	Lieut.-Gen. Sir Denis O'Connor, KBE, CB
1972	Major-Gen. W.D.E. Brown, CB, CBE, DSO
1978	Major-Gen. P.B. Foster, MC

APPENDIX III
DEPUTY COMMANDANTS AND GARRISON COMMANDERS, 1931-78

Garrison Commanders

1931	Captain E.M. Tyler, MC
1935	Bt. Major C.R.A. Wallis
1937	Major H.L.G. Burlton, MC
1939	Major H.A. Maconochie
1940	Major J.C.M. Mostyn, MC
1942	Col. H.G. Howson, CBE, MC, TD
1945	Col. W.E. Vaudry, MC
	Col. B.C. Trappes-Lomax, MC
1947	Col. B.G. Mason

Deputy Commandants and Garrison Commanders

1950	Col. F.N.W. Gore, OBE
1952	Col. G.C. Wells, MC
1954	Col. F.A. Bibra, DSO
1958	Col. J.M. Northen, MBE
1959	Col. B. Cocks, GM, TD
1963	Col. D.R.M. Owen, DSO, OBE
1964	Col. M.G. McComas, MBE
1968	Col. D.F. Wharry
1970	Col. E.A. Tremlett, OBE
1974	Col. G.C.K. Rowe
1976	Col. P.R.R. de Burgh, OBE

Deputy Commandant and Deputy Garrison Commander

1978	Col. J.M. Browell, MBE

APPENDIX IV
CAMP COMMANDANTS, SALISBURY PLAIN,
LARKHILL AND WESTDOWN PRACTICE CAMPS, 1899–1913

From 1899 to 1910 the camp was known as 'Salisbury Plain' although it was based on Larkhill and during this period a single commandant was appointed for the whole camp. From 1911 to 1913, two camps were established, one at Larkhill and the other at Westdown and a separate commandant was appointed for each.

1899	Lieut.-Col. H.B. Jeffreys
1901	Col. L.W. Parsons
1902	Col. L.W. Parsons, CB
1903	Col. F.H. Hall, CB
1904	Col. F.H. Hall, CB
1905	Col. F.H. Hall, CB
1906	Col. W.F.L. Lindsay, DSO
1907	Col. Sir G.V. Thomas Bart, CB, DSO
1908	Brig.-Gen. W.F.L. Lindsay, CB, DSO
1909	Brig.-Gen. B. Burton, CB
1910	Col. W.L.H. Paget, MVO
1911	Brig.-Gen. E.J. Phipps-Hornby, VC, CB (Larkhill)
	Brig.-Gen. J.P. Du Cane, CB (West Down)
1912	Brig.-Gen. N.D. Findlay, CB (Larkhill)
	Col. B.F. Drake (West Down)
1913	Col. B.F. Drake (Larkhill)
	Brig.-Gen. H.K. Jackson, DSO (West Down)

APPENDIX V
COMMANDANTS, SCHOOL OF INSTRUCTION FOR ROYAL
HORSE AND ROYAL FIELD ARTILLERY LARKHILL 1915–19

1915	Lieut.-Col. W.G. Thompson, RA
1916	Lieut.-Col. F.G.T. Deshon, RA
1917	Lieut.-Col. J.H. Gibbon, DSO, RA
1918	Lieut.-Col. H.A.W. Webber, RA
1919	Lieut.-Col. H.A.W. Webber, RA

APPENDIX VI
CHAPLAINS AT LARKHILL

CHURCH OF ENGLAND 1918–82

1918	Rev. G.H. Gore
1919	No record
1921	Rev. R.O. Lloyd
1923	Rev. J.A. Shiels
1926	Rev. H.R. Norton
1929	Rev. S.L.L. Webb
	Rev. D.A. Jones
1931	Rev. J.C.L. Isard
1933	Rev. R. Yale
1934	Rev. E.S. Dabbs
1936	Rev. H.L.O. Davies
	Rev. H. Greville Williamson
1938	Rev. N. Copeland, OBE
1940	Rev. A.G. Basker
	Rev. H.T. Boultbee
1942	Rev. E.A. Knight
	Rev. J.R. Beresford, TD
	Rev. J.B. Elliott
1945	Rev. S.W.G. Elvins
1946	Rev. T.J.C. Roberts, OBE
1949	Rev. H. Savage
1951	Rev. T.H. Lewis
1953	Rev. W.W.P. Rhys, MBE
1954	Rev. J.P. Stevenson, TD
1955	Rev. R.A. Ford, MBE
1960	Rev. D.S. Coey

1962	Rev. R.D. Ebbitt
1964	Rev. A.K. Thomas
1967	Rev. D.G. Bevan
1969	Rev. J.S. Westmuckett
1972	Rev. M.M. Martin
1973	Rev. I.R.C. Baillie
1975	Rev. S.I. McGee
1977	Rev. F.J. Preston, MBE
1979	Rev. P.T. Craig
1982	Rev. A.C. Carruthers

ROMAN CATHOLIC, 1969–82

1969	Rev. B. Jones
1970	Rev. M.J. Phelan
1971	Rev. P.P. Flavin
1972	Rev. G. Banks
1973	Rev. J. Moran
1975	Rev. D.N. McMillan
1976	Rev. P.P. Flavin
1978	Rev. L.J. Cosgrove
	Rev. F.J. Robson
1980	Rev. H.W.H.B. Martin
1982	Rev. J. O'Hara

Note

No records were available prior to 1969.

APPENDIX VII
DEPOT AND SUPPORT REGIMENTS, 1920–82

1920	15th Brigade, RFA
1921	7th Brigade, RFA
1922	1st Brigade, RFA
1924	25th Field Brigade, RA
1925	6th Field Brigade, RA
1928	2nd Field Brigade, RA
1930	26th Field Brigade, RA
1932	2nd Field Brigade, RA
1934	26th Field Brigade, RA
1937	9th Field Brigade, RA
1939	12th Field Regiment, RA
1940	98th Field Regiment, RA
1942	4th Field Training and Depot Regiment, RA

1946   124th Field Regiment, RA
1948   5th Regiment, RHA
1951   19th Medium Regiment, RA
1962   6th Field Regiment, RA
1966   25th Field Regiment, RA
1968   49th Field Regiment, RA
1971   26th Field Regiment, RA
1974   19th Field Regiment, RA
1979   2nd Field Regiment, RA
1982   The Support Regiment, Royal School of Artillery

APPENDIX VIII
THE ORIGINS OF THE ROYAL SCHOOL OF ARTILLERY

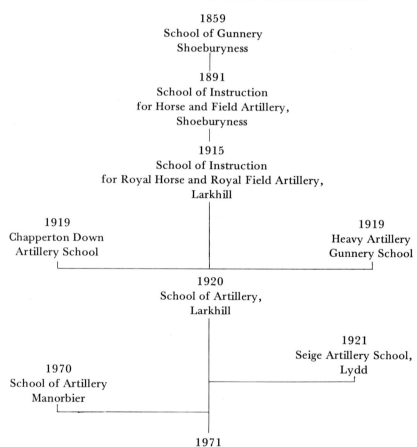

1859
School of Gunnery
Shoeburyness

1891
School of Instruction
for Horse and Field Artillery,
Shoeburyness

1915
School of Instruction
for Royal Horse and Royal Field Artillery,
Larkhill

1919
Chapperton Down
Artillery School

1919
Heavy Artillery
Gunnery School

1920
School of Artillery,
Larkhill

1921
Seige Artillery School,
Lydd

1970
School of Artillery
Manorbier

1971
Royal School of Artillery,
Larkhill

APPENDIX IX
SOME RA SCHOOLS AND PRACTICE CAMPS, 1778-1971

1778   The first gunnery school set up at the Royal Military Repository, Woolwich, by Sir William Congreve, the elder

1859   School of Gunnery established at Shoeburyness on 1 April 1859

1875   Okehampton Practice Camp formed on 2nd August 1875

1882   Lydd Practice Camp set up

1891   School of Gunnery for Horse and Field Artillery formed at Shoeburyness

1893   Buddon Practice Camp established between Dundee and Carnoustie

1899   Salisbury Plain Practice Camp opened at Larkhill and Westdown
       Glen Imaal Practice Camp established in Ireland

1900   Siege Artillery Branch of the School of Gunnery set up at Lydd
       Royal Military Repository at Woolwich closed in May 1900

1903   Trawsfynydd Practice Camp established near Ffestiniogg, Merioneth, North Wales

1912   Ad Fines Practice Camp (later named Redesdale) set up in Northumberland

1914   Approval given for the School of Gunnery for Royal Horse and Royal Field Artillery to move from Shoeburyness to Larkhill
       Pembrey Practice Camp acquired in Carmarthenshire

1915   School of Instruction for Royal Horse and Royal Field Artillery, established at Larkhill under the authority of ACI 120 of 12 February 1915

1916   The Overseas Artillery School, later renamed Chapperton Down Artillery School, was formed with its headquarters in Salisbury and its practice area at Chapperton down, west of the Tilshead–West Lavington road

1917   Central Siege School at Lydd recorded in the Army List for August 1917

1919   Amalgamation of the Chapperton Down Artillery School, the Heavy Artillery Training Centre and the School of Instruction for Royal Horse and Royal Field Artillery to form the School of Artillery, Larkhill

1920   The School of Artillery, Larkhill, formed on 1 January 1920

1921   Siege Artillery School, Lydd, joined the School of Artillery at Larkhill

1939   The School of Anti-Aircraft Defence moved from Biggin Hill to Manorbier, Pembrokeshire

1940   Practice Camp set up at Sennybridge, Breconshire

1942   Otterburn Ranges opened as an extension to Redesdale Practice Camp, Northumberland

1959   RA Guided Weapons Range established in the Outer Hebrides

1971   The School of Artillery, Manorbier, amalgamated with the School of Artillery, Larkhill, and moved to Larkhill. HM The Queen granted the prefix of 'Royal' to the School on 1 January 1971

APPENDIX X
LARKHILL DAYS AND ARTILLERY DAYS, 1962-82

In the following list of Larkhill and Artillery Days the names of the officers who took the salute are shown after the appropriate days, except in 1964 when other arrangements were made.

LARKHILL DAY

1962	27 July	Brig. P.J. Glover, OBE
	28 July	Gen. Sir Robert Mansergh, GCB, KBE, MC
1963	30 July	Brig. W.D.E. Brown, CBE, DSO, ADC
	31 July	Gen. Sir William Pike, KCB, CBE, DSO
1964	—	—
1965	30 July	Brig. J.A.T. Sharp, MC
	31 July	Gen. Sir Robert Mansergh, GCB, KBE, MC
1966	29 July	Brig. R.S. Streatfeild, MC
	30 July	Gen. Sir Robert Mansergh, GCB, KBE, MC
1967	4 August	Brig. R.S. Streatfeild, MC
	5 August	Gen. Sir Robert Mansergh, GCB, KBE, MC
1968	26 July	Brig. R.S. Streatfeild, MC
	27 July	Gen. Sir Robert Mansergh, GCB, KBE, MC
1969	18 July	Brig. G. de E. Collin, MC
	19 July	Gen. Sir Robert Mansergh, GCB, KBE, MC

ARTILLERY DAY

1970	17 July	Maj.-Gen. H.C. Tuzo, OBE, MC
	18 July	Gen. Sir Geoffrey Baker, GCB, CMG, CBE, MC, ADC
1971	16 July	Brig. P.B. Foster, MC
	17 July	F.M. Sir Geoffrey Baker, GCB, CMG, CBE, MC, ADC
1972	14 July	Brig. P.B. Foster, MC
	15 July	Gen. Sir Basil Eugster, KCB, KCVO, CBE, DSO, MC
1973	13 July	Brig. K.J. McQueen
	14 July	F.M. Sir Geoffrey Baker, GCB, CMG, CBE, MC, ADC
1974	12 July	Brig. K.J. McQueen
	13 July	F.M. Sir Geoffrey Baker, GCB, CMG, CBE, MC, ADC
1975	11 July	Brig. J.S. Badley, ADC
	12 July	F.M. Sir Geoffrey Baker, GCB, CMG, CBE, MC, ADC
1976	9 July	Brig. J.S. Badley, ADC
	10 July	F.M. Sir Geoffrey Baker, GCB, CMG, CBE, MC, ADC
1977	8 July	Brig. R.N. Ohlenschlager, MBE
	9 July	Gen. Sir John Gibbon, GCE, OBE
1978	14 July	Brig. J.D.W. Goodman
	15 July	Gen. Sir Harry Tuzo, GCB, OBE, MC
1979		Not held
1980	4 July	Brig. D.M. Jones
	5 July	Maj.-Gen. A.E. Walkling, CB, OBE
1981		Not held
1982		Not held

APPENDIX XI
GUNS AND EQUIPMENT OF HISTORICAL INTEREST
AT THE ROYAL SCHOOL OF ARTILLERY, 1982

Equipment	Location	Particulars
Two 16 pr, 12 cwt MKI, RML, heavy field pieces, 1872	In front of RA Mess	These were designed to supersede the 9 pr in Heavy Field Batteries. Issued in large numbers to Volunteer Field Batteries
Two 3 pr brass OML, SB guns	Inside front entrance of RA Mess	Presented by 1st Singapore Regiment RA to commemorate the service of the Royal Artillery on Blakang Mati, 1885–1958
18 pr Q.F. gun MKII. In service 1906–41	Inside entrance to School HQ	Inscribed with the names of 2 officers and 10 NCOs and soldiers of 135 Battery RFA. The gun was used in blowing an enemy saphead at Pilkem, 6 July 1915
Two 9 pr SB brass guns	Outside the Newcome Hall	Mounted on Field Carriage Pattern 1 1862. Reconstructed by REME Wing in 1967
Two 32 pr ML 'field pieces' 1806 and 1807	On either side of the main entrance to the Packway Mess	Built by Carron Ironworks, Falkirk, Scotland
Brass gun on wooden carriage	Outside the Guard Room	—
Thunderbird 2 Missile. In service 1956–77	Glover Road near junction with Bell Road	—
5.5 in. gun. In service 1941–80	Glover Road near junction with Bell Road	MK 1/1 carriage No. CA2280, manufactured by the Royal Ordnance Factory, Nottingham

Equipment	Location	Particulars
Russian 76 mm gun. In service 1939–45	Bell Road near junction with Glover Road	Captured by the Germans from the Russians and later captured by the British from the Germans in North Africa
Light anti-aircraft gun: 40 mm. No. 12 (Bristol Bofor). In service 1939–51	Bell Road, south of School HQ	–
25 pr gun-howitzer. In service 1940–69	As above	MKIII carriage with hinged trail for upper register shooting
17 pr anti-tank gun. In service 1943–51	As above	–
OQF 2 pr MK 10 on MKIIIA carriage. In service 1941–3	Gunnery Wing Equipment Branch	Barrel No. 35180 manufactured 1943, on carriage No. CA13275 built 1941
OQF 6 pr. In service 1942–6	As above	Built 1942 for proof and experiment only. Barrel No. 24013 manufactured by the Royal Ordnance Factory, Leeds
OQF 3.7 in. howitzer, MK1 on MK2 carriage. In service 1917–50	As above	Manufactured by the Royal Garrison Foundry
105 mm. Pack howitzer L3A1. In service (regular units) 1960–78	As above	Barrel No. 057072. Manufactured by Ota Melara, La Spezia, Italy

Equipment	Location	Particulars
'Sexton', SP OQF 25 pr MK 3/1. In service 1943–55	Gunnery Wing Equipment Branch	Barrel No. 106832. Manufactured by Armstrong Patent & Co. 1941
4.2 in. Mortar. In Service 1943–65	As above	SBML serial No. A6155 Barrel No. 1569. Manufactured by ACL Ltd, 1945
Two miniature replicas of Koelher guns	Outside HQ of 22 (Gibraltar 1779–83). Locating Battery RA at Horne Barracks	The barrels are from brass light guns of 1858. One barrel is inscribed 'F.M. Eardley Wilmot'
4.5 in. howitzer of the early 1800s	As above	—
Two Japanese Pack howitzers	Facing Watson Road and adjacent to the entrance to 22 (Gibraltar 1779–83) Locating Battery RA	No information is available regarding these howitzers but it is believed that they were given to the Battery by the RSA
Drone MQM-57. In service 1961–72	As above	A target surveillance aircraft controlled by short-range radio
Drone AN/USD 501. In service 1971–to date	As above	An unmanned surveillance drone, used for in-depth free-flight target surveillance. Nicknamed 'Midge'

APPENDIX XII
BUILDINGS AND ROADS BEARING COMMEMORATIVE NAMES

A number of individual buildings and barrack blocks, and most of the roads in the Larkhill Garrison area, have been named after officers who have been connected with the School or have served in the Royal Regiment elsewhere. The names are given below in alphabetical order and are followed by a brief note on the officer commemorated. In the case of those who served at the School of Artillery or the Royal School of Artillery, the rank shown is the highest which the individual attained and not necessarily that which he held whilst at Larkhill. This principle has also been followed in the case of honours and decorations.

BUILDINGS AND BARRACKS

Alanbrooke Barracks   Field Marshal The Viscount Alanbrooke, KG, GCB, OM, GCVO, DSO, Commandant School of Artillery, 1929-32, Master Gunner of St James' Park, 1946-56

Badley Library   Brigadier J.S. Badley, Commandant, Royal School of Artillery, 1974-6.

Collin Block   Major-General G. de C. Collin, CB, MC, Commandant, Royal School of Artillery, 1969-71

Hardy Block   Brigadier H.A. Hardy, MBE, MC, Commandant, School of Anti-Aircraft Artillery, 1967-70

Horne Barracks   General The Lord Horne, GCB, KCMG, Master Gunner of St James' Park, 1926-9

Mason House   Brigadier B.G. Mason, Garrison Commander and Officer i/c Administration, School of Artillery, 1947-50

Mears House   Brigadier G.G. Mears, CBE, DSO, MC, Commandant School of Artillery, 1947-9

Newcome Hall   Major-General H.W. Newcome, CB, CMG, DSO, First Commandant School of Artillery 1920-2

Roberts Barracks   Field Marshall The Earl Roberts of Khandahar, VC, KG, KP, GCB, OM, GCSI, GCIE, Master Gunner of St James' Park, 1904-14

Sharp Hall   General Sir John Sharp, KCB, MC, Commandant School of Artillery, 1964-6

Stirling Barracks   Brigadier-General W. Stirling, CMG, DSO, Commandant School of Artillery, 1922-6

ROADS

Alanbrooke Road   Field Marshall The Viscount Alanbrooke, KG, GCB, OM, GCVO, DSO, Commandant School of Artillery, 1929-32, Master Gunner of St James' Park, 1946-56

Armitage Square   General Sir Clement Armitage, KCB, CMG, DSO, Commandant School of Artillery, 1926-9

Bell Road   General Sir William Bell, KCB, Colonel Commandant RHA, 1865-73

Biddulph Road   General Sir Robert Biddulph, GCB, GCMG, Master Gunner of St James' Park, 1914-18

Bingham Road   Major-General Hon Sir Francis Bingham, KCB, KCMG, Colonel Commandant RA, 1931-3

Block Road   Major-General A.J.C. Block, CB, CBE, DSO, Commandant School of Artillery, 1956-9

Brackenbury Road   General The Right Honourable Sir Henry Brackenbury, GCB, KCSI, DIrector General of Ordnance, 1896-9

Brind Road General Sir John Brind, KCB, KBE, CMG, DSO, Colonel Commandant RA, 1936-47

Cator Road General Sir William Cator, KCB, Colonel Commandant RHA, 1865-6

Cocks Close Colonel B. Cocks, GM, TD, Deputy Commandant School of Artillery, 1959-63

Colquhoun Road Major-General Sir Cyril Colquhoun, KCVO, CB, OBE, Commandant School of Artillery, 1951-3

Congreve Road Lieutenant-General Sir William Congreve Bart, Colonel Commandant RA, 1803-14

Douglas Brown Walk Major-General W.D.E. Brown, CB, CBE, DSO, Commandant School of Artillery, 1962-4

FitzGibbon Square Brigadier F. FitzGibbon, DSO, Commandant School of Artillery, 1939-42

Foster Walk Major-General P.B. Foster, MC, Commandant Royal School of Artillery, 1971-3

Gardiner Road General Sir Robert Gardiner, GCB, KCH, Master Gunner of St James' Park, 1840-64

Glover Road Major-General P.J. Glover, CB, OBE, Commandant School of Artillery, 1960-2

Gore Road Brigadier F.N.W. Gore, CBE, Deputy Commandant School of Artillery, 1950-2

Goodbody Road General Sir Richard Goodbody, GCB, KBE, DSO, Commandant School of Artillery, 1949-51

Graham Square Brigadier Lord D.M. Graham, CB, DSO, MC, Commandant School of Artillery, 1934-6

Heath Square Major-General G.W.E. Heath, CB, CBE, BSO, MC, Commandant School of Artillery, 1945-7

Howard-Vyse Road Lieutenant-General Sir Edward Howard-Vyse, KBE, CB, MC, Commandant School of Artillery, 1953-6

Lawrence Road Brigadier-General Sir Henry Lawrence, KCB. Died of wounds in Lucknow while Military Commander all Troops in Oudh, 1857

Lawson Road Lieutenant-General R. Lawson, Colonel Commandant RA, 1807-16

Lightfoot Road Colonel J.G. Lightfoot, CB, Bombay Horse Artillery. His name was included in the list of distinguished Artillerymen which was inscribed on the panels in the Cadets Library at the Royal Military Academy in 1902

Mears Road Brigadier G.G. Mears, CBE, DSO, MC, Commandant School of Artillery, 1947-9

McNeill Road Major-General J.M. McNeill, CB, CBE, Commandant School of Artillery, 1959-60

McQueen Walk Major-General K.J. McQueen, Commandant Royal School of Artillery, 1973-4

Milne Crescent Field Marshal The Lord Milne, GCB, GCMG, DSO, DCL, Master Gunner of St James' Park, 1926-46

Northen Terrace Brigadier J. Northen, MBE, Deputy Commandant School of Artillery, 1958-9

Power Road   General Sir William Power, KCB, KH, Colonel Commandant RA, 1856–63

Pownall Road   Lieutenant-General Sir Henry Pownall, KCB, KBE, DSO, MC, Commandant School of Artillery, 1936–8

Ross Road   Field Marshal Sir Hew Dalrymple Ross, GCB, Master Gunner of St James' Park, 1964–8 (the first Artillery Field Marshal)

Shrapnel Road   Lieutenant-General H. Shrapnel, inventor of the shrapnel case shot, Colonel Commandant RA, 1827–42

Stirling Road   Brigadier-General W. Stirling, CMG, DSO, Commandant School of Artillery, 1922–6

Strangways   Brigadier-General T. Fox Strangways, CRA in the Crimea, killed at Inkerman, 5 November 1854

Tombs Road   Major-General Sir Henry Tombs, VC, KCB, Regimental Colonel of Artillery, 1872–5

Towell Road   Brigadier R.H. Towell, CBE, MC, Commandant School of Artillery, 1942–5

Wason Road   Lieutenant-General Sidney Wason, CB, MC, Commandant School of Artillery, 1938–9

Watson Road   Lieutenant-Colonel Jonas Watson, Master Gunner of Whitehall and St James's Park, 1710–41

Wells Close   Brigadier G.C. Wells, CB, MC, TD

Wells Road   Deputy Commandant School of Artillery, 1952–4

Whinyates Road   General Sir Edward Whinyates, KCB, KH, Colonel Commandant RHA, 1864–5

Willoughby Road   Lieutenant G.D. Willougby, Bengal Artillery. Famous for blowing up the magazine at Delhi, 11 May 1857, on the outbreak of the Indian Mutiny

Wilson Road   Lieutenant-General Sir Wiltshire Wilson, KH, Colonel Commandant RA, 1828–42

Wood Road   Major-General Sir George Adam Wood, CB, KH, CRA at Waterloo 1815

APPENDIX XIII
PLANTATIONS BEARING COMMEMORATIVE NAMES

In recent years a large number of plantations have been established on the ranges and in the Garrison area, and many of these have been named to commemorate either some of those who have been connected with School or with a particular event. In this appendix the plantations which have been so named, are arranged in alphabetical order together with a note as to their origin and the grid reference (GR) of their location. In the case of those who served at the School, the rank shown is the highest attained and not necessarily that which was held whilst at Larkhill. The same principle has been followed in the case of honours and decorations.

Alanbrooke's Plantations: West, Centre, East Field Marshal The Viscount Alanbrooke, KG, GCB, OM, GCVO, DSO, Commandant, School of Artillery, 1929-32, Master Gunner of St James's Park, 1946-56. GRs: 108451, 113452, 119451

America Wood To commemorate Americans who have been posted to the School since 1939. GR: 036498

Anniversary Plantation To commemorate the 50th Anniversary of the School in 1970. Planted in the shape of the Roman numeral L (50). GR: 133468

Australia Wood To commemorate Australians who have been posted to the School since 1939. GR: 033499

Badley Copse Brigadier J.S. Badley, Commandant, Royal School of Artillery, 1974-6. GR: 082486

Brown's Trees Major-General W.D.E. Brown, CB, CBE, DSO, Commandant, School of Artillery, 1962-4. GR: 095481

Canada Wood To commemorate Canadians who have been posted to the School since 1939. GR: 084485

Corke's Copse Major C.E. Corke, MBE, RA, Range Liaison Officer, 1948-55. GR: 056465

Crane's Folly Major H.S. Crane, MBE, RA ('Daddy' Crane), Range Officer, 1924-36, Mess Secretary, 1936-49. GR: 112461

Cutt's Copse Major A.L.D. Cutt, RA, Assistant Range Liaison Officer, 1946-60. GR: 126451

Ellis Copse Brigadier R.S. Ellis, CBE, MC, Instructor in Gunnery, 1925-27. GR: 124471

Glover's Plantation Major-General P.J. Glover, CB, OBE, Commandant, Royal School of Artillery, 1960-2. GR: 070472

Goodman Trees Brigadier J.D.W. Goodman, Commandant, Royal School of Artillery, 1977-9. GR: 089468

Horton's Folly Major T. Horton, DSO, MC, DCM, RA, Range Officer, 1925-48. GR: 112455

Johnson's Folly Mr D.D. Johnson, Cartographic Draughtsman on the staff of the Defence Land Agent, Durrington since 1974. GR: 083490

Jones Coed Bach Brigadier D.M. Jones, Commandant, Royal School of Artillery, 1979-82. GR: 093473

Jubilee Copse To commemorate the Silver Jubilee of HM Queen Elizabeth II. GR: 133445

Longden's Trees Lieutenant-Colonel J. Longden, RA, Senior Instructor, 1950-3. GR: 033489

Mathew Triangles Colonel A.W. Mathew, Chief Instructor in Gunnery, 1964-7. GR: 065470

Myford Park Lieutenant-Colonel R. Myford, RA, Range Liaison Officer, 1976-80. GR: 088473

Newcome's Gorse Major-General H.W. Newcome, CB, CMG, DSO, First Commandant, School of Artillery, 1920-2. GR: 118496

Norton's Hide Lieutenant-Colonel G.W. Norton, RA, Range Liaison Officer, 1968-76. GR: 057498

Ohlenschlager's Folly　Brigadier R.N. Ohlenschlager, MBE, Commandant, Royal School of Artillery, 1976–7. GR: 139460

Prendergast Wood　Colonel E.D.V. Prendergast, MBE, DFC, Chief Instructor in Gunnery, 1967–70. GR: 095469

Price's Covert　Lieutenant-Colonel J.H. Price, RA, Senior Instructor, 1963–6. GR: 113479

Rowe's Plantation　Colonel G.C.K. Rowe, Deputy Commandant, 1974–5. GR: 085477

Sharp's Plantation　General Sir John Sharp, KCB, MC, ADC, Commandant, School of Artillery, 1964–6. GR: 046478

Stacey Plantation　Major W.R. Stacey, RA, Range Liaison Officer, 1955–73. GR: 063466

Streatfeild Plantation　Brigadier R.S. Streatfeild, MC, Commandant, School of Artillery, 1966–9. GR: 046474

Taylor's Clump　Major A.O. Taylor, RA, Assistant Range Liaison Officer, 1960–4. GR: 036489

Wainwright's Pipe　Major-General C.B. Wainwright, CB, Instructor in Gunnery, 1930–32 and 1935–8. GR: 125467

Walker's Gorse　Major J.B. Walker, DSO, RA. Instructor in Gunnery, 1920–4. GR: 107502

Walker's Wood　Major H. Walker, RA, Assistant Range Liaison Officer, 1970–2. GR: 092478

Walton's Wood　Lieutenant-Colonel T. Walton, MBE, RA, Range Liaison Officer, 1960–8. GR: 044487

APPENDIX XIV
PLANTATIONS GROWING ON THE
LARKHILL AND WEST DOWN RANGES IN 1903

The following information is based on an Ordnance Survey map surveyed in 1872–84 and published in 1903 to a scale of 2 inches to 1 mile (1:31,680) and entitled *War Department Lands and Salisbury Plain* and on a map produced under the direction of the Director of Military Survey, published in 1980 to a scale of 1:25,000 (series GSGS 5294). New Copse is shown on a larger map of the same scale which was also surveyed in 1872–84 but not published until 1906.

Name on 1903 map	Grid reference	Information on 1980 map
Larkhill Range		
Alton Clump	126462	Marked but not named
Blackball Firs	097473	Marked and named
Box Iron	097482	Marked and named

Name on 1903 map	Grid reference	Information on 1980 map
Charlton Clumps (5 shown on map)	—	None shown on range
Fox Covert	084541	Shown as part of Scraggy Copse
Fox Covert	077508	Marked but not named
Fox Covert	110492	Shown as Enford Penning
Goods Clump	092466	Marked and named
Little Folly	091476	Marked and named
Old Farm Clump	102483	Marked and named
Robin Hood Ball (originally Robin Wood Ball)	107463	Marked and named Robin Hood Ball Clump
Round Acre	102538	Named but not marked
Round Covert	128472	Marked and named
Shrewton Folly	094484	Marked and named
Stone	091475	Marked but not named
Warren Plantation	099463	Marked and named
Wexland Hanging (originally Waxland)	116482	Marked and named
Wood's Butt	110463	Marked and named
West Down Range Barrow Plantation	060495	Marked and named
Downbarn Plantation	084470	Marked and named
East Down Plantation	056409	Marked and named
Gillum's Clump (marked but not named)	046537	Marked and named
Halfmoon Copse	075473	Marked and named
The Kernel (marked but not named)	059479	Marked and named
Long Plantation	060476	Marked and named
New Copse	027504	Marked and named
New Plantation	041557	Marked and named
Nut Park	056478	Marked and named
Old Plantation	051542	Marked and named

Name on 1903 map	Grid reference	Information on 1980 map
The Round O	061482	Marked and named
Urchfont Clump	054549	Marked but named Crate Wood
Warren Down Plantation	047518	Marked but not named
Weatherhill Plantation	054537	Named but not marked
West Down Plantation	050492	Marked and named
Witcombe Plantation	048542	Named but not marked
Young Plantation	066482	Marked and named

APPENDIX XV
FARMS EXTINGUISHED BY THE FORMATION
OF THE LARKHILL AND WEST DOWN RANGES

The following information is based on an Ordnance Survey map surveyed in 1872–84 and published in 1903 to a scale of 2 inches to 1 mile (1:31,680) and entitled *War Department Lands on Salisbury Plain* and on a map produced under the direction of the Director of Military Survey, published in 1980 to a scale of 1:25,000 (series GSGS 5294). Sloper's Farm is shown on a larger map of the same scale which was also surveyed in 1872–84 but not published until 1906.

Name on 1903 map	Grid reference	Information on 1980 map
Larkhill Range		
Compton Bake	099504	Site marked
Conock Hill Farm	065539	Site named
Enford Bake Farm	096492	—
Netheravon Bake	112466	Site named
Newfoundland Farm	107479	Site shown as Newfoundland Farm Wood
Rushall Down Farm	080504	—
Slay Down Farm	091503	—
Wexland Bake	111473	—
Wilsford Down Farm	074523	Site marked

Name on 1903 map	Grid reference	Information on 1980 map
West Down Range		
Candown Farm	043505	—
East Down Farm	054493	Site named
Eastcott Hill Farm	034543	Site named
Easterton Down Farm	063519	—
Easterton Hill Farm	038531	—
Fiddington Farm	034529	Site marked
Greenland Farm	068470	Site marked
Keeper's Farm	058473	Site named
Little Farm	029533	Site named
New Farm	034518	Site marked as 'The Octagon'
New Copse Farm	030502	Site marked
Phillpot's Farm	033521	—
Pond Farm	043525	—
Prospect Farm	074491	Site marked as 'Prospect Clump'
Sloper's Farm	022522	Site marked
Urchfont Hill Farm	051550	—

APPENDIX XVI
MASTERS, THE ROYAL ARTILLERY HARRIERS AND THE ROYAL ARTILLERY HUNT, 1907–82

THE ROYAL ARTILLERY HARRIERS

1907	Maj. J.G. Geddes
1908	Maj. G. Gillson
1909	Maj. E.S. Mairne
1910	Capt. C.L. Popham
1912	Capt. A.P. Heneage
1913	Maj. A.B. Bethell
1916	Capt. A.E. Hussey
1917–19	—
1919	Maj. R.G. Cherry, MC
1920	Capt. Sir Colin Jardine, Bart, DSO, MC
1924	Maj. C.E. Walker, DSO
1925	Maj. W. Scott Watson, MC

1928   Maj. C.P.J. Layard, MC
1933   Maj. W. Scott Watson, MC
1938   Maj. A. Drew
1939   Col. J.S.W. Galbraith

THE ROYAL ARTILLERY HUNT

1942   Lieut.-Col. Dean
1943   Maj. S.R. Edmunds
1944   Brig. J.H. Gibbon, DSO
1947   Lieut.-Col. L.H.O. Pugh, DSO
1948   Maj. J.M. Douglas
1950   Lieut.-Col. H.C.R. Gillman, MBE
1954   Maj. F.B. Edmeades, MC
1957   Maj. P.D.E. Riall
1961   Lieut.-Col. F.B. Edmeades, MC
1970   Lieut.-Col. F.B. Edmeades, MC   } Joint Masters
            Lieut.-Col. P.R. Heaton Ellis, OBE
1971   Lieut.-Col. P.R. Heaton-Ellis, OBE
1978   Maj. G.D.B. Thatcher

APPENDIX XVII
SOME NOTABLE EVENTS IN THE HISTORY OF
THE ROYAL SCHOOL OF ARTILLERY

This appendix does not include any events which relate solely to the Wings as these will be found in Chapter 9.

1897   Purchase of the first area of land for the ranges
1899   First practice camp held
1902   North and South Camps established on West Down for two cavalry brigades
1907   Royal Artillery Harriers formed
1910   The hangars which now adjoin Wood Road, built by the British and Colonial Aircraft Co. Ltd, Bristol, which later became The Bristol Aeroplane Co.
1912   Capt. E.B. Lorraine and S/Sgt. R.H.V. Wilson killed in a flying accident near Airman's Cross
1913   Maj. A.W. Hewetson, RFA, killed when his aircraft crashed on the airfield at Larkhill
1914   Erection of hutted camps began at Larkhill.
            Construction of the Larkhill Military Railway started
1915   School of Instruction for Royal Horse and Royal Field Artillery established at Larkhill
1916   No. 1 Balloon School, Royal Flying Corps, formed at Rollestone Camp and balloon hangars built

1919	Amalgamation of the Chapperton Down Artillery School, the Heavy Artillery Training Centre and the School of Instruction for Royal Horse and Royal Field Artillery immediately prior to the formation of the School of Artillery
1920	School of Artillery established
1921	Seige Artillery School, Lydd, moved to Larkhill and became part of the School of Artillery
1926	First Young Officer's Course held
1928	Larkhill Military Railway no longer in operation
1929	Improvements carried out to the Packway and trees planted on either side of it
1930-1	Hunter Trial Course laid out on Alton Down
1938	Garrison Church dedicated (21 May). Packway Mess opened. New Warrant Officers' and Sergeants' Mess opened
1941	Visit to HM King George VI and HM Queen Elizabeth (3 April). RA Mess formally opened
1942	RA Harriers became RA Hunt (Foxhounds)
1947	First race meeting held on the point-to-point course on Knighton Down (23 April)
1953	HM The Queen and HRH The Duke of Edinburgh attended the United Services Point-to-Point at Larkhill (21 February)
1958	HRH The Duke of Gloucester visited the School (8 January). HRH The Princess Royal visited the School (9 January)
1960	Foundation Stone of the new School buildings laid by Field Marshal Viscount Alanbrooke (27 September)
1961	The School adopted the badge of the Crown and Crossed Guns
1962	First Larkhill Day held
1966	The new school buildings officially opened by the Master Gunner, General Sir Robert Mansergh (6 October)
1968	The Roman Catholic Church dedicated (22 September)
1970	50th Anniversary of the formation of the School. First Artillery Day held which replaced Larkhill Day
1971	Amalgamation of the School of Artillery, Larkhill, with the School of Artillery, Manorbier, which then moved to Larkhill. HM The Queen granted the prefix of 'Royal' to the School (1 January). Visit of HRH The Duchess of Kent (6 May). The Wiltshire County Council granted the School the privilege of using the County Badge
1973	Visit to HM The Queen (3 April)
1974	The Close ('Bombard') OP built
1979	Visit of HRH The Prince of Wales (25 May)
1982	Formation of the Support Regiment, Royal School of Artillery

Index

The following points should be noted when using this Index. The names of many of the roads in the Garrison area and of a number of features on the ranges have been omitted. In general, the names of guns, vehicles and other equipment have not been included nor have the lists of names which appear under the Wings in Chapter 9. The Index does not cover the References or the Appendices and in some cases the initials 'RA' have been used in place of the words 'Royal Artillery'.

Absolon, WO2 S.J., 223
Adam, Gen. Sir Ronald, 80
Aerodromes,
    Lake Down, 36, 43
    Larkhill, 24-5, 30, 35
    Royal Naval, 36, 43
    Stonehenge, 36, 39, 43
Air Battalion RE, *see* Royal Engineers
Airborne Division, 6th, 83
Aircraft,
    Auster, 113
    Bristol Boxkite, 26
    Bristol Sociable, 28
    Farman biplane, 24
    Nieuport monoplane, 27
Airman's Cross or Corner, 27
Air OPs, 81, 85-6, 113, 171
Alanbrooke, FM Viscount, 62, 68,
        80, 82, 92, 102, 103-4, 106,
        192, 195, 197, 202, 227-8
Aldershot, 2, 20, 21, 26
Alexander, FM Viscount, 81
Allen, Bdr, P., 232
Allen, Capt. W., 219
Allied Command Europe (AMF), 124
Allis, Percy, 160
Almaza, 87, 91
Amesbury, 32, 39, 45, 59, 78, 176,
        185
'Anderson Sahib', 61
Anti-Tank,
    Compound, 40, 50, 119
    ranges, *see* Ranges
Ark, The, 63

Armitage, Gen. Sir Clement, 65, 102
Armstrong, Maj. B.H.O., 31
    huts, 32
Army Air Corps Centre, 216
    Cadet Force, 190, 207
    Council, 18, 31
    Education Centre, 222
    Group, 21st, 87, 88, 220
    Territorial Service (ATS), 78-9
Artillery Days, *see* Demonstrations
Artillery Training, Vol. II, 108
Assistant Instructor in Gunnery
        (AIG), 126
Atkinson, Rev. Col. R., 203
Australian Forces, 94, 215
Automatic Data Processing, 220

Badge of the School, 105, 118
Badley, Brig. J.S., 211
    Library, 211-12
Bagnall, Brig. J.G., 116
Bailey, Brig.-Gen. M.C., 120
Baker, FM Sir Geoffrey, 112, 120,
        121
Baker, WO2 (AIG) H.E., 231
Baker, Lt.-Col. R.S., 160
Balloons, 20-24, 26
Bands, 112, 219
    RA Alanbrooke, 111, 219
    RA Larkhill, 111, 114, 219
    RA Mounted, 120, 190, 219
    RA Portsmouth, 111, 219
Barbara Games and Gun, 227

Barber, Horatio, 24, 30
Barham, Rev. R.H.D., 177
Barracks,
    Alanbrooke, 59, 102, 189
    Bulford 'huts', 9
    Horne, 189, 219
    North, 59, 62
    Roberts, 14, 19, 35, 59, 107,
        189, 190, 191, 218
    Stirling, 146, 189
Bartholomew, Gen. Sir Wm., 94
Batchelor, Bdr. J., 233
Batteries
    G (Mercer's Troop), 95
    1 (The Blazer), 216, 232
    1 Warwickshire, 184
    54 RFA, 46
    65 (How) RFA, 24
    66 (How) RFA, 28
    104 RFA, 9
    131 RFA, 10
    878 RFA, 163
    6 Field, 168, 169
    22 Field, 168
    27 Field, 114
    39 Field, 168
    40 Field, 66
    50 Field, 168
    74 Field, 168
    96 Field, 168
    132 Field, 216, 232, 233
    176 Field, 216, 232
    271 Field, 187
    170 Light, 96
    18 Medium, 71
    236 Medium, 187
    1 Survey, 73
    192 Ind. Survey, 92-3, 104, 141
    22 Locating, 107, 117, 190, 191,
        211, 218, 232
    160 (Middleton's Coy), 107
    1 RA Practice Camp, 169
    2 RA Practice Camp, 169
    Hamilton, 35, 50, 51, 119
Battle of the Somme (film), 52
Battlefield Artillery Target Engage-
    ment System (BATES),
    126, 220
Bazeley, Maj. H.C., 129
Beagles, see Hunting
Belger, Sgt., 67

Belton Park, 31
Bennett, Bdr. D.R., 231
Bennett, Col. F.V., 65
Bennett, Maj. H.G., 171, 172
Benson, Lt.-Col. G.E., 146
Benson Prize, 146
Bingham, Col. the Hon. F.R., 18,
    186
Blackball Firs, 162, 175
Blackdown, 31
Blakenham, Viscount, 100
Blake, Gnr. K., 233
Blane, Capt. C.F., 195
Blears, Sgt. J.C., 233
Block, Maj.-Gen. A.J.C., 101, 153
Boer War, 11, 13, 20, 21, 42, 63, 226
Bombard OP, see Close OP
Böthling, Oberstleutnant J.W.K.,
    215
Botto, Craftsman, C.J., 233
Bowley, Bdr. R., 233
Bradbury, Gnr. M., 233
Brake, Brig.-Gen. H.E.J., 55
Bray, Lt.-Gen. Sir Robert, 107
Brayley, Col. Sir Desmond, 199
Brick road surfaces, 63
Brigades
    8th (How) RFA, 24, 28
    2nd Field, 215
    6th Field, 168, 215
    12th Field, 168
    19th Field, 168
    24th Field, 168
    25th Field, 215
    26th Field, 66, 215
    6th Medium, 191
    3rd South Midland, 184-5
    4th South Midland, 182-3
    68th South Midland, 187
    3rd West Lancashire, 184
    59th (4th West Lancashire)
        Medium, 187
Bristol Aeroplane Co., 25
Bristol Flying School, 25, 26, 30
British Aircraft Corporation, 25,
    and Colonial Aircraft Co., 24, 109
    Army of the Rhine, 92, 122, 164
    Expeditionary Forces, 52, 62,
        73, 75, 77, 164
Brooke, Brig. A.F., see Alanbrooke,
    FM Viscount

Brooke-Popham, ACM Sir Robert, 29
Browell, Col. J.M., 50
Browell, Brig.-Gen. W.B., 50
Brown, Capt. A.V., 166
Brown, Lt.-Col. Tod, 4
Brown, Maj.-Gen. W.D.E., 68, 107
Browning, Lt.-Gen. F.M., 83
Brunker, Gen., 52
Buckley, WO1 (RSM) W.A., 123
Bulford, 9, 24, 33, 42, 87, 197, 208,
    224
Bunty's Folly, 177–8
Burnett-Stuart, Gen. Sir John, 65,
    68, 202, 203
Burnyeats, Lt. H.P., 195
Bushell, Cpl. S.D., 233
Burroughs, BSM (IG), 131
Bustard, Great, 180
    Inn, 7, 13, 16, 159

Cadets, see Army Cadet Force
Calibration,
    Screen, 163–4
    Troops, Nos 1 to 5, 164
Cambridge, Duke of, 2
Campbell, J.C.M., 201
Campbell-Bannerman, Sir Henry, 12
Camps,
    Bustard, 14, 16
    Durrington, 14, 17
    Fargo, 14, 16, 17, 31, 45, 185
    Fargo Hutted, 85
    Hamilton, 16, 17, 31
    Larkhill, 14, 17, 18, 19, 55–6
    Pond Farm, 14, 16
    Rollestone, 7, 14, 16, 17, 31, 36,
        61, 68, 123, 173, 184, 223
    RFA Practice, 13
    West Down, 13, 46
        North, 13, 17, 45–6
        South, 13, 17
Canadian Forces, 37, 45, 54, 85–6,
    94, 169
    School of Artillery, Shilo, 86, 107
    IGs, 85, 94, 214
Casey, R.G., 82
Cashmore, BSM (IG), 131
Catterick, 31, 75, 96
Cavalry at West Down, 13
    polo ground, 160

Cecil, Gnr. D., 233
Central Flying School, 26
Chalons-sur-Marne Artillery School,
    107, 232
Chapman, Lt.-Col. G.P., 139
Chapperton Down, 58, 163
    Artillery School, see Schools
Chateaudun, 87
Cherwell, Lord, 82
Chilcot, F., 171
Chivers, A., 103
Chivers, E., 39
Chivers & Sons, Messrs W.E., 39,
    42–3, 51, 103–4, 108
Churches,
    Garrison, 13, 35, 40, 41, 54, 98,
        189, 190, 204
        Anniversary service, 114, 116
        Dedication, 203
        Flags, 204
        Foundation stone, 65, 202
        School collect, 205
        Windows, 105, 204, 205
    Roman Catholic, 190
        Dedication, 205
        Foundation stone, 205
        Old church, 205
Churchill, Mrs Odette, see Hallowes,
    Mrs
Churchill, Sir Winston, 82, 204, 232
Clarke, WO2 (AIG) E.R., 231
Clarke, Lt. P.T.N., 66, 68, 70
Clarke, W.S.H. ('Nobby'), 201
Cleeve, Lt.-Col. S.M., 75
Clewell, Maj. R.M., 214
Close OP, 122–3, 179
Cockburn, G.B., 24, 30
Cocks, Col. B., 170, 171, 203
Collin, Maj.-Gen. G. de E., 114, 117,
    122, 232
Collingwood, Brig. S., 81
Colquhoun, Gen. Sir Cyril, 98
Combined Cadet Force, 12
Commander RA (South), 220
Communications, battery, 11
Congreve, Sir Wm (the elder), 5
Connaught, HRH Duke of, 193
Conservation, 178–80
Cooper, Capt. F.A.L., 199
Coronation of HM Queen Elizabeth II,
    98, 124

Corps, XII, 87
Coulloumme-Labarth, Gen., 232
County badge, grant of, 118, 119
Couper, Lt. J.M., 48
Couper, Maj. T.F., 48
Craigie, Maj. A.J., 233
Crane, Maj. H.S. ('Daddy'), 166, 199
Crisp, Gnr. S., 233
Curtis, I.E., 201

Darlington, Lt.-Col. I.G., 215
Dartmoor, 2–4
Defence Land Agent, 159, 178, 190, 224
de Gaulle, Gen. C.A.J.M., 232
Delahaye, Lt.-Col. J.V., 74
Demonstrations and exercises
    'Ambassador', 98, 100, 229
    Artillery Days, 105, 112-3, 165, 199, 229, 231
    'Avon Express', 124, 165, 231
    Joint Services, 104, 105, 106, 165
    Larkhill Days, 98, 105, 106, 107, 112-13, 165, 229-31
    'Scapa', 229
    Staff College, 161
    'Ubique', 91–2
    'Young Ambassador', 98, 100, 106, 229
Denbigh, Earl of, 12
Deolali, 87, 91
Dept of the Environment, 190, 226
Depot Brigade/Regiment, 215
de Vallett, Lt.-Col. M., 215
Directors of Music, 219
Director RA, 211, 212, 220
Dorset Imperial Yeomanry, 12
Dowell, S/Sgt. S., 231
Drones, 117, 165
Drought, Col. G.E., 169
Drought's Flagstaff, 169
Druid's Lodge, 36-7, 39, 40, 166
Drummer Jones, 176-7
Duke of Edinburgh's Own Gurkha Rifles, 233

Eardley-Wilmot, Maj.-Gen.F., 2, 4
Earle, Brig. E., 80

Eboli, 87
Edinburgh, HRH Duke of, 98
Edmeades, Lt.-Col. F.B., 114
Edwards, Lionel, 197
Edwards, R.W., 199
Eisenhower, Gen. D.D., 232
Ell Barrow, 175
Ellershaw, Lt.-Col. W., 47
Etherington, Maj. J.L., 85
Eugster, Gen. Sir Basil, 118
Evans, Capt. G.E., 219
Evelyn, John, 7
Excellent, HMS, see Royal Navy
Exercises, see Demonstrations

Fairclough, Col. J., 106
Falklands campaign, 232-3
Fallon, Maj. M.H., 233
Family, Housing and Welfare Service, 206
Fargo
    Ammunition Depot, 16, 23, 36, 85
    camp, see Camps
    military hospital, 23, 36, 39, 45
    plantation, 14, 28, 36, 39, 43
Farnborough, 25, 26, 29
Figheldean House, 91
Fildes, Denis, 195
Firbank, Messrs J.T., 32
Fishing, 210
FitzGibbon, Brig. F., 46, 74, 81, 82, 161
Flags, 232
    School flag, 118, 232
    in Garrison Church, 204
Flower show, Garrison, 206
Flying at Larkhill, see Larkhill
Forbes, W.A., 195
Ford, Mrs G.G., 59, 60
Forestry, 178
Fort Sill, 107, 204, 232
Foster, Maj.-Gen. P.B., 121, 122
Foster, Mrs P.B., 119
Fournier, Chef d'Escadron B., 232

Fox-Strangways, Brig.-Gen. T.,
    62
Freeman, Lt.-Col. G.G., 207
French Army, The, 2, 20, 71,
    107, 232
    Liaison Officers, 213, 215
Fulton, Capt. J.D.B., 24, 26,
    28, 30

Gale, Gen. Sir Richard, 83
Games and recreations, 100,
    106, 110, 116, 171,
    208
Garrison, *see* Larkhill
Geddes, Maj. J.G., 208
Gee, Col. E.E., 131
Gell, Maj. P.M., 174
German Army, 107, 124
    Liaison Officers, 213, 215
Germany, 164, 219
Gibson, L/Bdr. A., 233
Gillett, Maj.-Gen. Sir Peter,
    160-1
Girls Venture Corps, 208
Gladstone, Capt. G.V., 227-8
Gloucester, HRH Duke of, 101
Glover, Maj.-Gen. P.J., 116
Golf course, 160
Gorton, Rt. Hon. T., 118
Gould, John ('Taffy'), 160
Graham, Brig. Lord Malise,
    67, 102, 160
Greene, Maj. W., 145
Greenlands Farm and camp,
    16, 45, 49, 50, 65,
    164, 166-8, 171-2,
    173, 192
Greig, Lt.-Col. R.B., 199
Greyson Brothers, The, 197
Gridded oblique photographs,
    84
Grimm, Oberstleutnant G., 215
Guides, *see* Scouts
Guild of St Helena, 204, 207
Gun Club, The, 123, 189
Gunn, James, 195
Gunner, 60
Gunner, The, 65
Gunner's ABC, The, 15
Gunnery Staff, 214
Guy, Lt.-Col. J.R., 111, 134

Haining, Gen. Sir Robert, 161
Haldane, Viscount, 12, 181
Hallowes, Mrs Odette, 94
Hamilton, Gen. Sir Ian, 50
Hamilton battery, *see* Batteries
Hamwell, Capt. J., 195
Harding, FM Lord, 93-4, 99
Harris, Maj. D.J., 114
Harrison, Lt.-Col. W.R.E., 160
Hay, Maj.-Gen. E.O., 8
Headlam, Maj.-Gen. Sir John, 9
Heath, Maj.-Gen. G.W.E., 102,
    160, 208
Heaton-Ellis, Lt.-Col. P.R., 122
Heavy Air Defence Compound,
    40, 50, 119
Heavy Artillery Gunnery
    School, *see* Schools
Henderson, L/Bdr. K., 233
Hewetson, Maj. A.W., 28, 63
Hicks, Capt. B.E., 219
Hicks, Capt. W.A., 131
Hill, Brig, T.W.R., 169
Hilton, Col. R., 81, 129
History of Gunnery Wing, A,
    134
Hoare, Sir Richard, 175, 176
Hobday, Col. E.A., 15
Holiday, Gilbert, 197
Honourable Artillery Company,
    12, 181-2
Horton, Maj. T.F. ('Tom'),
    166, 169, 171
Howard-Vyse, Lt.-Gen. Sir
    Edward, 102, 201
Hull, FM Sir Richard, 100
Hulse, Capt. A.E., 208
Hunter Trials, 110, 160, 208,
    209
Hunting,
    Larkhill Beagles, 209, 210
    RA Hunt, 208
Hussey, Capt. A.E., 208

Idar Oberstein, 107
Indian Army, 77
    officers to RA, 92
Ingoldsby Legends, The, 177
Ironside, Gen. Sir Edmund,
    74, 82
Ismay, Lord, 82

Italian Army demonstration,
      101

Jackson, L/Bdr. J., 233
Jackson, Sir John, 32
Jeffreys, Lt.-Col. H.B., 10
Johnson, President L.B., 232
Jones, WO2 C.S., 232

Kadir Cup, The, 195
Kemp-Welch, Miss Lucy, 195,
      197
Kennedy, Maj. J.W., 171
Kenny, Capt. T.A., 219
Kent, HRH Duchess of, 118
'Kilbary', 195
King, HM,
   George V, 37, 38, 45
   George VI, 81-2, 96, 195
King's Cup, HM The, 187
King's Prize, HM The, 185,
      187
King's Troop, RHA, The, 71
Kitchener, FM Lord, 32, 38,
      45
Knowles, G., 82

Lancashire Field Artillery, 181
Land classification, see
      Schedule lands
Lansdowne, Marquis of, 8
Larkhill,
   acquisitions, 5, 6, 7, 8
   balloons at, 20-4, 26, 68
   Dramatic Society, 207
   flying at, 24-6, 28, 29, 30,
      35
   Garrison, 59-63, 98, 102-4,
      107, 189-210
   military railway, 30, 32-40,
      52
   OCTU, 73, 74-5
   Royal School of Artillery,
      see Schools
   Royal visits, 81-2, 101,
      118, 120-2, 125
   School of Artillery, see
      Schools

School of Instruction,
      see Schools
Larkhill Days, see Demonstra-
      tions
Latham, Col. H.B., 136
Lawrence, Maj. P.J., 215
Learey, Sgt. D.P., 233
Library, see Badley
Lindsay, Col. W.F.L., 13
Lindsell, Lt.-Gen. Sir Wilfrid,
      94
Lines
   Dickson, 59
   Newcome, 72
   North, 59
   Roberts, 59
   Stirling, 59
Little, Maj. J.E., 210
Locomotive 'Queen Mary',
      37-8, 68
Lomax, S/Sgt (AC) H, 231
Longmoor, 31
Loraine, Capt. E.B.,
Lund, Lt.-Gen. Sir Otto, 78,
      80
Lydd, 5, 6, 56

Macleod, Maj. R.E., 61
McCoy, M., 199
McCrae, Col. John, 53
MacKay, Capt. D.H., 219
McKeever, Sgt. A., 231
McMahon, S/Sgt. P., 233
Manorbier, see Schools
Mansergh, Gen. Sir Robert,
      112
Maps,
   Andrew, J. and Drury, A.,
      175
   Cary, J., 175
   Ordnance Survey, 7, 12, 14,
      19, 39, 40, 49, 68,
      160, 175-6, 190,
      205
   Speed, John, 175
Marshall, Gen. George, 82
Marshall, Maj.-Gen. G.H., 8
Martin, Sgt. F.C., 232
Mason, Brig. B.G., 52
Matchan, J., 176-7

Mears, Brig. G.G., 102, 116
Mechanisation, 71
Medical and Dental Care, 190
Messes
    'A' Mess, 53, 108-9, 190-1
    'B' Mess, 191
    'C' Mess, 191
    Greenlands Farm, 192
    Packway, 19, 64, 85, 190,
        191
    RA, 13, 35, 38, 59, 108,
        160, 189, 190,
        193-201
        construction of, 64,
            191-2
        Mess Secretaries, 199
        Mess Staff, 199, 201
        pictures, 68, 101, 114,
            122, 195, 199
        silver, 118, 193-5
        special events, 86, 88,
            89, 92, 112, 113, 120,
            124, 125, 193
    RA - The Packway, 191
    Survey Company, 191
    Warrant Officers and
        Sergeants, 64, 108,
        113, 192-3, 201-2
    West Down Camp, 192
Meteorological office, 223-4
Michel, J.D., 32
Middle Wallop, 90
Military Lands Act, 1892, 8
Military Traction Engines and
    Lorries, 1858-1918,
    42
Militia (1939), 72, 181
Milne, FM Lord, 86, 88, 195
Ministry of Defence, 159, 179,
    211, 218, 220, 222,
    223
    Conservation Groups, 179
Mitchell Hill Trophy, 171
Montgomery, FM Viscount,
    88, 94

Napoleon Bonaparte, 20
National Artillery Association,
    4, 185-8
National Servicemen, 95

Navy, Army and Air Force
    Institutes (NAAFI),
    107, 108, 123, 171,
    189, 190
Neil, L/Bdr. A., 233
Neill, The Ven. Archdeacon
    I.D., 105, 203
Netheravon, 8, 9, 30, 160, 176
Newcome, Maj.-Gen. H.W.,
    48, 50, 60, 61, 106,
    116
Newcome, Maj. J., 116
Newcome's Gorse, 177
Newcome Hall, The, 108, 114,
    118, 120
Newfoundland Farm, 9, 166
Newton Tony, 32
Nicholson, Sir Cameron, 100
Nicholson, WO M., 231
Norman, Lt.-Col. P., 120
Norrie, Orlando, 101, 195
North Atlantic Treaty Organi-
    sation (NATO), 124

O'Connor, Lt.-Gen. Sir Denis,
    112, 114
Officer Cadet Training Unit
    (OCTU), 73, 74-5
Officer Training Corps, 12
Okehampton, see Practice
    camps
Oldfield, Maj. R., 64
Ordnance Survey, see Maps
Otterburn, 164
'Overlord', Operation, 83, 87
Overseas Artillery School, see
    Schools
Owen, Gen. Sir John, 5
Owen, Lt.-Col. W.A., 131

Packhorse Inn, 190, 207
Packway, The, 12, 13, 14, 16, 35-6,
    39, 40, 42, 54, 61, 63,
    74, 189, 205
Packway Hall, 206-7
Paget, Gen. Sir Bernard, 82
Pasquier, Lt.-Col. J., 215
Parsons, Lt.-Gen. Sir Lawrence, 10,
    12, 150

Parsons, Maj. C.G., 118, 120
Pauls, HE Rolf. F., 124
Payne, C.J., *see* 'Snaffles'
Paynter, Lt. W.D., 195
Perceval, Col. C.P.W., 73
Phillips, Capt. Mark, 209
Phipps-Hornby, VC, Brig.-Gen. E.J., 11
Photographic Research Branch, 88
Pickard, Maj. E.C., 92
Pierret, Maj. C.P.F., 78, 131
Piggot, Lt.-Col. H.L., 62, 190
Pinkney, Maj. A.R., 114, 219
Plain Talk, 117–18
Point-to-point course, 93, 94, 97, 98, 110, 114, 120, 122, 199, 208–9
Police,
    Ministry of Defence, 190, 224, 226
    County, 190
Polo ground, 160
'Pom-pom' guns, 13
Power, H. Septimus, 199
Practice camps, 1–6, 10, 11, 52, 169
    Ad Fines (Redesdale), 5, 181, 188
    Buddon, 187
    Glen Imaal, 5, 22
    Lydd, 5, 6, 183
    Okehampton, 3, 4, 5, 10, 18, 181, 183, 188
    Pembrey, 183
    Trawsfynydd, 5. 181, 188
Pratt, Maj.-Gen. F.W.H. ('Ambrose'), 70, 139, 145, 146
Pratt, WO2 (BSM) H.W., 231
Pratt, WO2 (CSM), W.G., 231
Primary School, Larkhill, 190, 206
Prince of Wales, HRH, 125, 185, 193
Princess Anne, HRH, Mrs Mark Phillips, 209
Princess Royal, HRH, 101, 195
Profumo, Rt. Hon. J., 107
Proof and Experimental Establishment, 173, 214, 222, 232
Property Services Agency, 159, 178
Publications, 86, 99
Pugh, Capt. G.M., 233
Purey-Cust, Maj. R.B., 166

Queen, HM,
    Elizabeth II, 98, 120–2, 193, 195, 199
    Elizabeth, The Queen Mother, 81–2
    Mary, 37
    Victoria, 185
Queen's Cup. The, 187
Queen's Prize, The, 185
Quick barrage, 81

Radnotti, Maj. D.L., 215
Railway mounted howitzers, 87, 166
Railways,
    Amesbury & Military Camp Light, 32
    Larkhill Military, 30, 32– 40, 52
    London & South Western, 32, 33
Ramus, Lt.-Col. P. de N., 169
Range detachments, 52, 65, 75, 87, 104, 168–73, 216
Range Liaison Officers, 172, 213
Ranges,
    Anti-Tank, 125, 162–3
    Conservation areas, 178–9
    Deployment areas, 160
    Imber, 170, 171
    Impact areas, 159
    Larkhill, 7, 8, 12–14, 16, 18–19, 22, 52, 64, 87, 125
    Miniature, 125–6
    West Down, 5, 6, 7, 8, 9, 11, 12–14, 16, 18–19, 73, 87
Redhorn Hill, 7, 12, 13, 16, 159
Regiments,
    5th RHA, 95, 191, 210
    2nd Field, 113, 199, 215
    6th Field, 215
    12th Field, 169
    25th Field, 215
    26th Field, 215
    39th Field, 216
    49th Field, 114
    124th Field, 209
    18th Medium, 215, 228–9
    12th Air Defence, 233
    47th Guided Weapons, 100
    1st Survey, 73, 218
    2nd Survey, 218

40th Survey Training, 73, 79
4th RA Training, 91
Maritime Regiment, 226
Support Regiment, RSA, 190,
191, 211, 215–216
Regiments, Composition of, 102
Renton, Capt. F.A., 219
Reprographics, see Schools, Royal
School of Artillery
Rhyl, 31
Richards, Brig. J.H.W.G., 62, 63, 199
Roberts, VC, FM Lord, 45
Roberts Memorial Prize, 146
Robertson, Maj. F.M., 199
Robertson, Sgt. E.C., 231
Robin Hood Ball, 174–6
Rollestone, 7, 12, 14, 16, 23
artillery range, 16
balloon hangars, 22, 23, 209
camp, see Camps
Rolls, Hon. C.S., 24
Rowell, Drv., 58
Royal Aircraft Establishment, 94,
104, 173, 222–3, 232
Royal Aircraft Factory, 20
Royal Air Force, 23, 24, 105, 123,
125, 173, 201
balloon centre, 23
No. 3 (Fighter) Squadron, 29
Royal Armaments Research and
Development Establishment
(RARDE), 99, 173
Royal Army Dental Corps, 206
Royal Army Medical Corps, 206
Royal Army Ordnance Corps, 25,
173
Royal Artillery,
Gold Cup, 195
Guided Weapons Range, 101
Gunnery Training Establishment,
122, 214
Hunt, see Hunting
Hunt Pony Club, 209
Liaison Officers, 226
Mess, see Messes
Saddle Club, 91, 109, 208, 209
Sales Demonstration Team, 213,
216, 218
School of Survey, see Schools
Target Operation Group, 173,
223

Work Study Group, 107
Royal Corps of Signals, 96
Royal Electrical and Mechanical
Engineers, 98, 108, 114,
204, 232
Royal Engineers, 55, 173
Air Battalion, 20, 21, 22, 26, 27,
28, 30, 35, 37
Balloon Company, 26
Commander, RE, 63, 191, 226
Royal Flying Corps, 22, 23, 26, 28,
29, 30, 43
Royal Marines, 55, 61, 86, 105
Royal Marine Artillery, 226
Royal Military Academy,
Sandhurst, 146
Woolwich, 1, 75, 144–5
Royal Naval Air Service, 36, 43
Royal Navy, 165, 176, 201, 226–9
HMS Dryad, 227
HMS Excellent, 79, 105, 226–7
HMS Powerful, 226
HMS Vanguard, 227–9
Royal School of Artillery, see
Schools
Royal Visits, see Larkhill
Ross, W., 203
Ryan, Brig. D.F., 39, 210
Ryan, Gnr. M., 233

Saddle Club, see Royal Artillery
Safety officers, 66
St Alban, 203
St Anthony, 205
St Barbara, 105, 203, 205
St Elegius, 204
Salisbury Plain, 1, 2, 5, 7, 11, 54
Salvation Army, 40
Schedule lands, I, II and III, 159–60
Schools,
Central Flying School, 26
Chapperton Down, 48–50, 54, 55,
61, 106
Coast Artillery School, 93
Heavy Artillery, 6, 54–5
Royal School of Artillery,
Charter, 211
Courses, 212
Exchange IGs, 214–15
Headquarters staff, 213

Library, Badley, 211, 212
Reprographics, 211, 212, 213
School Booking Centre, 213
Terms, 212
School of Anti-Aircraft Artillery,
    93, 104
School of Artillery, Larkhill,
    Amalgamation with Manorbier,
    116
    Anniversary, 50th, 112–16,
    197–8
    Badge, 105
    Courses, 56, 73–4, 75, 83, 90,
    104, 106, 109, 125
    Formation of, 55
    Foundation stone laid, 102–4
    Opening (1966), 108
    Overseas students, 95
    Prefix 'Royal' conferred, 116
    Rebuilding, 107–8
School of Artillery, Manorbier,
    104, 106, 112, 116
School of Infantry, 81, 173, 216
School of Instruction, Larkhill,
    46, 47, 49
School of Railway Artillery, 75
School of Survey, 79, 84, 91
Siege Artillery School, 6, 56
Scott, Brig. M.F., 153
Scott, Maj. G.D.C., 214
Scouts and Guides, 98, 207–8
Selby-Lowndes, Brig. M.W.W., 168,
    169
Sennybridge, 164
Sergeant-Major Instructor in Gun-
    nery (SMIG), 126
Seymour, WO2 (AIG) F.A.G., 231
Sharp, Gen. Sir John, 207
Sharp Hall, 206, 207
Shilo, see Canadian Forces
Shoeburyness, 1, 2, 4, 5, 8, 9, 17,
    65, 185, 211
    partial transfer to Larkhill, 8,
    17–18, 47, 82
Shooting, Game, 210
Short Bros Air Services, 223
Shrapnel, discontinuance of, 67
Shrewton, 8, 16, 32, 171, 176
Siddell, Bdr. B.M., 231
Simcock, Lt.-Col. W., 214
Slessor, Lt. H., 68, 70

Slim, FM Sir William, 96
Slim, WO1 (RSM) G.E., 114
Smith, Col. S.C., 17–18, 186
Smith, G.J., 118
Smith, Pte, Phyllis M., 199, 201
Smith, Reggie, 201
Smith, 'Smudger', 104
'Snaffles', (C.J. Payne), 197
South West District, 211–12
Stadward, Maj. E.G., 199
Staff College, Junior Division, 216
STANOC, 190, 220
Stanton, Messrs A.H., 203
Starner, Col. R.A., 232
Steel Houses, The, 62
Stoep, The, 63
Stonehenge, 7, 36, 39, 223
Strangways, 35, 62, 82
Sultan of Muscat and Oman, HM
    The, 101
Sun gap at Larkhill, 24
Survey Company, RA, 191
Sussex Artillery Volunteers, 185
Suther, Lt.-Col. P., 55
Swinton, Capt. K., 233
Syrencote House, 8, 82–3

Taylor, Lt.-Col. H.M., 84
Technical Advisor in Gunnery
    (TAIGR), 99
Technical Instructor in Gunnery
    (TIG), 96, 124
Templer, Brig. C.R., 20
Templer, Brig. J.R., 20
Templer, Maj. L.R.B., 20, 21, 42
Territorial Army, 4, 5, 12, 17, 18,
    71, 73, 92, 94, 96, 181–8
Thicknesse, Lt.-Col. H., 136
Thompson, Col. R.G.R., 199
Thompson, Miss A., 59
Thompson, RQMS G.W., 59
Thorold, Rev. E.H., 65, 203
Tickle, Rt. Rev. G.W., 111, 205
Tidworth, 42, 53
Tilshead, 8, 16, 18, 170, 171, 176,
    223
Times, The, 110, 180
Toombs, VC, Maj.-Gen. Sir Henry,
    146
Toombs Prize, The, 146

Totterdown House, 94
Towell, Brig. R.H., 73, 102
Traction engines, 42, 51
Training Development Team, RA, 123, 220, 222
Trawsfynydd, *see* Practice camps
Trees, woods and plantations, Anniversary Plantation, 114
Coronation plantings, 98, 124
Larkhill Copse, 190
On the ranges, 177–8
Packway, The, 63, 190
Tuck, Brig. P.H.J. ('Friar'), 195
Tullock, Brig. D.C.C., 169
Tullock, Maurice, 197
Tuzo, Gen. Sir Harry, 112

Uniacke, Maj. R.J., 210
Unit Training Officer (UTO), 123
United Kingdom Land Forces, 94, 122, 210, 212, 220
United States Army, 169, 220
Display by, 107
Fort Sill, 107, 204, 232
IGs, 94, 214–14
Women's Army Corps, 120

Victory over Japan ('VJ Day'), 88

Wagon Lines Club, The, 107, 123
Walsh, A.S., 207
Wanklyn, Miss Joan, 38, 68, 114, 122, 199
War Department/Office, 1, 18, 24, 42, 160, 190, 202, 224
Warren, Gnr. A., 233
Wason, Lt.-Gen. S.R., 73, 82, 102
Webb, Brig. C.M.F., 122
Weldon, Lt.-Col. F.W.C., 195
West Down, *see* Camps and Ranges
West Lavington, 8, 164, 173, 223, 232
Westmuckett, Rev. J.S., 114
Whale Island, 79, 226
Whitney, Dr R.J., 85
Wilkinson Cane, 231–2
Williams, Gnr. J., 233
Wilson, Maj. W.A., 45–6
Wilson, S/Sgt. R.H.V., 27–8

Wings, The, 127–58, 211, 212
Administrative, 117, 123, 141–3, 172, 216
Air Defence, 116, 117, 155–7
Air, 81, 84, 88, 90, 129–30
Anti-Tank, 81, 127, 129
Counter-Bombardment, 91, 96, 100, 106, 143
Equipment, 81, 84, 85, 90, 104, 130–2
Guided Weapons, 109, 148–50, 157–8, 207, 212, 213, 233
Gunnery, 84, 90, 94, 104, 117, 122, 132–5, 164, 172, 212, 213, 224
Headquarters, 79, 84, 127
Locating, 96, 106, 117, 122, 150, 165, 224
Observation, 90–1, 96, 106, 140–1
Radar, 88, 139–40
REME, 96, 109, 114, 117, 120, 153–5, 213, 233
Signals, 117, 150–3, 213, 238
Survey, 84, 91, 138–9
Tactics, 84, 88, 90–1, 99, 117, 136–8, 212–13
Young Officers, 144–8, 211, 213
Wiltshire County Council, 118, 119
Wiltshire Educational Authority, 206
Women's Royal Army Corps, 99, 108, 111, 112, 118, 120, 189, 216, 218–19, 232
Wood, VC, FM Sir Evelyn, 8, 11
Woodhouse, Lt.-Col. E., 38–9
Woolwich, 1, 75, 164, 202
Arsenal, 20
Repository, 5, 6
Rotunda Museum, 88

Youens, The Ven. Archdeacon J.R., 114
Young artillerymen, 91
Younger, Maj.-Gen. J.E.T., 60
Young Men's Christian Association, 40, 54, 206, 207
Young Officers, 110
Branch, 57
Courses, 57, 94
Quarters, 108
see also under Wings